AF646471

THE AESTHETICS OF WONDER

The Aesthetics of Wonder

NEW FINDINGS IN SANSKRIT ALAṄKĀRAŚĀSTRA

A. V. Subramanian

Delhi
MOTILAL BANARSIDASS
Varanasi Patna Bangalore Madras

First Published: Delhi, 1988

MOTILAL BANARSIDASS
Bungalow Road, Jawahar Nagar, Delhi 110 007

Branches

Chowk, Varanasi 221 001
Ashok Rajpath, Patna 800 004
24 Race Course Road, Bangalore 560 001
120 Royapettah High Road, Mylapore, Madras 600 004

© MOTILAL BANARSIDASS. ALL RIGHTS RESERVED

ISBN: 81-208-0444-9

PRINTED IN INDIA
BY JAINENDRA PRAKASH JAIN AT SHRI JAINENDRA PRESS, A-45 NARAINA INDUSTRIAL AREA, PHASE I, NEW DELHI 110 028 AND PUBLISHED BY NARENDRA PRAKASH JAIN FOR MOTILAL BANARSIDASS, DELHI 110 007.

PREFACE

Sanskrit aestheticians have undoubtedly made some notable contributions to the field through their discovery of the concepts of *rasa*, *dhvani* and *aucitya*. Indians have generally done well in the field of abstract thinking and some of the finest minds have been at work in aesthetics till about a thousand years ago. I should confess, however, I am not quite pleased with the state of the discipline we have inherited; my discontent arises from three causes; many ideas which have only their age to recommend them have persisted without challenge, have even gained greater glamour on account of their age and the fact that their progenitor was a *muni*; secondly, in quite a few areas, there has been little of innovative work done while there has been no dearth of thinkers in the field who spent their lives in polemical activity relating to a handful of concepts which were possibly glamorous and very much in fashion, like the *dhvani* theory; and lastly, excepting for a flicker or two, there has persevered a stupefying state of intellectual stagnation in aesthetics over the last nine hundred years.

One such inadequately explored area, surprisingly, is the nature of the sentiments and how they are evoked and how they afford pleasure to the dilettante. This, indeed, is the heartland of Sanskrit aesthetics and it is amazing, how, despite the prolific attempts at interpreting Bharata's *rasa sūtra*, there still remains a great deal of a misty fog over this part of the field. I do not think Bharata *muni*'s basic concept of *sthāyibhāva* generating sentiments on being acted upon by excitants explains the process. It has obviously been accepted without question, much like a religious dogma and has never been critically examined, in its fundamentals. To bring in a wholly unknown, a distressingly vague term like *sthāyibhāva* as the foundation of the *rasa* theory is merely to explain the unknown in terms of the equally unknown. Unless *sthāyibhāva* is explained and understood in terms of something known, either in our traditional lore or in terms of western science, I shall continue to be dissatisfied, I shall persevere in the feeling that the basis of the appeal of literature is yet to be properly understood.

If this is the position of the central axiom on which the *rasa* theory is based, it is no wonder the *rasas* themselves have received sketchy treatment in the books on aesthetics. While the sentiments of love, heroism and pathos have been recognised to be the dominant ones, it must be apparent that even these have not been systematically analysed on the basis of authentic aesthetic experience. It is therefore not surprising that the lesser sentiments like wonder and humour have received little attention: indeed, the writers appear to lose all interest when they come to this part of the discussion and append the sketchiest of notes about them, just in order that the passage may not look incomplete.

Clearly, there was a widespread tendency to accept ideas blindly without question, in the field of aesthetics. Why this should be so in this field, while in philosophy, where one would expect such abject acceptance, new ideas flowered in such brilliant efflorescence is wholly beyond me. One reason why works of master-thinkers like Bhaṭṭatouta are unavailable while those presenting the existing knowledge without any innovation are still available may be that people were moved to copy school textbooks more because of the greater demand: it was difficult labour copying books by hand and only the books badly needed were multiplied manually. This theory, if true, reflects little credit on the society which allowed the best works of its most brilliant thinkers to be lost on account of lack of interest and pure laziness. Further, even text-book writers would have referred to other views prevalent in the field and would not have suppressed important schools of thought. It is therefore clear that for this neglect of vast areas of aesthetics, one has to postulate lack of innovativeness, a tame acceptance of hoary theories and a tendency to get lost in the minutiae of polemics.

Today the position is no better. Printing has revolutionised the spread of knowledge and universities have multiplied: the Government in India and the private foundations in the west spend vast sums of money over research in Sanskrit. But, unfortunately, we see little fruitful work of an original type being done anywhere. There is little tendency to question age-old beliefs in academic circles though the air outside is thick with the clatter of iconoclasm. A doyen among Indian Indologists was quoted in the newspapers sometime ago as saying that the scope for research in Sanskrit is fast getting reduced today. The truth seems to be that original, innovative work is yet to start in a few fields. Clearly the deadening inertia of nine centuries lies over us like a miasma, still.

Among the least researched themes in aesthetics is the sentiment of wonder. The neglect is wholly on the part of the *ālaṅkārikas*: for the poets have made extensive use of wonder to spice their works. The first feature of wonder that claims our attention is how it is excited, fanned up; the older writers took into account only the physical excitants of wonder like miracles and supernatural phenomena; a later writer very casually added "clever and twisted sayings" to the list of excitants. The reader will find in this work quite a large number of new (or newly recognised and labelled) categories of excitants with suitable illustrations from the entire range of Sanskrit literature. In an effort to bring some order to this part of the work, an attempt has been made to analyse these excitants under three classes, though the writer quite readily concedes that some of them may be shown under more than one class: this has been presented under the entry 'excitants' in the subject index appended. An earnest endeavour has been made to present only the more interesting and significant *vibhāvas* and the temptation to make the list numerically impressive has been resisted, though the reader may have a passing feeling that this part of the work has been rather overdone.

The work then goes on to examine the literary benefits accruing from a delineation of the sense of wonder. Seeing that it can only be ancillary and never the dominant sentiment in any work, if poets still evoked it extensively, as noted earlier, there must be considerable literary benefits derivable from its portrayal and there has been no effort made previously, in two millennia, to study them. So an important part of the work is devoted to a consideration of these manifold literary advantages arising from the evocation of this sense.

There is a hesitancy on the part of Sanskrit researchers to seek the help of western science in solving problems of Sanskrit aesthetics. But if we make careful provision for the wide differences in concept, approach and procedures in the east and the west, we would discover that startling but wholly reasonable new explanations can be had by a sensible application of some western scientific concepts to problems in Sanskrit aesthetics. The last part of the work records the results of one such sally where some recent discoveries in neuropsychology are shown to throw brilliant light on the very nature of the sense of wonder. It would be accepted that this exercise throws open wholly new gateways through which the modern aesthetician can sally forth on exciting tours of discovery. If the present work serves to clear some part of the fog that lies over the field so that earnest thinkers can look upon the exciting new land that lies ahead and feel the urge to march forward, it would have amply fulfilled its purpose.

I am grateful to M/s. Motilal Banarsidass who have brought out this book to their customary high standards. As in all my literary endeavours, Śrī P.S. Rāmamūrti has rendered invaluable help in my writing this and in making it ready for the press. I owe a debt of gratitude to Dr K. V. Sarma, Professor of Sanskrit, Adyar library, Madras for having schooled me in the techniques of referencing, indexing and other academic modalities in which this writer, alas, is so notably deficient.

A.V. Subrmanian

Mylapore
Madras-600 004
1987

CONTENTS

Chapter I

WHAT WE KNOW OF WONDER TODAY

The sentiment of wonder is spectacular, demonstrative, showy: it has nothing of the shrinking violet about it: it is dramatic, it is domineering, it demands undivided attention, shutting out all other rival voices. With these unique qualities, particularly valuable in plays, one would expect the sentiment of wonder to have attracted much more attention among Sanskrit aestheticians than it has. Judging from the prolific production of works on aesthetics, one would expect very much more of original work to have been done on this sentiment: but the sad reality is that excepting two refreshingly innovative thinkers, the rest of the very large number of writers have wholly neglected this sentiment and little work of fresh innovation has been done on it in the last two thousand or more years after Bharata Muni's pioneering work.

It is always difficult to assign reasons why innovative work was not done in any field. One reason might be that once the sentiment of wonder was relegated to the lesser level, that of an ancillary sentiment, its fate was sealed and people did not want to waste their time on it. A more potent reason seems to be that after Ānandavardhana propounded his *dhvani* theory, his successors allowed themselves to be so completely dominated by it that they spent their time either opposing it or supporting it with some additional matter of their own. While it speaks highly of the calibre of Ānandavardhana and Abhinavagupta, it does not reflect much credit on the writers who followed them, who allowed themselves to be dazzled by the brilliance of the theory.

Rājaśekhara in his *Kāvyamimāmsā* speaking of the scarcity of truly innovative poets says,

सन्ति श्वान इवासंख्याः जाति भाजो गृहे गृहे ।
उत्पादका न बहवः कवयः शरभा इव ॥

[IV Chapter]

The statement that there is never a surfeit of original innovators is true of all fields of human endeavour. Many Sanskritists felt impelled to write works on aesthetics without having anything new to impart: naturally their works have proved to be rehashes of those of their predecessors. Some, like Mammaṭa were able to produce competent school text-books, at best. After the great spurt of activity in this field in Kashmir over a period of perhaps two hundred years around the end of the first millennium after Christ which produced a certain number of fresh concepts, there was only Jagannātha Paṇḍita rising as a lone star of originality who shed fresh light on the subject: a thousand years could produce only one *utpādaka*, a creative thinker if we discount the case of Nārāyaṇa on the grounds that no work of his has come down to us.

Let us now quickly recapitulate the existing ideas relating to the sentiment of wonder before we venture into uncharted territory. In his pioneering work, the *Nāṭyaśāstra*, Bharata recognised it as one of the eight sentiments ruling the field, assigning surprise (*vismaya*) as its *sthāyibhāva.*

He seems to have recognised in a general way the importance of wonder for he says in the 21st chapter that the presentation of the story should be done in such a way as to produce a sense of wonder: **आश्चर्यवदभिख्यानम् ।**

Abhinavagupta in his commentary the *Abhinavabhārati* furnishes a short list of circumstances which may evoke this sentiment:

> **स च दिव्यजनदर्शनेप्सितमनोरथावाप्त्युपवनदेवकुलादिगमनसभाविमानमायेन्द्रजालसंभावनादिभिः विभावैरुत्पद्यते ।**

[VI Adhyāya]

It may be seen that Abhinavagupta legislated mainly for the kind of wonder generated by physical uniqueness of the type purveyed by miracles. Little thought was given to other kinds of uniqueness. The great aesthetician, however, says briefly in another place that surprise is generated by **असंभवद्वस्तुप्रदर्शनम् ।** (VI Chapter). This is a very general classification, it is true: but the way it has been worded, quite a large number of cases can be brought under its wide wingspan. It is also to be noted that a large number of categories we are going to recognise later on will fall outside its scope.

The most significant contribution to the study of the sentiment of wonder was made by Ācārya Nārāyaṇa who appears to have written a work on aesthetics. The work is now lost to us and his highly original concept on wonder is available only in the quotation found in the 3rd *paricchēda* of Sāhityadarpaṇa written by his great great grandson Viśvanātha. These are the three lines (a verse and a half) attributed to Nārāyaṇa.

रसे सारश्चमत्कारः सर्वत्राप्यनुभूयते ।
तच्चमत्कारसारत्वे सर्वत्राप्यद्भुतो रसः ।
तस्मादद्भुतमेवाह कृति नारायणो रसम् ॥

The Ācārya identified *camatkāra* as the basic ingredient of all the rasas: now this quality of *camatkāra* is purveyed by the sentiment of wonder. So the Ācārya concludes that the sentiment of wonder is the chief or even the only sentiment there is. Mahāmahopādhyāya S. Kuppuswāmy Śāstri coined the word rasa-synthesis and calls Ācārya Nārāyaṇa's theory the adbhuta-synthesis.

Clearly the Ācārya gave a high position of importance to the sentiment of wonder: but it is not clear if he felt it could be the main, dominating sentiment of any work. In fact, nothing more is known of his views except the three lines quoted by Viśvanātha who did not, himself, consider this concept of sufficient importance that deserved to be developed. We have also here to condemn the lack of judgment of the Sanskritists of that era in general who allowed the work of this original thinker to perish by neglect: a similar case of a great work being allowed to perish is the Kāvyakautuka of Bhaṭṭatouta from which we get brief glimpses in the references made by his loyal, admiring pupil, Abhinavagupta. It is as mystifying as it is unfortunate how quite ordinary, uninspired pot-boilers have survived while great works of innovators have been forever lost to the world.

We now come to the brilliant innovator Jagannātha Paṇḍita of Āndhra Pradēsh whose work the *Rasagaṅgādhara*, despite its recondite diction deserves a much wider readership. In his discussion of the implications of his own definition of poetry, he has a strikingly original thing to say which is of interest to all those who want to understand the true role of the sentiment of wonder in literature. He defines poetry as रमणीयार्थप्रतिपादकः शब्दः काव्यम् । He then proceeds to explain the word 'ramaniya' [I (Kāvyalakṣaṇa)] as a factor that generates an unworldly pleasure of an elevated nature, employing the word '*lōkōttara*': this word, itself, according to Jagannātha is equivalent to '*camatkāra*' which can be rendered in English as something bright and flashing, something that causes surprise.

The word *lōkōttara* and its variant *lōkōttirṇa* have been used by Ānandavardhana and Abhinavagupta in a general manner: Jagannātha works it into his basic concept of what constitutes a poetical work, supplying a clarification that *lōkōttara* is what furnishes surprise, that it is meant to exclude worldly statements that may give pleasure without any claim to being literature, ike "you have just got a male issue" and "I shall present you with wealth".

A fuller discussion of the implications of the word '*lōkōttara*' will be undertaken elsewhere in this book. But it is important here to note that Jagannātha allots a pivotal role to surprise among the constituents of poetry, that, according to him, it is precisely its capacity to purvey an elevated level of surprise that distinguishes poetry from other writing.

Apart from these writers who made significant contributions in the field, we can refer to two more aestheticians before we conclude. One is Kuntaka who considered that *vakrōkti* is the very soul of poetry: and he defined *vakrōkti* in this manner:

वक्रोक्तिरेव वैदग्ध्यभङ्गी भणितिरुच्यते।

[Vakrōktijīvita, Kārikā I/11)

This *vakrōkti* has come to have additional significance at the hands of Kuntaka: it has a strong element of unusualness, even a waywardness that is artistic. Kuntaka uses the words *camatkāra* and *atiśaya* in the *kārikā* and *vṛtti* associated with the work, in his attempt to explain the scope of this key word. So Kuntaka's concept can be considered to be similar to that of Jagannātha only from the viewpoint of the place accorded to unusualness among the ingredients of poetry.

Unfortunately this cannot be said of Bhānudatta the author of Rasataraṅgiṇī to whom reference is being made here for a different reason. He has nothing original to contribute regarding the nature of poetry nor does he say much that is new about the diverse excitants (*vibhāvas*) of the sentiment of wonder beyond this:

अथ अद्भुतरसस्य विभावाः मायेन्द्रजालार्थलाभादयः ऊहनीयाः

[II *taraṅga*]

अत्युक्ति भ्रमोक्तिचित्रोक्तिविरोधाभासप्रभृतयः अद्भुता एव

[VII taraṅga]

It may be seen that the writer, without adding any new thought has clarified the concepts of Bharata and other predecessors: perhaps, with his emphasis on expression (ukti) he may be credited by sympathetic critics with having thrown the doors open for other kinds of surprises than the purely physical. However, he did not consider this field worth any further examination, obviously.

Bhãnudatta, earlier, thinks it fit to make a statement which is somewhat puzzling:

भृंगारादौ चमत्कारदर्शनाद्यत्र मनोविकृतिः
अङ्गतया भासते तत्र भृंङ्गारादयः एव रसाः
प्राधान्येन यत्र भासते तत्राद्भुत एव रसः ।

The first part of the statement is very clear: where the other sentiments dominate and wonder merely reinforces them, it plays only an *aṅga* or accessory role. He then goes on to say that it becomes the *aṅgi* or the dominant *rasa* when it outshines the other sentiments. Theoretically this statement is all right, though there is little of original contribution in it, since this is merely a routine application of the rule governing dominant and accessory sentiments. But the reader is curious to know if there is a single instance in Sanskrit literature of the sentiment of wonder becoming the aṅgi rasa. One recent writer regards Śaktibhadra's Āścaryacūḍāmaṇi as the play where this sentiment is dominant: one feels he has allowed himself to be misled by the title: for, clearly the sentiment of wonder is not the dominant rasa in it, indeed this sentiment can never be the dominant one in any work of literature. A scientific examination confirms what experience has already found—that this sense of wonder has necessarily to play a subordinate role in any work and to evoke it continuously over long periods will be to court disaster.

CHAPTER 2

THE EXCITANTS OF THE SENSE OF WONDER

Despite the almost total neglect of the sentiment of wonder by Sanskrit aestheticians, the poets have very sensibly made excellent use of this admirable device. They make use of diverse methods (called *vibhāvas*) to evoke the sentiment and an analytical study of these methods is as necessary as it is interesting. The high ingenuity with which they evoke it can be an absorbing study in itself and it is a pity Sanskrit aestheticians with some honourable exceptions have denied themselves and their readers this genuine intellectual diversion. Such a study is a very important part of the field of aesthetics too: it throws considerable light on the moot questions of aesthetics, it reveals what is going on in the dimly-lit corners of the poet's mind, it uncovers many of the secrets of the process of poetry-making. And we have to bear in mind that a poet's mind remains today the least explored part of man's world, by the side of which the darkest Africa must be regarded as exhaustively explored and fully mapped.

In this chapter, an attempt will be made to analyse the many categories of factors which can serve to evoke the sentiment of wonder: and these categories will all be illustrated with examples from Sanskrit works. This subject has been cooking in the present writer's mind—conscious and subconscious—for over three years and the number of categories has grown steadily. He has made an earnest attempt to merge some categories and reduce the number, in order to escape the criticism that he is guilty of over-categorisation, a peculiarly Indian failing. The intelligent reader will be able to discern the differences—mostly obvious and only in occasional cases, somewhat subtle: and it is hoped the present writer will not be lampooned for multiplying the categories. His shortcoming—if it is considered such—will, it is hoped, be understood as a case of reaction against the near-total neglect of the subject in the past and forgiven by the gentle reader.

There is no particular hard and fast rule according to which these categories have been arranged except that those more frequently employed by the poets will be discussed in the earlier part of the chapter. Examples have been selected not only from the classical poets but from lesser practitioners of the art and even from what is generally regarded as devotional literature: aphoristic stanzas have been freely used.

The categories discussed here are many and are wide-ranging, but an overview will indicate that a single quality can be discerned that is common to most of them and that is that of unexpectedness. A wag said, "I love surprises—as long as I am ready for them." The point is, of course, that the essence of surprise, its unexpectedness is destroyed if it is anticipated, if you are ready for it. Expectation is merely a projection into the future of what you know now. The essence of surprise is that the new phenomenon is outside the ken of knowledge of the person who is exposed to it and is therefore something he could not have expected or figured out in advance.

As surprise relates to an area beyond that covered by our daily experience, some of the categories analysed may be a little abstract: in order to make them easier to understand, certain examples from the contemporary world have been furnished. Many of them, it will be found, have a strong element of humour in them, but this is incidental: they have been used here for their element of surprise classifiable under the particular categories and it is hoped that they will help the reader in a hurry to comprehend the point. If, in addition, they make the passage lighter and more enjoyable, the present writer will not be dismayed, as he does not believe that a work of research, to secure academic respectability should necessarily be dull.

2.1. *Supernatural occurrences*

This is one of the few categories enlisted in the laconic passage in the *Abhinavabhāratī*: it can be seen that it is the most basic and common among the excitants of the sentiment of wonder that can be encountered. To say that supernatural occurrences excite wonder is just a tautological truth like the famous statement of Calvin Coolidge's that when many people are out of work, unemployment results. Miracles and supernatural phenomena in defiance of the established laws of nature are not a matter of everyday occurrence, they were not, even in the earlier epochs; and they have always evoked the deepest wonder from the onlookers: indeed they were made to occur only with the objective of convincing, through shock and surprise, the sitters-on-the-fence. They were freely used by divine beings and by god-men: and as Sanskrit literature is thickly peopled by gods and godmen, miracles are the commonest excitants of surprise one can meet with.

We find supernatural phenomena in the plays of Bhāsa, Kālidāsa and Bhavabhūti and the major epic poems. Naturally we do not find them in the social play of Śūdraka (the *Mṛcchakaṭika*) and the political play of Viśākhadatta (the *Mudrārākṣasa*). Bhāsa makes characters of Lord Nārāyaṇa's weapons in the Dūtavākya and the Bālacarita and Bhavabhūti fills the last act of his *magnum opus* with supernatural occurrences like the appearance of the *jṛmbhaka* weapons and the cleaving of the waters of the Gaṅgā. Kālidāsa has a number of such occurrences in his *Śākuntala* in the IV, the V, the VI and the VII Acts and his *Vikramōrvaśiya* is chockful of them as Ūrvaśī is a divine courtesan who practises magic and Purūravas can journey at will (like Duṣyanta) in the upper worlds.

A verse has been quoted in the *Subhāṣitaratna bhāṇḍāgāra* as an example under the sentiment of wonder, which we may savour here. It describes Lord Nārāyaṇa who, appearing as a dwarf and obtaining a grant from Mahābali grows to a colossal size silencing the asuras who were earlier inclined to ridicule Him:

किं क्रमिष्यति किलैष वामनः
    यावदित्थमहसन्त दानवाः ।
तावदस्य न ममौ नभस्तले
    लङ्घितार्कशशिमण्डलः क्रमः ॥ [379/14]

Similar verses about Kṛṣṇa and Narasiṁha have been quoted by the writers on poetics as illustrative of this sentiment.

Supernatural occurrences are powerful excitants of wonder and in plays they constitute excellent theatre. But the greatest poets have been very chary about using this device: for indiscriminate use of this powerful device makes for incredibility, particularly among the elite sections of the spectators. Great poetry appeals on account of its ease of universalisation: and miracles, being beyond the ken of the experience of most men in any epoch, prove recalcitrant material defying universalisation. In fact, the greater the wonder potential of a device, the greater is the difficulty in its getting universalised. Wonder has several important uses which will be discussed in Chapter III; but great poets take particular care to use it only where it is warranted: and where it is needed, they use it to evoke wonder, for a few seconds only, overcoming the temptation to overportrayal.

2.2 *Surprise twists in the plot*

Poets and playwrights in Sanskrit drew their plots from the two famous epics the Rāmāyaṇa and the Mahābhārata or from that storehouse of fascinating stories, the Kathāsaritsāgara. A very small number of works were based on the poets' own fabrication like the Mālatīmādhava: some like the Mudrārākṣasa were drawn from history.

But even where the plot was taken from the epics, the playwright had the sanction of dramaturgists to alter it to suit the exigencies of rasa delineation or character portrayal. This sanction was later verbalised by Dhanañjaya in his Daśarūpaka.

यत्तत्रानुचितं किंचिद् नायकस्य रसस्य वा ।
विरुद्धं तत् परित्याज्यं अन्यथा वा प्रकल्पयेत् ॥ [III/24]

This permissive provision has been widely utilised by the master dramatists to great advantage.

The best illustration is provided by Kālidāsa in his greatest work. Kālidāsa took the plot for his play Śākuntala from the Mahābhārata. The story as given in the epic is flat, insipid and the hero's repudiation of Śakuntalā is presented in such a cavalier, amateurish manner that the reader would not be in a position to sympathise and identity himself with the hero. No one but a genius could have identified the makings of an immortal play in this bland, unconvincing puranic story. And in order to breathe artistic life into it Kālidāsa had to introduce surprise twists in the story.

One is the episode of the curse of Durvāsas: curses and short tempered hermits were dime-a-dozen in those days and they may have appealed to the gallery but not to the box: so this curse episode, though without much of a surprise potential must be regarded as a device thought up by the gifted playwright to salvage the character of the hero whose repudiation of Śakuntalā now becomes a little credible.

Another is the whisking away of the helpless girl by Mēnakā to the heavenly regions. For, consider the context in which this becomes necessary: the king remains unconvinced that she is really his wife and her people have left for the penance-grounds without her. Śakuntalā is in a singularly anguished state. The chief *purōhita* of the king offers a solution to the problem: he will look after the girl in his house till she delivers the child and by studying its marks, it can be verified whether it is genuinely the child of a great king. The king accepts the suggestion as there seems to be no alternative. But, for the dilettante of the dramatic art this is a particularly unattractive solution. So, in order to rescue the play from such an inartistic ending, Kālidāsa introduces a surprise twist here making Mēnakā come down and take her away to Hēmakūṭa.

This has considerable dramatic advantages over the bland priestly solution. The king's memory is restored on his seeing the ring: now he does not know where she is and therefore he pines for her, raising the emotional level of the play: this would not have been possible if the other solution had been adopted as the king knows she is living in the priest's house. From the spiritual view-point too this alternative chosen by the playwright is the more appropriate: the love of the two was based, earlier, on pure physical attraction and hence no union resulted: Śakuntalā, living in heavenly penance grounds performs austerities and Duṣyanta too burns up his sins in the fire of sorrow, penitence and self-criticism; and the union that ensures at the end is lasting and is productive of great good to the country as it is now securely based on spiritual means.

But, from the viewpoint of the spectator there is a sudden twist in the story at the end of the V Act and it has mystery, there is a supernatural phenomenon, the whole thing is sudden and dramatic: the spectator does not know what has really happened to the unhappy girl: so this is a real surprise twist and constitutes an excellent example of this category. All that was said earlier in this section is the critic's attempt to lay bare the mental workings of the poet faced with some problems: the average theatre-goer does not know these and is bound to register surprise at the episode.

A second instance is provided by Bhavabhūti in his Uttararāmacarita. He takes up a natural tragedy from the old epic and in deference to dramatic tradition converts it into a comedy, reuniting Rāma and Sītā. From the way the playwright has handled the plot, the spectators will be surprised at the big change in the fortunes of the main characters: Sītā is restored to a grateful Rāma through the good offices of semi-divine beings. This is a change of major dimensions and the problems besetting the poet in encompassing this which must have been formidable have been analysed in a monograph "The innovative genius of Bhavabhūti" CPR Foundation, 1, Eldams Road, Madras 18, by the present writer. The fact that he introduces the twist with a surprise-laden series of supernatural events and its implications are discussed in Chapter III.

Indians have taken little interest in history and the average theatre-goer may have just heard of the names, Chāṇakya and Candragupta. The story is handled very adroitly by Viśākhadatta and the spectator is constantly kept on the alert, shocked and surprised by the many curious turns of the complex plot. Though the spectator does not know the story in advance (as he certainly knows the Rāma story), he is led or misled by the master playwright to expect certain events and when they do not happen and events not expected take place, he is surprised.

Plays like the *Mudrārākṣasa* and the *Mṛcchakaṭika* and the *Mālatīmādhava* based on scarcely known stories are rare in Sanskrit. Most playwrights took the kernel of their plot from the extremely well-known epics but they introduced a number of surprise twists in the plot to inject interest and also to reinforce their character and sentiment-delineation. Hence this constitutes a fecund source of surprise in Sanskrit.

2.3 *Unique, even perverse reactions of characters*

When a stimulus in the shape of the spoken word or an action assails a character in literature, its reaction can often be predicted, if the character-portrayal has been efficiently done. But human nature is complex and not always and wholly divinable and not every time subject to the rules of logic. Hence a character may come out with an unexpected reaction which, if it is not altogether preposterous shocks the reader.

A chain-smoker friend said, "I have recently been reading a lot of magazine articles on the evils of smoking. I happened to come across a book full of illustrations showing the badly corroded lungs of a smoker. It was terrible, just to look at those pictures and I have been extremely unhappy after such reading sessions. So, I have decided to stop-reading!" In this case the normal, expected reaction, of course, is that he has decided to stop smoking: when he announces his decision to stop reading (which, when you come to think of it, will wholly relieve his unhappiness, though his health may not improve) there is surprise followed by amused laughter.

J.K. Galbraith recounts a joke against the Russians in his "A life in our times". The sociology department of Moscow university made the discovery that there was widespread corruption in many branches of Government and in the Government-managed distribution agencies. A wing of the secret police conducted an experimental check in one of the peripheral departments and confirmed the report. The Government was obviously very annoyed and reacted quickly and decisively—it ordered the closure of the university's sociology department.

In this instance too, though the reaction is unusual, unexpected and certainly perverse, it is not unnatural, given the attitudes of totalitarian administrations everywhere. Here, in order to meet the criticism, the Government could have totally eradicated corruption—which takes some doing—or silence the critic—which it promptly did.

We have a number of instances of this category in Sanskrit. In Vālmīki's Rāmāyaṇa, while Rāma is camping in Citrakūṭa along with Sītā and Lakṣmaṇa, Bharata comes with his army to the place intending to restore the throne to Rāma. To Lakṣmaṇa who is impetuous by nature and whose entire capacity for love is used up in his affection for Rāma, this arrival of the usurper with his army looks extremely suspicious and he runs in excitement to Rāma not only to report but to see his permission to fight the enemy and destroy him.

Given Lakṣmaṇa's great love for Rāma, his reaction is fully in accord with what we would expect. But what of Rāma who has been cheated out of the most resplendent throne in the world by Bharata's mother who executed this classic piece of chicanery only that her son may ascend it? Did he fall in with Lakṣmaṇa's proposal, did he support his scheme for battle?

Rāma's reaction comes out with an exclamation of surprise: he asks: "Why are you talking of bows and arrows when the noble Bharata is on his way to our place? Why this sabre-rattling when he is announced?"

To the puzzled Lakṣmaṇa, Rāma makes this wonderful observation: "You think he is coming to kill us and secure the throne for himself! When he comes to me, O Lakṣmaṇa, and if I ask him to hand the kingdom over to you, you will find he agrees readily." In his overflowing affection for Bharata, Rāma is a little harsh with the devoted Lakṣmaṇa, saying things meant to hurt him a little. But what a reaction, noble beyond compare, not to be expected by the average reader even of Rāma! The passage in Vālmīki's simple, effective language is this:

महेष्वासे महाप्राज्ञे भरते स्वयमागते ।
किमत्र धनुषा कार्यं असिना वा सचर्मणा ॥ [97/2]
उच्यमानोऽपि भरतः मया लक्ष्मण तत्त्वतः ।
राज्यमस्मै प्रयच्छेति बाढमित्येव वक्ष्यति ॥ [97/18]

Bhāsa presents this same reaction of Rāma in his Pratimānāṭaka with a verve and freshness that enhance the sense of wonder evoked in the reader. This verse is addressed to Bharata himself:

वक्षः प्रसारय कवाटपुटप्रमाणम्
आलिङ्ग मां सुविपुलेन भुजद्वयेन ।
उन्नामयाननमिदं शरदिन्दुकल्पम्
प्रह्लादय व्यसनदग्धमिदं शरीरम्॥ [IV/16]

But let us go back to Vālmīki for another illustration. Rāma is camping with all his monkey hordes ready for the war with Rāvaṇa when Vibhīṣaṇa, Rāvaṇa's brother, deserts him and arriving at Rāma's camp sends word to him seeking sanctuary. Rāma holds a council of war seeking advice from his monkey allies. Chieftain after chieftain gets up to counsel him against admitting the rākṣasa. Sugrīva opens his big mouth to counsel Rāma against trusting anyone who has wronged his brother. Rāma smiles at this and turns to Hanumān who praises Vibhīṣaṇa's values and advocates his admission adding that he would be a useful ally.

Now Rāma begins to speak: his whole thinking on the subject looks radically different. Most of the counsellors had advised rejection saying that Vibhīṣaṇa was unreliable and Hanumān had advocated admission on the grounds that he was a noble person and might prove useful. Now Rāma says he should be admitted, basing his arguments on the highest ethics according to which everyone irrespective of his shortcomings should be offered sanctuary if he seeks it : all considerations of the qualities of the suppliant become irrelevant in the light of this higher morality. These are the famous words of Rāma ringing down the corridors of time as the credo of incarnate God:

सकृदेव प्रपन्नाय तवास्मीति च याचते ।
अभयं सर्वभूतेभ्यः ददाम्येतद् व्रतं मम ॥

[Yuddha Kāṇḍa: 18/33]

Even those by now familiar with the unique nobility of Rāma will be surprised at this reaction. Now the surprise is further reinforced by his announcement that he is prepared to offer sanctuary even to Rāvaṇa if he only seeks it, shocking his contemporaries as much as all the millions of Hindus who read and reread the great epic even to this day, with the dizzy moral heights he scales with ease.

आनयैनं हरिश्रेष्ठ दत्तमस्याभयं मया ।
विभीषणो वा सुग्रीव यदि वा रावणः स्वयम् ॥

[Yuddha Kāṇḍa 18/34]

In the former instance he welcomed Bharata effusively: it may be argued that Rāma was singularly unambitious and the loss of something he never valued high did not exacerbate him. But he was an ardent lover, his love for Sītā shines as the resplendent ideal of a man's love for his wife in the Hindu mind. A confirmed celibate like Hanumān was obviously repelled by the lamentations of Rāma at the loss of his wife. If Rāma could talk without rancour and offer to forgive not only Vibhīṣaṇa but Rāvaṇa himself who had plunged him to the nadir of suffering by abducting Sītā, the reader, after his initial high crest of surprise has ebbed away, will conclude rightly that no man is big enough to contain such vaulting forgivance, that this is, truly and transcendentally, a divine quality.

Kālidāsa provides a good illustration for this category in the III Act of his Śākuntala. In the earlier two Acts, Duṣyanta's ardour for Śakuntalā is adroitly painted as beyond anything he himself had ever experienced (and he was certainly one with a history of a large number of romantic entanglements). But as in all such cases, the lover is yet unsure if his love is returned. In this frame of mind he walks up in the shade of the trees intending to join Śakuntalā who can be seen lying on the ground being ministered to by her faithful friends. But the scraps of their conversation which he happens to catch stir up his curiosity: he stations himself behind a tree near them and listens eagerly to what they are saying.

As he had half suspected, the subject of their conversation is the love-sickness of Śakuntalā: her friends earnestly importune her to tell them who has caused it. Śakuntalā is very shy and hesitant, naturally; but, yielding to the sustained pressure from her bosom friends she is obviously very near the point where she would come out with the truth.

Having brought the spectator to this point, other playwrights would have proceeded to report Śakuntalā's revelation without further ado; but not Kālidāsa. At this point Kālidāsa shifts the focus to Duṣyanta to record his observation which will spring a big surprise even on the veterans among the spectators. For these are the lover's words:

पृष्टा जनेन समदुःखसुखेन बाला
नेयं न वक्ष्यति मजोगतमाधिहेतुम् ।
दृष्टो विवृत्य बहुशोऽप्यनया सतृष्णं
अत्रान्तरे श्रवणकातरतां गतोऽस्मि ॥ [III/10]

In his present frame of mind, the king would have been prepared to give up his throne in exchange for a message confirming that he indeed was the fortunate person who ruled her heart. Śakuntalā was certain to speak out her mind to her intimate friends, encouraged by the feeling that they were alone in the penance woods. And indications have not been wanting in the past few days about where her affections lay.

And yet he feels his reading of her heart may be wrong, may be prejudiced: it may be that he has put a favourable construction on some innocuous remarks and gestures of the girl: she might have lost her heart to a young man of the penance grounds from her own social milieu. And if this is true and she speaks out her heart, he would find himself flung to the deepest hell of anguish. Her pronouncement in the next seconds could make him the happiest man alive, certainly—but the terrible alternative that could not be ruled out could make him instantly the most miserable creature on earth.

Therefore he is moved to declare that he dreads hearing her

innermost feeling expressed in the clearest terms. What an unusual, even unique reaction from a lover! And withal, how natural, how psychological, how much in keeping with human nature under stress this is!

Kālidāsa obviously thought highly of this reaction, for he used it with necessary changes in his Vikramōrvaśīya also. When Urvaśī gets converted into a creeper owing to the operation of a curse, King Purūravas goes searching for her, now mistaking the deer to be his love on account of the similarity of the eyes and taking the river to be she because of the grace of movement and the froth on the water looking like white silk. For this passage, Kālidāsa is heavily indebted to the long-held poetic convention in the country equating beautiful women to various flora and fauna on the basis of similarity of qualities: the passage is highly stylised and is redeemed from mediocrity only by the superlative versification of the master.

At the end of this passage, perhaps on account of the repeated disappointments suffered by him, the king decides to close his eyes and continue his search using only his tactile sense. Now he happens to touch the self-same creeper; and as he is wearing the miraculous gem the sangamamani, the effect of the curse gets instantly annulled and Ūrvaśī appears.

The king's eyes are closed but he has only to open them to feast upon the lovely form of his beloved. But no! he is very reluctant to open his eyes for fear that this too might prove a disappointment, even though the thrill caused by touching her clearly indicates that she has indeed been restored to him The moment of truth with its one-in-a million possibility of frustration is dreaded so much, it is postponed consciously. If Duṣyanta had been afflicted by the fear of hearing, Purūravas is stymied by the fear of seeing. Let us savour the verse.

समर्थये यत्प्रथमं प्रियां प्रति ।
क्षणेन तन्मे परिवर्ततेन्यथा ॥
अतो विनिद्रे सहसा विलोचने
करोमि न स्पर्शविभावितप्रियः ॥ [IV/39]

2.4. *Excessive reaction to stimulus*

This category is related to the previous one as the reaction of a character is the source of surprise in both: while under the earlier one, we studied the unique, even perverse nature of the reaction, here we propose to study the degree of the emotion associated with it, especially when it is excessive. On the basis of our experience we learn to expect a certain extent of emotion in a character's reaction to stimuli: when it is far in excess (and this excessive reaction is not unnatural, does not appear contrived) surprise is occasioned in the reader.

In the VI Act of Śākuntala the moment the king sees the ring brought to him by the fisherman, the effects of the sage's curse are dispelled and he realises with a sense of shock how he had wronged the poor girl. This and the realisation of how he had turned away the loveliest girl in the world whom he had wedded secretly, push him down to the deepest despondency. But the mental state of the king, as described by the chamberlain is likely to cause surprise as it is in excess of what the average spectator would expect:

> **रम्यं द्वेष्टि यथा पुरा प्रकृतिभिर्न प्रत्यहं सेव्यते**
> **शय्याप्रान्तविवर्तनैर्विगमयत्युन्निद्र एव क्षपाः ।**
> **दाक्षिण्येन ददाति वाचमुचितामन्तः पुरेभ्यो यदा**
> **गोत्रेषु स्खलितस्तदा भवति च व्रीडाविलक्षश्चिरं ॥** [VI/5]

The king hates what is delightful. This is most surprising as Duṣyanta normally is a great lover of the good things of life, a dilettante, a connoisseur. Now the more surprising thing is that nature itself reacts to this changed mood of the king and desists from displaying all its pleasantest aspects on the advent of the spring season:

> **चूतानां चिरनिर्गतापि कलिका बध्नाति न स्वं रजः**
> **संनद्धं यदपि स्थितं कुरबकं तत्कोरकावस्थया ।**
> **कण्ठेषु स्खलितं गतेऽपि शिशिरे पुंस्कोकिलानां रुतं**
> **शङ्के संहरति स्मरोऽपि चकितस्तूणार्धकृष्टं शरम् ॥** [VI/4]

Rāvaṇa the very embodiment of arrogant self-assurance gets the shock of his life when Rāma lands with his monkey hordes in the very soil of Laṅkā—a development, the like of which had not happened till that moment. But Rāma is a human stripling and his army ranks are manned by mere monkeys—so to Rāvaṇa, this invasion should not loom as a great source of trouble. But Rāvaṇa reacts excessively to the challenge in a verse in the Hanumannaṭaka, memorable on account of its high poetic value and of the fact that Ānandavardhana has paid tribute to it.

न्यक्कारो ह्ययमेव मे यदरयस्तत्राप्यसौ तापसः
सोप्यत्रैव निहन्ति राक्षसकुलं जीवत्यहो रावणः ।
धिक् धिक् शक्रजितं प्रबोधितवता किं कुम्भकर्णेन वा
स्वर्गग्रामटिकाविलुण्ठनवृथोच्छूनैः किमेभिर्भुजैः ॥ [XIV/6]

Rāvaṇa's truculence is the subject-matter of a stanza in Prasannarāghava: here again, Rāvaṇa is portrayed in an unusual mood, a case of seemingly excessive reaction. Rāvaṇa is infatuated with the beauty of Sītā but is unable to make any progress in making her accept him. Obstacles sharpen the appetite, particularly of haughty, self-assured people like Rāvaṇa for whom nothing in the three worlds has till now been unobtainable. Sītā's obduracy makes Rāvaṇa humble for the first time in his life: in his own words the describes to Sītā how the most truculent of his ten heads which refused to bow before his most adored God, Śiva Himself is now paying homage to her, seeking her love. It is a verse with a complex conceit that can be composed only by a Sanskrit poet of unusual mental powers:

यत्संतुष्टवतः पुरा पुरभिदश्छेदोत्सवच्छेदिनः
न क्रोधादनमन्नवोद्गतशिरःश्रेणौ नमन्त्यामपि ।
एतत्ते दशमं शिरो मम नमत्त्वत्पादपाथोजयोः
अव्याजं मिथिलेन्द्रपुत्रि भवतीं प्रेमातुरं याचते ॥ [VI/25]

When excessive reaction is being discussed, Bhavabhūti comes to the mind as a high-priority claimant for he revelled habitually in excessive portrayal, particularly of pathos. The stanzas uttered by Rāma in a frenzy of self-accusation at the end of the I Act after he had decided to banish Sītā (like verses 43, 45, 46/49) and many stanzas in the III Act of which verses 31, 32 and 35 may serve as representative specimens, will do duty here as good illustrations.

Among the stanzas quoted by the ālaṅkārikās as illustrations are two which express excessive (but not necessarily perverse) reactions of two girls to the stimuli of love: while their authorship is uncertain, the verses themselves are nicely sculptored and are worth quoting. One is as follows:

अङ्गासङ्गिमृणालकाण्डमयते भृङ्गावलीनां रुचं
नासामौक्तिकमिन्द्रनीलसरणिं श्वासानिलाद्गाहते ।
दत्तेयं हिमवालुकापि कुचयोर्धत्ते क्षणं दीपताम्
तप्तायःपतिताम्बुवत् करतले धाराम्बु संलीयते ॥
[Kuvalavānanda N.S. Edition page 86]

A girl in love who is unable to be with her lover for any reason is traditionally supposed to develop considerable heat in the body. There are poems describing this, Kālidāsa himself having referred to the effect of heat generated by separation on the body of the beloved in the Śākuntala. This stanza paints an extreme picture of almost incandescent heat in the body which makes the stalks of lotus placed on her to cool her, turn black and the white pearl in the nose ornament turn into a blue emerald and a piece of camphor placed in the breast as a coolant burst instantly into flame and drops of water evaporate, the moment they come into contact with her palm. Physiologists may protest saying that the human system is not designed to contain so much heat but the aesthetician may nod his approval after overcoming the initial shock of incredulous surprise.

In another poem a woman deeply in love with Kṛṣṇa laments the inadequacy of her faculties to enjoy His qualities in the fullest measure. For when she looks at Him she wants all her other faculties to be turned into eyes so that she could see Him as He should be seen: similarly, when hearing the stories concerning Him she wants to be all ears (in the literal sense of the expression) and she desires ardently that all her other senses and organs to metamorphose into the mouth when conversing with Him. This is the stanza.

मुरारिं पश्यन्त्याः सखि सकलमङ्गं न नयनम्
कृतं यच्छृण्वत्या हरिगुणगणं श्रोत्रनिचितम् ।
समं तेनालापं सपदि रचयन्त्या मुखमयम्
विधातुर्नैवायं घटनपरिपाटीमधुरिमा ॥

It is not man only that can react excessively: God loves man more than man can ever love God: in His infinite compassion for suffering man and in His zeal to succour him, He makes His eyes which are the chief agency for the expression of compassion take over the functions of His other organs. As the first step in this process, Lord Raṅganātha's eyes have gone very far indeed in the direction of His ears—otherwise how explain His overly elongated eyes? The stanza is by Parāśara Bhaṭṭa, one of the most brilliant poets of the Tamil Vaiṣṇava school.

कृपया परया करिष्यमाणे
सकलाङ्गं किल सर्वतोऽक्षि नेत्रे ।

प्रथमं श्रवसी समास्तृणाते
इति वैध्र्येण विबन्ति रङ्गनेतुः ।।

[Raṅgarājastava I/98]

2.5. *Extraordinary displays of personal qualities*

Gods are brought in as characters in epic poems and plays and men of extraordinary valour, generosity and beauty of form like Raghu, Duṣyanta and Nala frequently appear as heroes. The verses in works of dramaturgy laying down the required qualities in heroes are utopian, they are just a list of all that is the brightest and the best without regard to either realism or even to the question whether such unrelieved goodness will make for good art: fortunately the greatest playwrights introduce some infirmity of character into their heroes' make-up to make them credible and interesting.

However it can be seen that in Sanskrit there are frequent occasions where characters are shown displaying extraordinary personal qualities. And with the known tendency of all eastern poets to hyperbole, we can expect larger-than-life portraits splashed in the brightest colours the poets can mix. Such displays evoke surprise from the ordinary reader on account of their unfamiliarity, even rarity, their falling outside the pale of everyday experience.

Let us go to the vēdas for the first examples of this category. These hymns of the vēdas—some of them composed by genuine poets—are full of the wonder of an unsophisticated people at the very dawn of human civilization: they are expressive of the wonder the ṛṣis felt at the extravagant displays of nature like lightning and thunder and hurricane which inspired them into an awed admiration laced with surprise: we can feel these qualities in some of the vedic hymns. In the second maṇḍala devoted to the hymns of the members of Ghṛtsamada's family we have a hymn devoted to Indra: the ṛṣi tells the people in awe and wonder how great and powerful Indra is. It was he who steadied the trembling earth, controlled the whimsical mountains and extended the heavens and supported them. "Know the mighty architect of all this, O people, to be Indra!" he expostulates. The mantra is this:

यः पृथिवीं व्यथमानामदृंहत्
यः पर्वतान्प्रकुपिताँ अरम्णात् ।

यो अन्तरिक्षं विममे वरीयो
यो द्यामस्तभ्नात् स वजनास इन्द्रः ॥ [II/12/2]

The ṛṣi seems to have had some apostates and doubting Thomases in his hand: he exclaims in surprised disgust, "People unaware of Indra's might and glory ask, 'Where is he?' Some even go to the length of denying his very existence. He is the destroyer of the armies, the cattle and the wealth of the enemy. Have faith in him, O people ! Realise he is Indra!"

यं स्मा पृच्छन्ति कुह सेति घोरम्
उतेमाहुर्नैषो अस्तीत्येनम् ।
सो अर्यः पुष्टीर्विज इवा मिनाति
श्रदस्मै धत्त स जनास इन्द्रः ॥ [II/12/5]

The hymns on hurricanes and heavy downpours of rain also contain very graphic descriptions of nature at her awesome best but they are not quoted from as there is a certain hesitancy in using the concept of personal qualities with regard to them: many of these deities like vāta are very imperfectly anthropomorphised and it is difficult to speak of personal qualities with regard to them. But despite this technical objection, they can be enjoyed by the painstaking reader with the aid of a good translation as evocatory of the sense of wonder.

From the vedas we have to step down to the story of Rāma: Rāma's sixteen wonderful qualities, difficult to find individually and impossible to find all coexisting in any other person are such as to evoke wonder. When Khara the lord of Janasthāna sends an army of fourteen thousand soldiers to crush Rāma, Rāma fights the army alone, commissioning Lakṣmaṇa to look after Sītā. But to the rākṣasas ranged against him, there arose an illusion that there were fourteen thousand Rāmas in the field each dealing with one-rākṣasa. This is the simple verse in Raghuvaṃśa reporting the wonderful exploit.

एको दाशरथिः कामम्
यातुधानाः सहस्रशः ।
ते तु यावन्त एवाजौ
तावांश्च ददृशे स तैः ॥ [XII/45]

Rāma's deceptively young and handsome frame conceals an astounding prowess. Paraśurāma who is generally portrayed as vain, boastful and impetuous in Rāma plays confesses at the end of a duel (in Mahâvīracarita) that he had been taken in by the delicate features of the young adversary: he was now witness to the most astounding act of valour of Rāma which was out of the earth: with a deep sense of wonder he lauds Rāma's feat of valour in a good stanza, succeeded by a prose passage where he uses the word āścaryam!

अप्राकृतस्य चरितातिशयस्य भावैः
अत्यद्भुतैर्मम हृतस्य तथाप्यनास्था ।
कोप्येष वीरशिशुकाकृतिरप्रमेयम्
माहात्म्यसारसमुदायमयः पदार्थः ॥ [II/39]

No human could have broken the Lord's bow and vanquished him, Paraśurāma. So he concludes he is incarnate God come down to succour the world.

त्रातुं लोकानिव परिणतः कायवानस्त्रवेदः
क्षात्रो धर्मः श्रित इव तनुं ब्रह्मकोशस्य गुप्त्यै ।
सामर्थ्यानामिव समुदयः सञ्चयो वा गुणानां
आविर्भूय स्थित इव जगत्पुण्यनिर्माणराशिः ॥ [II/14]

The element of surprise in these stanzas owes less to the undoubted valour of the prince and more to Paraśurāma's failure to recognise divinity face to face. The old warrior's present sense of wonder redeems him from the depth to which he had fallen, despising and insulting Rāma in a long passage of doubtful taste and even more doubtful poetic merit.

In the fifth Act of Uttararāmacarita, Candrakētu is shown registering shock and surprise at the incredible valour of Lava, the boy of the hermitage, who, single-handed, is able to contain the onslaught of Rāma's army: he uses the word āścaryam twice and during the course of the passage mouths the possibility that Lava may be a scion of the line of the Raghus and not the son of a hermit.

मुनिजनशिशुरेकः सर्वतः संप्रकोपात्
नव इव रघुवंशस्याप्रसिद्धप्ररोहः ।
दलितकरिकपोलग्रन्थिटंकारघोर-
ज्वलितशरसहस्रः कौतुकं मे करोति ॥ [V/3]

Rāma performs wonderful feats of valour in the field of battle in Laṅkā: at the height of his triumph, when Rāvaṇa stood deprived of his chariot and weapons, shorn of all his glory and at the mercy of his foe, Rāma does not mow him down as everyone expected him to do but sends him away graciously to recoup and report back in the field for a fresh duel in the morning. The great devotee of Viṣṇu and the first disciple of Rāmānuja, Srīvatsāṅka Miśra (better known as Kūratu Ālvār) becomes almost speechless with wonder at this quality of Rāma: indeed he declares he is unable to classify it properly or describe it adequately.

यत् तादृशागसमरिं रघुवीर वीक्ष्य
विश्रम्यतामिति मुमोचिथ मुग्धमाजौ ।
कोऽयं गुणः कतरकोटिगतः कियान् वा
कस्य स्तुतेः पदमहो बत कस्य भूमिः ॥

[Atimānuṣastava]

God's ineffable love and compassion for His devotees are dramatically brought out in many well-composed verses: one of them deals with Rāma's ready, even impetuous acceptance of Vibhīṣaṇa who forsakes his evil brother and seeks sanctuary with Rāma: this is by Rāmabhadra Dīkṣita, the well known author of play *Jānakipariṇaya*: the verse is in the *pṛthvi* metre which somehow captures the impetuous hurry of the decision.

अशोधितकुलक्रमं पुनरपृष्टजातिक्रियम्
नयानयविचारणाविधुरमस्तशङ्काकणम् ।
उपयुषि विभीषणे झटिति दत्तमस्याभयम्
मयेति समुदीरिता भगवतो गिरः पान्तु नः ॥

[Rāmastava Karṇarasāyana]

Similar is the impetuous haste of the Lord in rushing to the succour of the elephant Gajēndra which was losing the battle with a crocodile and clearly at the end of its tether. Venkatādhvarī the author of the *Visvagunādarśacampū* describes this in a memorable verse that is alive with the sense of hurry in every syllable:

लीलालोलतमां रमामगणयन् नीलामनालोकयन्
मुञ्चन् किंच महीमहीश्वरमयं मञ्चं हठाद्वञ्चयन् ।
आकर्षन् द्विजराजमप्यतिजवाद्धा हन्त लोकान्तरात्
गोप्तुं शौरिरुदित्वरत्वर उदैत् ग्राहग्रहार्तं गजम् ॥ [2/18]

In similar manner the Lord's descent as half-lion, half-man to save His great devotee Prahlāda from his father gets balladized by the same poet who presents in it a quaint reason for God's unusual appearance.

वैकुण्ठो महताहताखिलमहारम्भं मदेनोच्चकैः
चण्डं खण्डयितुं हिरण्यकशिपुं वेतण्डमुत्कण्ठया ।
सैंहं वेषमशेष भीषणमहो गृह्णन् त्वरागौरवात्
प्रह्लादव्यसनासहिष्णुरुदगादाकंण्ठकण्ठीरवः ॥ [2/19]

The precipitous descent of the Lord to succour a devotee stimulates the reverent wonder of Parāśara Bhaṭṭa: his poetic effusion breathes the very nervous hurry of the Lord in memorable words set to the appropriate metre, the *pṛthvi*:

अतन्द्रितचमूपतिप्रहितहस्तमस्वीकृत—
प्रणीतमणिपादुकं किमिति चाकुलान्तःपुरम् ।
अवाहनपरिष्क्रियं पतगराजमारोहतः
करिप्रवरबृंहिते भगवतस्त्वरायै नमः ॥

[Raṅgarājastava II/57]

There is a hymn to Lord Śiva called Śivamahimnastōtra celebrated for its bold, original concepts and its verbal felicity: the work is ascribed to a gandharva called Puṣpadanta. In one of the stanzas in it, the cosmic dance of the Lord is described in ecstatic language and the cataclysmic effects it is bound to have on matter in all the universe anticipated with an escalating sense of wonder. Let us savour the fine piece.

मही पादाघाताद्व्रजति सहसा संशयपदम्
पदं विष्णोर्भ्राम्यद्भुजपरिघरुग्णग्रहगणम् ।
मुहुर्द्यौर्दौःस्थ्यं यात्यनिभृतजटाताडितजटा
जगद्रक्षायै त्वं नटसि ननु वामैव विभुता ॥ [16]

The epics in Sanskrit fairly teem with semi-divine beings and gifted men like Arjuna, Karṇa, Duṣyanta: Sanskrit poets love to paint characters larger-than-life making them even larger in the process. Hence, surely, this category must be the most prolific among all the excitants of wonder we shall be considering.

2.6 *Exorbitant claims*

Many people we meet display a tendency to make exorbitant claims about their personal achievements. To many, the little things they or their children do, the insignificant features of their village, town or district appear big enough to boast of: to some even their diseases, their problems appear inflated and have to be bragged about. But, when this boast steps out of the realms of probability, it evokes surprise.

A Texan came to me and said, "We Texans are given to exaggeration: we are all terrible liars. People must have told you a Texan mosquito can carry you, bed and all away to a distant place: it is obviously untrue, it is a typical Texan exaggeration. Actually two Texan mosquitos are needed to fly away with a person, bed and all". Even the highly balanced version of this Texan has a marginal exaggeration which causes a certain amount of surprise. Literature is full of examples of this foible.

Kālidāsa presents Madana the god of love as a boastful person inclined to make exorbitant personal claims: there is a purpose to this, for Madana wants to ingratiate himself into Indra's favour by promising the impossible. Kālidāsa achieves several objectives through this passage: he paints Manmatha, god of love as over-confident and apt to think lightly of the terrible dangers that lie await in the path he has chosen to tread: then by showing that this god gets reduced to ashes by the Lord, he paints up the greatness of his hero.

Moreover, his epic poem is a tale of love and it is an excellent poetic device to portray the omnipotence of the god of love, even if it be in his own unbridled words. And the fact that he does indeed subjugate the redoubtable Śiva for a moment making the poet exclaim in surprised disbelief,

हरस्तु किंचिद् परिलुप्तधैर्यः
चन्द्रोदयारम्भ इवाम्बुराशिः ।
उमामुखे बिम्बफलाधरोष्ठे
व्यापारयामास विलोचनानि ॥

[Kumārasambhava, III/67]

shows that cupid's claims were not wholly hollow but had a substratum of truth.

But to the reader reading canto III for the first time, the claims of Madana evoke surprise at their unrestrained extravagance. In one of the stanzas (III/6) he claims he can corrupt any person even if that person has received instruction at the feet of the great moralist Uśanas, by making him feel deeply the pangs of love. In another (III/9) he advises Indra to retire his weapon the *vajra*, claiming that he can annul the animus of his adversaries by making them fear the anger of helpless women for whom they will have developed an overwhelming passion.

Rising to a crescendo, his claims now involve Lord Śiva Himself: Śiva's two qualities—his self-control in matters of the heart and his fiery temper are both well known. Despite this and despite the fact that cupid wields such seemingly fragile weapons as flowers for arrows and has only the spring season as his ally, he now claims he can agitate the mind of Hara Himself. The verse may be enjoyed here:

तव प्रसादात्कुसुमायुधोऽपि
    सहायमेकं मधुमेव लब्ध्वा ।
कुर्यां हरस्यापि पिनाकपाणेः
    धैर्यच्युतिं के मम धन्विनोऽन्ये ॥ [III/10]

Among the four classes of heroes type-cast in the works on dramaturgy, the dhīrōddhata is given to making exorbitant personal claims. He is by definition an egotist, a haughty, opinionated person, much given to singing his own praise according to Daśarūpaka:

दर्पमात्सर्यभूयिष्ठो मायाच्छद्मपरायणः ।
    धीरोद्धतस्त्वहंकारी चलश्चण्डो विकत्थनः ॥

[Daśarūpaka II/5]

Examples of this type are Bhīma, Duryōdhana and Aśvatthāman in Vēnīsamhāra, Paraśurāma in all the Rāma plays and Rāvaṇa, above everyone else. Playwrights fulfil themselves by portraying these characters in the loudest colours they can call to their aid. In addition, there was the well-established custom in those days of heroes indulging in a session of *viravāda* as a preliminary flexing of muscles, during which a good deal of tall claims was indulged in.

Only one instance will be cited here as a specimen of this kind of writing. It is taken from the *Āścaryacūḍāmaṇi* where the eagle, Jaṭāyus discovers Rāvaṇa taking away Sītā, the daughter-in-law of his intimate friend, Daśaratha; Jaṭāyus now flings a *viravāda* at the kidnapper, which is reproduced below:

वक्त्राण्येतानि तेऽद्य प्रलयघनरुचः पिङ्गकेशानि रोषात्
    भृङ्गाणीवाञ्जनाद्रेर्दवदहनशिखादीपितानीव रात्रौ ।
उत्कृत्योत्कृत्य चञ्च्वा झटझटिति गलत्सांद्ररक्तारुणानि
    प्रत्यक्षं क्षत्रियायाः दश दशशु दशग्रीव दिक्षु क्षिपामि ॥ [IV/II]

It may be noticed that the poet has succeeded in producing the intended impact of a terrible threat, through the selection of an appropriately involved metre and the prolific use of the harshest-sounding letters in the Sanskrit alphabet.

Let us end this section with the strident words of self-praise from Rāvaṇa, the king of all the braggarts. When the adverse happenings engineered by Rāma were hesitantly pointed out by the devoted wife Mandōdarī (in Bhavabhuti's Mahāvīracarita) Rāvaṇa's soaring ego goes lovingly over his past exploits of endurance and religious zeal in one and the valour of his arms in another notable stanza which are worth reproducing here.

उत्पुष्यत्गालधननिस्फुटप्रसर्पत्-
प्रत्यग्रक्षतजझरीनिवृत्तपाद्यः ।
हर्षाश्रुप्रचुरमधुस्मितस्फुट श्री-
वक्त्राब्जार्चितचरणः शिवः प्रमाणम् ॥ [VI/14]

श्रुतं मे जानाति श्रुतिकविरथाज्ञां सहचरः
स शच्या धैर्यं चाशनिरथ यशोऽदस्त्रिभुवनम् ।
बलं कैलासाद्रिः किमपरमहो साहसमपि
क्षरत्कीलालाभ्यःस्नपितचरणः खण्डपरशुः ॥ [VI/15]

The first thing to be noted in regard to both the verses is that the claims made therein are wholly true and in that sense do not deserve to be labelled exorbitant: but it takes a braggart constantly to remind his nearest of his own exploits: it is wholly out of taste and it reveals the protruding ego of the speaker.

The earlier poem, set in the less common praharshini metre presents a sonic reproduction of the rhythmic gushing of blood from the severed blood vessels of the tough-minded votary in his gruesome worship of his favourite deity.

In all these cases, the boastful claims will normally induce an amused incredulity and not wonder if they emanate from the mouths of ordinary persons. But the calibre and the known history of the actual achievements of characters like Paraśurāma and Rāvaṇa lend a certain credibility to them, making the reader sit up and take notice, impressed in spite of himself. It is the quality of these characters that enables these claims to overleap the walls of disbelief to turn on the gushing fountain of wonder in the reader's mind.

2.7 *A new twist to an old concept*

In an old civilization like India's there is bound to be a large body of axioms, moral aphorisms, social concepts, myths and legends, the meaning of which is widely known in the society, even to the unlettered. Poets can recycle these to yield a startlingly different meaning which does not, however, appear preposterous. In such cases there is a quality of unexpectedness, often a downright cheekiness, a rebellious radicality about the twist, that is very much intended by the author, that evokes instant surprise.

Let us see some examples. "When a child asks difficult questions, invention is the necessity of Mother"—this involves only the physical redistribution of the words of the proverb "necessity is the mother of invention" but this redistribution of words gives a new twist to the meaning, in fact a different meaning altogether.

"Jane" moaned her husband, "You promised you wouldn't buy another new dress. What made you do it?"

"Dear", she replied, "the devil tempted me".

"Why didn't you say: 'Get thee behind me, Satan?" her husband enquired.

"I did," the woman replied sweetly, "and then he whispered over my shoulder: 'My dear, it fits you just beautifully at the back'."

Nīlakaṇṭha Dīkṣita, the later-day humorist poses the questions, "Why are the Gods respected? What is the factor which makes them popular?" and replies pointing to a factor missed by all the wordy theologists—that it is the fact that they are rich that makes them universally respected, their prosperity being a thing that is admitted in the Scriptures, though not quite in the way the Dīksita presents it.

लक्ष्मीश इति गोविन्दो मेरुधन्वेति शङ्करः ।
हिरण्यगर्भ इत्येव ब्रह्मापि बहु मन्यते ॥ [Sabhārañjana śataka 90]

Dress is obviously all important as a factor lending social acceptability, even status. This is proved by the way the Ocean solved his problem: he had a beautiful daughter called Lakṣmī to marry off, he also had a terrible poison to get rid of. He found Lord Nārāyaṇa well dressed, in yellow silk and gave his daughter in marriage to him. Lord Śiva then hove into view with his raw hide garment and without any compunction the Ocean gave him the poison. This plausible-looking story is the result of the turning of an old *purāṇic* legend inside out and it serves as an excellent example of this category.

किं वाससा तत्र विचारणीयम्
वासः प्रधानं खलु योग्यतायाः ।
तीताम्बरं वीक्ष्य ददौ स्वकन्याम्
चर्माम्बरं वीक्ष्य विषं समुद्रः ॥

[Subhāṣitaratnabhāṇḍāgāra, 180/888]

There are innumerable stanzas in Sanskrit which have found their way into the many anthologies of aphoristic verse where old legends and myths are given a new twist. Śiva's poverty is a recurrent theme: only three verses out of the many are quoted as specimens from the Subhāṣitaratnabhāṇḍāgāra:

को नाम नानुवृत्तिं सुमहानपि धनवतः कुरुते ।
वित्तेश भवनभित्तेः समीपमुपसेवते शम्भुः ॥ [धनिप्रशंसा, 68/7]

न विद्यया नैव कुलेन गौरवं
जनानुरागो धनिकेषु सर्वदा ।
कपालिना मौलिधृतापि जाह्नवी
प्रयाति रत्नाकरमेव सत्वरम् ॥ [धनिप्रशंसा, 68/12]

वासश्चर्म विभूषणं शवशिरो भस्माङ्गलेपः सदा
ह्येको गौः स च लाङ्गलाद्यकुशलः संपत्तिरेतादृशी ।
इत्यालोच्य विमुच्य शंकरमगाद्रत्नाकरं जाह्नवी
कष्टं निर्धनिकस्य जीवितमहो दारैरपि त्यज्यते ॥ [71/76]

Correspondingly Nārāyaṇa as the husband of Lakṣmī, Goddess of Wealth comes in for laudatory mention as a person of means with the customary supercilious indifference of the rich to the sufferings of others.

लक्ष्मीवन्तो न जानन्ति
प्रायेण परवेदनाम् ।
शेषे धराभरक्लान्ते
शेते नारायणः सुखम् ॥

[Subhāṣitaratnabhāṇḍāgāra, 67/2]

Rivers go down to mix with the sea as a natural phenomenon. The serpent Śeṣa is believed to hold up the earth on his hood.

All these separate facts are twisted to yield the result desired by the poet—which was to show that rich people are indifferent to the sufferings of others and the poor receive bad treatment from everyone, even from their wives. To a society steeped in the myths, these twisted interpretations will engender surprise.

2.8 *An arrestingly different principle developed—radically different from popular concepts*

We find sometimes—such instances are not unfortunately too common—a new principle is derived or freshly developed with brilliance (and not with mere sophistry) taking off from a widely known concept: it is startlingly different from popularly held ideas, in quite a few cases it is just the opposite of these: but the listener or reader has no difficulty in appreciating the reasonableness of the new proposition, after an initial threshold period of shock and wonder. Thus, in proportion to its variance from popular concept it evokes the sense of wonder as an initial reaction before acceptance by the listener or reader: and, though instances of this category are not common in life, they are to be found in numbers in the writings of gifted poets and playwrights.

This category should be distinguished from the previous one from two standpoints. One is that all the cases classifiable under the earlier one are those where there is a definite contrived attempt to twist an old concept to yield a bright new significance which is not necessarily an addition to the sum total of the world's knowledge. A second feature is that the old concept is not necessarily rendered untrue and replaced by the new: often, the old idea still continues to reign, the new being only a whimsically contrived product forged to dazzle and surprise.

This category is thus substantially different: the new idea is expected to reign supreme, quite replacing the old. And clearly there is no contrived attempt here at twisting an old concept, it is not a case of recycling but of inspired creation.

We may examine a few modern examples before we enter the domain of Sanskrit literature. Thoreau asked, anticipating today's anti-pollutionists, "What is the use of a house if you haven't got a tolerable planet to put it on?" replacing forever the old concept of the individual being regarded as a self-sufficient unit with the much broader one of interdependence.

"A person who knows no fear has no imagination" suggests

the new idea that fear is not all that bad, that fear is the penalty we pay for having a lively imagination.

The great philosopher J. Kṛṣṇamūrty (who died recently) contributed this: "when our hearts are empty, we collect things." Not only those who collect china or stamps have empty hearts: those who love to gather money, who spend their lives adding to a growing store of wealth have empty loveless hearts.

"One of the most difficult things to give away is kindness—it is usually returned"; Harry Truman's "It is what you learn after you know it all that really counts"; "The time to relax is when you don't have time for it"; "Love is an egotism of two"; "If you realise that you aren't as wise today as you thought you were yesterday, you are wiser today"; "Love endures only when the lovers love many things together and not merely each other"; "True courage is not only a balloon for rising but also a parachute for falling"; "peace comes not from the absence of conflict in life but from the ability to cope with it"; "The important thing in life is not belongings but belonging" and "Growth for the sake of growth is the ideology of the cancer cell" are all good illustrations of this category where an arresting new idea replaces the old from which it sprang.

Sanskrit literature fairly bristles with examples: the one that comes most readily to the mind is the statement Kālidāsa makes in the Mēghadūta, on which the greatest critics of the west and east have showered tributes as representing "a higher morality": this is in justification of the yaksha's decision to request a passing cloud to carry his message to his wife.

याच्ञा मोघा वरमधिगुणे नाधमे लब्धकामा ।

[Pūrvamēgha 6]

Kālidāsa's doctrine advocates the making of requests only to the noble-minded: for, even where they are not in a position to grant the request, they will try their hardest to help the suppliant in other ways: in any case, there is no possibility of harm coming to him as a result. If, on the other hand, a request is made of the wicked, it may even be granted: but experience teaches us that they invariably exploit the suppliant, laying him under their debt forever: they often expect him to help them in their evil designs, thus leading him down the road to moral degradation. This, of course, is directly at variance with the universally held belief that requests should be made only where they are likely to be granted, without regard to the character of the potentate approached: and consequently it evokes surprise.

Kālidāsa had this rarest quality of examining popular concepts deeply and coming out with variations which shock and surprise the routine-minded reader. But again, as an instinctive poet he was able to fight against the temptation to introduce contrariness for its own sake, merely for the shock it provides the unwary reader without regard to the question whether it is in accord with human experience. Not many even among the acknowledged masters possess this quality. Kālidāsa provides another excellent example of this category in the Vikramōrvaśīya: in Act II, when Urvaśī's maid reports her mistress's love-sickness to the king, the king replies to her pointing out that he too suffers on the same account, adding a generalisation that such suffering is universally common to all lovers: he then soars to wonderful heights making the startling observation that if love triumphs at the end it is on account of this suffering which melts the hearts of the lovers which can now get securely welded together.

पर्युत्सुकां कथयसि प्रियदर्शनां ताम्
आर्तं न पश्यसि पुरूरवसं तदर्थे ।
साधारणोऽयमुभयोः प्रणयः स्मरस्य
तप्तेन तप्तमयसा घटनाय योग्यम् ॥ [II 16]

After the factual observation that the maid has only eyes to notice Urvaśī's suffering and that she cannot see how he himself is tormented by the same love-disease, the king permits himself a general observation that as love should be mutual (otherwise it will be one-sided and is not classifiable as love at all), suffering also should visit both the parties involved. For most poets this would be the ultimate in mentation and they would have stopped there with a sense of triumph. But not Kālidāsa, who now takes, not a mere step, but quite a leap forward. For he makes the king say, "This suffering that is the lot of lovers everywhere plays a vital role in consummating the love. For, if two pieces of iron have to be soldered, they both have to be heated to a very high temperature."

The analogy is wonderfully apt, as it always is with Kālidāsa: but apart from the metaphor, the generalised concept suggested here is a strikingly original contribution to the world content of thought on the theme of love. For, where others have thought lovers got united at the end despite their suffering, the master affirms that only on account of their anguish does their love get requited ! This suffering is not something that poets add to make their work deep and artistically satisfying (though it does perform these services); in the thinking of the king of poets, this anguish becomes an indispensable agency that unites the hearts by burning up, as it were, their divisive individuality, by breaking up the separating barriers, by pulverising their little suspicions and selfishnesses: this suffering moulds them into a homogeneous togetherness. And who will dispute that this revolutionary new message is better learnt by the spectator on account of the shock of surprise with which it is passed on.

An unusual idea (similar to that used by Kālidāsa in his Meghadūta) has been pressed into commission by the poet Bhāravi in his *Kirātārjuniya.* Yudhiṣthira deputes a certain forest-dweller to find out and report to him the activities of Duryōdhana. The latter performs his task with thoroughness and in his extended report he describes how the villainous Duryōdhana is trying hard to earn a good name among his people by doing good acts. He adds a generalisation that friendship with the bad should be avoided: one should have relations only with the good: he then adds a startling note that these relations with the good may sometimes sour but even then, we should continue to deal only with the good, even enmity with the good being far preferable to fiiendship with the wicked:

तथापि जिह्मः स भवज्जिगीषया
तनोति शुभ्रं गुणसंपदा यशः ।
समुन्नयन् भूतिमनार्यसंगमात्
वरं विरोधोऽपि समं महात्मभिः ॥ [I/8]

Parāśara Bhaṭṭa to whom we have already referred was a highly gifted, innovative religious poet who devoted his very short life to the worship of Lord Raṅganātha of *Śrīraṅga.* In his hymn on his favourite deity, he has sculptored a stanza that, for sheer innovative brilliance, stands unrivalled in the entire range of devotional literature. He says, "Lord; you did show your compassion when dealing with villainous people like Kākāsura and Śiśupāla: but as they had certain good qualities too, co-existing with the bad your compassion had a certain difficulty in entering and engulfing them. In my case, there can be no such obstacle in the shape of good qualities impeding the course of your compassion which can therefore flow with ease and engulf me !"

बलिभुजि शिशुपाले तादृगागस्करे वा
गुणलवसहवासात्त्वत्क्षमा संकुचन्ती ।
मयि गुणपरमाणूवन्तचिन्तानभिज्ञे
विहरतु वरदासौ सर्वदा सार्वभौमी ॥

[Raṅgarājastava II/97]

The popular understanding of the nature of compassion is blown to smithereens by Bhaṭṭa in this. Everybody naturally believes that God would find it easier to show His compassion in the case of those with predominantly good qualities than in the case of thorough-bred rascals. Bhaṭṭa says just the opposite—and what a wonderfully gracious significance it reveals—and how much in accord it is with God's intentions in so far as we can know them ! Compassion, according to this gifted minstrel is of a most unusual nature, coming to play not where there are plenty of good qualities but where there is a lack of them: it is a very special device in God's hands with which He is able to welcome the most wicked, the totally lost, the irredeemable. It is of less relevance in the case of good people and is totally useless when dealing with the truly saintly.

So, for God's compassion bad qualities act like a magnet, attracting it to them: and, by the same token good qualities must act as a repellant driving it away. Normal people have a mixture of good and bad qualities: God's compassion, attracted by the bad traits in them, however, gets impeded in its flow into them by the presence of the good traits in them. In the case of the unmitigatedly wicked, the gates of the heart are wide open and compassion can dance its way merrily in, with none to question.

The present writer has found that this verse used in the course of lectures has an electrifying effect on the brightest members of the audience and a puzzling effect on the others and he even feels it can be used to divide people into different grades of intelligence without the aid of elaborate intelligence tests. But there is no doubt at all that all the sections of all audiences were shocked and surprised at this daring innovation—which becomes not only quickly acceptable but quite elevating to the more gifted among them on account of the wonderful way it explains the laws and the priorities of God.

Vedânta Deśika composed a hymn of a hundred verses on God's quality of compassion: in some of them he presents brilliant new viewpoints that surprise the reader initially but eventually get accepted by him on account of the deep insight they help him to have concerning religion and the ways of God and the relationship between Him and man. In one of the initial verses he says that though God has many great qualities, most of them, in fact, like His erudition, His valour are more to be regarded as defects: the reason is that God has assumed these qualities only to be able to attract man to the right path and help him to find and reach Him: and these very noble qualities of His are actually forbiddingly great in the eyes of ordinary men who are most likely to shy away from them. Thus these divine traits are in reality functioning as defects in so far as fulfilling His intentions. But the presence of the single quality of compassion among them redeems all of them, making them function as good traits attracting man to God. The verse is simple and direct:

वृषगिरिगृहमेधिगुणाः
बोधबलैश्वर्यवीर्यशक्तिमुखाः ।
दोषा भवेयुरेते
यदि नाम दये त्वया विनाभूताः ॥

[Dayāśataka 15]

Now Deśika goes ahead to present a wonderfully egalitarian dispensation provided by the Lord's compassion levelling Him down to be on the same level with the humblest of His devotees who are levelled up by the same quality. He furnishes, a list of three devotess in Rāmāyaṇa, the hunter Guha, Sugrīva, the monkey chief and Śabarī, the huntress and likewise four from the Bhāgavata similarly humble and low-placed, like the penurious Kucēla, the deformed dispenser of perfumes, the unsophisticated cowherdesses of Nandavraja and the flowerseller of Kamsa's capital. Now all these received in abundant mesure the grace of the Lord sitting in His unscalable heights in Tirupati hills. What is the result? The result is the same as is seen after severe floods over terrain full of ups and downs: the land now appears level, the ups having disappeared along with the downs. In fact the earth from the ups has been carried by the floodwaters to fill the downs. In a similar way, the gaping difference in level between God and man is totally destroyed when His compassion begins to flow, the blessed devotee enjoying an equality of level with Almighty God. This is the well-composed verse in Dayāśataka.

निषादानां नेता कपिकुलपतिः काऽपि शबरी
कुचेलः कुब्जा सा व्रजयुवतयो माल्यकृदिति ।
अमीषां निम्नत्वं वृषगिरिपतेरुन्नतिमपि
प्रभूतैः स्रोतोभिः प्रसभमनुकम्पे समयसि ॥

[Dayāśataka 65]

Another arresting new idea has been presented by Nīlakaṇṭha Dīkṣita in his Śāntivilāsa. Experience tells us and the biographies of great men confirm that usually a long apprenticeship is needed for success in any field: and as the pursuit of the spiritual goal which is emancipation of the soul is admittedly the toughest of all human endeavours one would expect it would need efforts sustained over a very long period, perhaps several life-times. There are clear statements confirming this in the Hindu works on philosophy and religion: the Bhagavadgītā specifically states that a person attains to Godhead after several lifetimes of hard spiritual endeavour.

But Dīkṣita points out that it need not necessarily be so, in every case: for, if the quality of spiritual practice is of the highest and the dedication of the practitioner total, he can achieve emancipation even in a matter of a few minutes, as the famous king Khaṭvāṅga did. Doubting Thomases without faith, even though blessed with a long life may not accomplish anything: the criterion here is not the duration of the spiritual endeavour; it is the extent of sincere dedication that counts. This radical idea has been worked into a lovely, well-constructed verse, worth quoting:

यस्त्वत्यन्तव्यवसितमतिः संजिघृक्षेत धर्मम्
खट्वाङ्गदेरिव न किमलं तस्य यामार्धमायुः ।
दुष्पाण्डित्यादपहृतमतिः यः पुनः संशयात्मा
कस्मै तस्य प्रभवतु वृथा काकवद्दीर्घमायुः ॥

[Śāntivilāsa 34]

2.9 *An unexpected sequel to a step taken*

When a step is taken to achieve a certain purpose and the sequel is very different, even opposite to what was intended (in some cases), the unexpectedness fuels a charge of surprise: the greater the variance of the sequel from what was expected, the greater is likely to be the quantum of surprise.

This is a prolific category and examples abound in Sanskrit literature. Kālidāsa unfolds the tragedy of Indumatī's sudden death on a garland of divine flowers falling on her from Nārada's lute. A garland of flowers does not look a killer and Aja, the bereaved husband, reeling under the shock, asks pathetically why the same garland does not kill him when placed on his own chest:

स्रगियं यदि जीवितापहा
हृदये किं निहिता न हन्ति माम् ।
विषमप्यमृतं क्वचिद्भवेत्
अमृतं वा विषमीश्वरेच्छया ॥

[Raghuvaṁśa VIII/46]

The explanation is, of course, that owing to that ubiquitous and uniquely Indian institution of a sage's curse, Indumatī was destined to live on the earth as a human till she came into contact with divine flowers on which she would leave the earth to resume her place among the divine dancers. This is revealed to Aja and to the readers only at the end of the canto: and the falling of the divine wreath having the totally unexpected sequel of killing the queen must cause a good deal of surprise.

Rāvaṇa tried to lift the Kailāsa mountain for reasons that had to do with his Himālayan ego: it was not clearly an act calculated to propitiate the Lord. And, as a matter of fact the first reactions on the denizens of the mountain are wholly adverse, as is evident from the graphic picture painted by Sri Harṣa in his Priyadarśikā. But Pārvatī, rattled at the sudden quaking of the hitherto solid mountain impulsively embraces her lord, affording Him considerable pleasure, the more so as the embrace was wholly unexpected. Sri Harṣa is a competent versifier rather than an inspired poet and his compositions are always musical and superficially pleasing: this verse is a good example of his craftsmanship.

कैलासाद्रावुदस्ते परिचलति गणेषूल्लसत्कौतुकेषु
क्रोडं मातुः कुमारे विशति विषमुचि प्रेक्षमाणे सरोषम् ।
पादावष्टम्भसीदद्वपुषि दशमुखे याति पातालमूलम्
क्रुद्धोऽप्याश्लिष्टमूर्तिर्भयघनमुमया पातु तुष्टः शिवो वः ॥

[Priyadarśikā I/1]

Ascetics living in the forests create and sustain an atmosphere of love and compassion for all living things. However, kindness may go too far and advantage may be taken even by notoriously timid animals like the deer whose fear of man has been banished totally. When the wives of the ascetics keep rice spread on a plate as an offering to the gods, they discover that the deer had been at it in their absence: and worse still, a deer is noticed still lunching on it in total disdain of the women. The annoyed women take up a stick to drive it away: but such is the total absence of fear among them, the deer thrusts its muzzle to smell the brandished stick exploratorily, to find out if that too is edible. The women are exasperated and the ascetics who look on the scene are amused. This is the scene of idyllic peace as described by Lakṣmaṇa in Murāri's Anargharāghava.

बालेयतण्डुलविलोपकदर्थिताभिः
एताभिरग्निशरणेषु सधर्मिणीभिः ।
तत्त्रसहेतुमपि दण्डमुदस्यमानम्
आघ्रातुमिच्छति मृगे मुनयो हसन्ति ॥ [II/20]

In Indian literary tradition, woman seldom strays from the narrow path of virtue but man often does: and, when he is caught and punished by the offended wife, we should expect the former to be properly penitent and the latter, triumphant. The punishment, indeed, is intended to show to the philanderer that transgression does not pay. But in a poem from the immortal Amaru, we have quite the opposite sequel: the wife cries while she beats the husband, himself wreathed in smiles ! The poem is exquisite and should be rolled about in the tongue.

कोपात्कोमललोलबाहुलतिकापाशेन बद्ध्वा दृढम्
नीत्वा वासनिकेतनं दयितया सायं सखीनां पुरः ।
भूयोप्येवमिति स्खलन्मृदुगिरा संसूच्य दुश्चेष्टितम्
धन्यो हन्यत एव निह्नुतिपरः प्रेयान्रुदत्या हसन् ॥ [9]

The overwrought lady tells him during the beating, "Do not let this happen again !" Nothing in the expression or the behaviour of the lothario could have afforded much hope to the wronged woman, however: for the rogue is cheerfully unrepentant: most of Amaru's heroes will be found to have broken many of the scriptural commandments but all of them are charming, charismatic to a degree.

Amaru has a hero in another stanza who perhaps on account of a minor transgression has earned the anger of his lady. She quarrels with him and is not disposed to talk to him: provocatively she talks to her girl-friend when he is around. But since her anger is quite mild, she does not remove her feet when he is clearly about to fall at them seeking her pardon: on the other hand, she covers them with the end of her saree. She avoids looking at him and when the memory of a witty remark made by him earlier provokes her to a smile she conceals it with an effort. "It is not only the loving, affectionate relationship with her that is lovely to experience: even tiffs of this type are indeed delightful !"

आशंक्य प्रणतिं पटान्तपिहितौ पादौ करोत्यादरात्
व्याजेनागतमावृणोति हसितं न स्पृष्टमुद्वीक्षते ।
मय्यालापवति प्रतीपवचनं संख्या सहा भाषते
तोन्व्यास्तिष्ठतु निर्भरप्रणयिता मानोऽपिरम्योदयः ॥ [47]

This is married love: premarital love differs in some essential aspects from that after marriage: for one thing, the lover at the premarital stage looks a very different proposition from the strident, self-confident male apt to transgress the moral law with impunity: he is diffident, unsure of himself and feels unwell and sighs a great deal. The reign of the god of love is supreme and this delicate subtle feeling called love lays the lover low, destroys his courage. So ruminates Makaranda, observing Mādhava closely, after he had been smitten with love for Mālatī. All this surely was not intended or even anticipated when love had begun to sprout.

There is a similar poem in Tamil declaring that the fiery warrior of many battlefields has been rendered timid, diffident, his valour and courage now a thing of the past, all the result of his meeting the doe-eyed maiden from the hamlet on the hill. This is the Sanskrit verse:

गमनमलसं शून्या दृष्टिः शरीरमसौष्ठवम्
श्वसितमधिकं किं त्वेतत्स्यात् किमन्यदितोऽथवा ।

भ्रमति भुवने कन्दर्पाज्ञा विकारि च यौवनम्
ललितमधुरास्ते ते भावाः क्षिपन्ति च धीरताम् ॥
[Mālatīmādhava I/20]

The spring season is a pleasant time of the year with its special musical effects in the shape of bird music and the cool southern breeze blowing: these however prove extremely painful to those afflicted by the pangs of separation. Not only nature's agencies but the well-meant efforts of maids and servants to help these unhappy people prove counter-productive: sandal paste feels hot and lotus stalks irksome. This is a familiar traditional concept in India made use of by all the poets, major and minor inclusive of Kālidāsa (Śākuntala III/3). Let us savour in passing a verse from Bhartṛhari's Śṛṅgāraśataka.

मधुरयं मधुरैरपि कोकिला–
कलरवैर्मलयस्य च वायुभिः ।
विरहिणः प्रहिणस्ति शरीरिणो
विपदि हन्त सुधापि विषायते ॥ [82]

The same composer of popular aphorisms has a good stanza on the unique conduct of noble people whose action bears the opposite kind of fruit from the one which people would expect from it.

नम्रत्वेनोन्नमन्तः परगुणक थनैः स्वान् गुणान् ख्यापयन्तः
स्वार्थान्संपादयन्तो विततपृथुतरारम्भयत्नाः परार्थे ।
क्षान्त्यैवाक्षेपरूक्षाक्षरमुखरमुखान् दुर्मुखान् दूषयन्तः
सन्तःसाश्चर्यचर्याः जगति बहुमताः कस्य नाभ्यर्चनीयाः ॥ [Niti 60]

There is another *niti* verse from an unknown writer which also sings of the quaint way the good react to prosperity which does not have the effect it usually has on the worldly.

अहो किमपि चित्राणि चरित्राणि महात्मनाम् ।
लक्ष्मीं तृणाय मन्यन्ते तद्भरेण नमन्त्यपि ॥
[Subhāṣitaratna bhāṇḍāgāra, Page 46, Sajjana praśamsā]

A fine example of a wholly unexpected sequel to a step taken causing delighted surprise, though this sequel is fully explicable in the light of Indian literary tradition is furnished by an unknown poet. He describes the efforts of a high-born maiden at gathering flowers from an *aśoka* tree. Finding some blossoms in the lowest branch of the tree she gathered them without effort: then, as she needed some more, she decided to climb up on the lowest branch so as to reach an upper branch. But the moment she stepped on the lowest branch, she discovered, to her joy, that the same branch, totally bereft of any bloom, not moments before, had suddenly put on fresh flowers again. She did not therefore have to reach up to the upper branches after all—but how did this miracle happen? This sudden efflorescence is in full conformity with Indian literary tradition according to which an *aśoka* tree blooms when kicked by a high-born damsel. But even those steeped in tradition would have experienced a flash of surprise at this quick service afforded by the *aśoka* tree, the way the stanza has been composed.

उच्चित्य प्रथममधःस्थितं मृगाक्षी
पुष्पौघं श्रितविटपं गृहीतुकामा ।
आरोढुं पदमदधादशोकयष्टौ
आमूलं पुनरपि तेन पुष्पिताऽभूत् ॥

[Kuvalayānanda N.S. Edition, page 140]

We shall now enjoy two stanzas from the pen of unknown poets, anthologised in the Subhāṣitaratnabhāṇḍāgāra. Marriage is a state to which lovers rush with rosy visions of unmitigated bliss: but in the sequel, it may not prove blissful at all, it may turn out to be quite irksome—not only to mortal man but even to the highest of the immortals, to the Hindu Trinity, even! This is recounted in one of them.

शंभुस्वयंभुहरयो हरिणे क्षणानाम्
येनाक्रियन्त सततं गृहकर्मदासाः ।
वाचामगोचरचरित्रविचित्रिताय
तस्मै नमो भगवते कुसुमायुधाय ॥ [262/12]

The second stanza which will occasion more than a modicum of surprise is about the reaction of a thief who inadvertently enters a very poor house: the travails of the family so move the burglar that he departs presenting the family with what he has taken from another house!

वासःखण्डमिदं प्रयच्छ यदि वा स्वाङ्के गृहाणार्भकम्
रिक्तं भूतलमत्र नाथ भवतः पृष्ठे पलालोच्चयः ।
दम्पत्योरिति जल्पितं निशि यदा चोरः प्रविष्टस्तदा
लब्धं कर्पटमन्यतस्तदुपरि क्षिप्त्वा रुदन्निर्गतः ॥ [70/63]

In the field of religion, too, such unexpected sequels are met with, Śaṅkarācārya (if, indeed, he is the author of the hymn Saundaryalaharī) sings exquisitely of the contrary effects of nectar and poison, respectively on the devas and on Lord Śiva, putting down the latter effect to Goddess Pārvatī wearing a pair of ear ornaments, the traditional symbol of a woman whose husband lives long.

सुधामप्यास्वाद्य प्रतिभयजरामृत्युहरिणीम्
विपद्यन्ते विश्वे विधिशतमखाद्या दिविषदः ।
करालं यत्क्ष्वेलं कबलितवतः कालकलना
न शम्भोस्तन्मूलं तव जननि ताटङ्कमहिमा ॥
[Saundaryalaharī 68]

In another, Kṛṣṇa is the God praised, but it looks more like a dismal record of God's failure. He incarnates Himself only to blot out the mental confusion (*mōha*) of people but as Kṛṣṇa, He succeeds only in whipping up more of it through His bewitching beauty of person.

मोहं जगत्त्रय भुवामवनेतुमेतद्
आदाय रूपमखिलेश्वर देहभाजाम् ।
निस्सीमकान्तिरसनीरधिनामुनैव
मोहं प्रवर्धयसि मुग्धविलासिनीनाम् ॥
[Kuvalayānanda N.S. edition p. 104]

2.10 *A statement made in juxtaposition with another conveys a startlingly different meaning*

We experience startled surprise in life when two statements are made by different persons in chronological contiguity and they yield a radically different meaning from what was meant, when heard in quick succession.

In a Canadian city a pedestrian found a huge hoarding put up by a church group with the legend, "Jesus, the light of the world." He also found that the Energy Conservation Board of the area happened to have put up this slogan, just under the legend about Jesus: "Turn off that light !"

Over the main gate of a church were inscribed these words in big letters: "Gateway to heaven". Below them, in smaller lettering was the instruction, "In winter, use the other gate".

Slogan on the back of a truck: "Nation on the move !" Just below that, this injunction had been painted; "Speed limit. 40 kilometres per hour."

In a town in England, there were two butcher shops opposite each other, in the same street. One of them carried this information: "We supply sausages to the queen!" The rival shop responded with: "God save the queen!"

There seems to be no need to elaborate on these examples. The point has been made that two statements made (by different people) with a certain signification separately now mean something startlingly different, when put in juxtaposition either in space or in time.

Realising the terrific dramatic advantages inherent in this device, the better playwrights in Sanskrit have made good use of it in their plays: the device is technically known as *patākā-sthānaka* and is defined thus:

प्रस्तुतागन्तुभावस्य वस्तुनोऽन्योक्तिसूचकम् ।
पताकास्थानकं तुल्यसंविधानविशेषणम् ॥

[Daśarūpaka I/14]

In plays, the juxtaposition can only be in time: the device is handled in this manner. A character makes a statement and before the echoes of the last words die down, another character enters excitedly making an impetuous announcement which is not related to the earlier one in the mind of this second character. But this second one heard within seconds of the earlier produces a very different impression than intended by either character: this startlingly different impression is made on the characters present on the stage as well as the spectators in the theatre. The chance juxtaposition of two statements conveying a dramatically new signification is the essence of the matter: it can have great dramatic value but it is a pity its potential has not been realised by more playwrights.

Among the more astute playwrights who have exploited this device is Bhāsa, the oldest known of them all. In his play the Pratijñāyaugandharāyaṇa, King Pradyōta is shown conferring with his chief advisors on the question of whom his daughter

Vāsavadattā should wed. He wonders, aloud, which of the great princes of India would be the fittest person to marry the highly accomplished and beautiful Vāsavadattā.

अस्मत्सम्बद्धो मागधः काशिराजो
वाङ्गः सौराष्ट्रो मैथिलः शूरसेन : ।
एते नानार्थैर्लोभयन्ते गेणैर्मां
कस्ते वैतेषां पात्रतां याति राजा ।।

[Pratijñāyaugandharāyaṇa-II:8]

Before the echoes of the last line (meaning "Who, among these appears worthy of the honour?") die out, in rushes the chamberlain, obviously in considerable excitement, shouting, "The king of the Vatsās!"

King Pradyōta is shocked and disbelievingly demands, "What, the king of the Vatsās?" as everyone knew the running feud between the two kings and it was unthinkable that Vāsavadattā would be given in marriage to Udayana, the king of the Vatsās. The chamberlain now realises his indiscretion and apologises for it, putting it down to his eagerness to convey good news to the king. For, what he had to report was that Udayana had been taken prisoner by Pradyota's minister.

But, whatever his intentions, the mischief had been done: for apart from the king and his courtiers, the spectators have heard the dramatic announcement "The king of the Vatsās" made immediately after Pradyōta's question and seemingly in reply to it; and they would have emotionally accepted the idea of prince Udayana marrying Vāsavadattā—for the impression burnt into their consciousness with the aid of the emotion with which the second statement had been made is not likely to be much affected by the subsequent explanation of the chamberlain: logic seldom prevails over emotion, in literature, as in life.

Bhavabhūti makes excellent use of this device in the greatest play he ever wrote, the Uttararāmacarita. In the first Act of this play of which the main sentiment is the pathetic, the playwright makes Rāma utter this verse in euphoria at the unparalleled conjugal bliss he has been blessed with.

इयं गेहे लक्ष्मीरियममृतवर्तिर्नयनयोः
असावस्याः स्पर्शो वपुषि बहुलश्चन्दनरसः ।
अयं बाहुः कण्ठे शिशिरमसृणो मौक्तिकरसः
किमस्या न प्रेयो यदि परमसह्यस्तु विरहः ।। [I/38]

The stanza ends with this reflection that everything about Sītā is most desirable except separation from her, the last word of it being "separation" (*viraha*). Scarcely is the last word out of his mouth when a palace official announces "It/he has arrived!" arrived !"

देव उपस्थितः ।

The last word uttered by Rāma, i.e. "separation" along with these said by the official, heard together, as they are bound to be, would clearly suggest to the audience the idea that separation from Sītā has taken place.

The palace official was announcing the arrival of Durmukha the spy and Rāma would be taking the decision to banish Sītā in a matter of moments after hearing his report. This, therefore, constitutes excellent dramatic anticipation: the spectators who have till now been treated to unmitigated conjugal bliss would sustain a mild shock of surprise at this sudden (and unintended) prognostication of tragedy.

A lesser instance—lesser on account of the flawed manner in which it has been contrived—occurs in the Venisamhara. In the II Act, Duryōdhana in the course of an amorous passage recites this stanza ending in the words "my thigh", addressed to his wife Bhānumati.

लोलांशुकस्य पवनाकुलितांशुकान्तं
त्वद्दृष्टिहारि मम लोचनबान्धवस्य ।
अध्यासितुं तव चिरं जघनस्थलस्य
पर्याप्तमेव करभोरु ममोरुयुग्मम् ॥ [II/23]

A palace official enters excitedly, exclaiming, "Broken, broken!" The significance that the king and the queen and the spectators will get from this sequence of statements is that Duryōdhana's thigh has been broken. In the context of Bhīma's terrible vow to break Duryōdhana's thighs, this looks ominously prophetic and makes for good theatre: the flaw lies in the fact that it is a bit unnatural for the official to come exclaiming "Broken!" when all he had to communicate is that a flagmast has been broken. It is not a serious enough event for an experienced palace official to break into the king's bed chambers when the king is with the queen, to announce in excitement: and it is most unnatural for him to omit the subject and merely say "Broken; Broken". The astute playwright who had realised the dramatic potential of this device clearly was tempted to harness this somewhere in his play and somehow manoeuvred it in here.

2.11 *A perverse reversal of ethical standards*

Here we enter deep waters: we are face to face with the ugly visage of crime, we shall be dealing here with a true criminal mentality. The wary reader will, however, quickly find out that we shall not be dealing with routine mindless criminals: this section is wholly concerned with the workings of a capable mind which can see and logically present crime as quite ethical, not in accord with the accepted code of the rest of the world but from the viewpoint of their own individual value-system. The ease and total confidence with which these gifted villains pursue their own ethical values, setting at naught the cherished values universally in application are bound to evoke surprise in the reader and in the spectator.

Śarvilaka, the erudite brahmin thief of Mṛcchakaṭika makes several observations in the III Act of that admirable play which place him in the special category described above. Very early in the proceedings he calls into question the disapprobation with which people view thieving: in his own opinion, a life of crime with the independence it can confer is preferable to a life of servility and he quotes the shining example of Aśvatthāman who assassinated the *Pāṇḍaıa* princes in their sleep.

कामं नीचमिदं वदन्तु पुरुषाः स्वप्ने च यद्वर्धते
विश्वस्तेषु च वञ्चनापरिभवश्चौर्यं न शौर्यं तत् ।
स्वाधीना वचनीयतापि हि वरं बद्धो न सेवाञ्जलि-
मर्गो ह्येष नरेन्द्रसौप्तिकवधे पूर्वं कृतो द्रौणिना ॥ [III/41]

Hereabouts he makes a number of statements which signify his evaluation of his own vile trade more as a fine art involving considerable skill developed through years of apprenticeship. He tells himself that when people see the hole he has made in a wall, they praise his skill as an artist. Indeed he expatiates like a professor in a university on the various methods of making holes in walls, making use of involved technical parlance and pays obeisance to the great teachers of yore who have composed manuals on the gentle art of house-breaking. At the height of his cynicism, he compiles a list of uses to which a brahmin thief can put his sacred thread during the course of the practice of his trade: the stanza is truly unique and is very much worth enjoying.

एतेन मापयति भित्तिषु कर्ममार्ग-
मेतेन मोचयति भूषणसंप्रयोगान् ।
उद्‍घाटको भवति यन्त्रदृढे कपाटे
दष्टस्य कीटभुजगैः परिवेष्टनं च ॥ [III/16]

Throughout the long passage which is in the form of a monologue, there is little reference to the moral aspect of the calling and Śarvilaka displays no scruples, no ethical sense at all: at one point he is about to kill the *vidūṣaka* and desists only because it is not necessary ! In only one place does he refer to thieving as an unworthy deed (*akārya*) which he ruefully declares he is forced to perform in order to obtain the release of his girl-friend Radanikā. In the caste-dominated society of Śūdraka's times, such a character must have shocked many an orthodox spectator: this and the many scenes where gamblers, profligates and prostitutes have a free run demonstrate as vividly the supreme realism of Śūdraka as they betoken the moral laxity of his times.

For an even more total reversal of ethical standards, we have to come down the centuries to the Rāma play, the Āścaryacūḍāmaṇi. In this unusually innovative play, the most original feature is the portrayal of Rāvaṇa. In the V Act, after Rāvaṇa had abducted Sītā and secreted her away in his pleasure garden, his wise and intrepid minister tries to reason with him, bringing up various aspects of his master's dastardly crime in a manner seldom seen in courtiers. He first tries to impress Rāvaṇa with the prowess of Rāma whose enmity it may prove dangerous to acquire. Rāvaṇa laughs it away, saying that a mere man can do him no harm. The minister is quick to point out that he is not a mere man but Lord Nārāyaṇa Himself, come down in human form. Rāvaṇa recounts the story of his laying siege to the heavens and defeating Indra and derisively asks where Nārāyaṇa was hiding when his elder brother (Indra) was being sorely pressed !

जित्वा ज्यायांसं स्वात्मनो देवराजं
स्वर्गे रक्षोभिर्दूषिते मामकीनैः ।
शच्यां त्रस्तायामप्सरोभिश्च सार्धं
विष्णोरेतावान् विक्रमः क्व प्रलीनः ॥ [V:12]

Then comes the most significant homily of the minister: he points out to Râvaṇa that this desire of his for a married woman is bound to create a scandal in the three worlds particularly because he is the great grandson of the Creator and he enjoys a high pedigree in the dharmic field. Râvaṇa's reply is cynical, tricky, mischievous: he argues that his coveting a married woman cannot be such a bad thing, in the eyes of *dharma* for Indra himself is styled reverentially as the lover of Ahalyâ (married to Gautama) in the *Vedic* mantras calling him to come down and accept the proffered oblations in sacrifices! The verse constitutes a great exercise in sophistry and is worth reproduction here.

कृतवान् विधिना शतं क्रतूना-
मभिधेयो वचसामकर्त्तृकाणाम् ।
मरुतां पतिरग्रजस्त्रिधाम्नो
हरिराह्वानमहल्यया किमेति ॥ [V:16]

This sophistry of Râvaṇa reaches its zenith in the next passage. Till now, his arguments have been seemingly based on belief in the inviolability of the *dhârmic* code by which the rest of the world is guided. Now he proceeds to repudiate the code of *dharma*, the universal moral law by which all men through the ages are bound: he claims that this code does not apply to strong and virile men like himself, dismissing the moral law as the crutch and support of weaklings! For cynical disdain of universally accepted principles, for sheer audacity, there are few passages in all Sanskrit literature to equal this:

यदि सुरपदकाङ्क्षा वज्रिणो वज्रपातात्
असिरविकृतधारः चन्द्रहासः सखा मे ।
तव विरमतु धर्मः साधनं दुर्बलानाम्
बलवत इव पथ्यं सर्वमस्मद्विधस्य ॥ [V/17]

This wholesale repudiation of the universally accepted code must have caused audible gasps of astonishment from the spectators of earlier epochs, particularly in this country where, whatever was the actual practice, the law had been inviolable. One generally sees villains in life and literature, proclaiming that their actions are in the strictest accord with the guiding principles of dharma: here is a unique case of a villain who is startlingly honest in the matter: for he proclaims with impunity that the law does not apply in cases like his, that, in fact, he is above it, that the correct criterion for judgment in worldly transactions is might and not morals! Śaktibhadra anticipates by several centuries the essence of the Marxian dictum that the existing moral law is legislated only for one set of people and therefore does not apply to the rest.

2.12 *Presenting good and virtuous conduct as bad or ineffective*

We have seen in the previous section how villains can present "the worse to appear the better reason". Now we shall examine the opposite process at work—for villains can often pour unmitigated scorn on virtuous conduct causing surprise and consternation among the more orthodox spectators. The roots of a villain's behaviour are difficult to trace: such contrary behaviour may stem from his own innate dislike of or contempt for the established law: it may arise from a pragmatic and calculated attempt to wean a *dhārmic*-minded character away from a morally ordained life, in self-interest. A third type of illustration may be the result of a mood of sheer contrariness of a poet who loves puckish fun and does not mind shocking some of his readers.

In Vālmīki's epic, the Rāmāyaṇa, Rāma, exiled for fourteen years extends a solemn promise to the harassed ascetics of Dandaka to rid the woods of the demons and goes about it with such determination that it rings alarm bells in the enemy ranks. News is carried by Śūrpaṇakhā to Rāvaṇa in a manner which underscores the demons' total preoccupation with their own destructive role; for what must be hailed as a salutary act of benevolence to society is represented in an aggrieved tone of complaint as calamitously adverse tidings!

ऋषीणामभयं दत्तं कृतक्षेमाश्च दण्डकाः ।
धर्षितं च जनस्थानं रामेणाक्लिष्टकर्मणा ।।

[Āraṇyakāṇḍa: 33:13]

If we remember that the Rāmāyaṇa is an epic with a very pointed, typically Indian moral tone and the readers and listeners were wholly wrapped up in the *dhārmic* appeal of the work, such an unusual and uncontrived cynicism must have evoked agonised gasps of astonishment. The present writer has personally seen such a reaction perhaps only slightly muted, even in these sophisticated, cynical times when talented lecturers expatiate on this passage in their discourses.

The very innovative characterisation of Rāvaṇa by Śaktibhadra in his Rāma play was referred to earlier. As part of this, the playwright introduces a dialogue between him and Sītā imprisoned in his pleasure garden. Rāvaṇa's prime objective is to persuade her to accept him as husband or lover.

When he realises that constancy is one of the cardinal qualities of chaste women, he derides Sītā's claim to that quality, she being the daughter of the earth who, in Sanskrit tradition, becomes the spouse of every succeeding king.

He then helps himself to an observation of such concentrated cynicism that even the (now) hardened spectators who have listened to his credo in the earlier part of the Act would gasp in disbelief. For Rāvaṇa invites Sītā to pair up with him if her objective is to attain to the heavens through her austerities: for, he can take her to the heavenly regions with none to block his progress, in exercise of the right earned by his martial prowess. On the other hand, her obstinately morbid perseverence in the austerities imposed by chastity is now acting as a padlocked door keeping her away from instant enjoyment of heavenly amenities:

स्नात्वा गङ्गापयसि विहितोपायना कल्पवृक्षैः
कैलासे वा शिखरिणि वने नन्दने वा मनोज्ञे ।
दुष्प्रापां वः सुतनु तपसा निर्विश स्वर्गलक्ष्मीं
पातिव्रत्यं परिध इव ते स्वर्गमार्गं रुणद्धि ॥

[Āścaryacūḍāmaṇi x: 27]

Sītā gives a spirited rejoinder saying she would gladly follow Rāma even to hell, meaning clearly that heaven must surely be a most disagreeable place nowadays if it is frequented by the ilk of Rāvaṇa! This too is evocative of the sense of wonder, as few characters, even villainous in those classical times could be heard to declare that they prefer hell to heaven.

We shall now enjoy a naughty verse composed by an obviously fun-loving poet who was not overawed by the general solemnity of the climate.

इन्दुर्यत्र न निन्द्यते न मधुरं दूतीवचः श्रूयते
नालापा निपतन्ति बाष्पकलुषा नोपैति कार्श्यं वपुः ।
स्वाधीनामनुकूलिनीं निजवधूमालिङ्ग्य यत्सुप्यते
तत्किं प्रेम गृहाश्रमव्रतमिदं कष्टं समाचर्यते ॥

[Sarasvatīkaṇṭhābharaṇa—Publication Board, Assam edition, page 285]

The idea that a man should have frequent forays away from homely love and the wife should waste away in anguish and that this is true bliss and not the staid life of a faithful householder is certainly not advanced as serious counsel; but the fact that an Indian poet could write this kind of stuff and get away with it (with the verse zealously preserved for posterity) is a favourable commentary on the level of tolerance of what is usually looked upon as a hide-bound society.

2.13 *A display of audacity, a cheerful disregard of public prejudices*

There are quite a few people—men, usually—in any society who wish to say and do audacious things, not because they are criminals at heart but generally for the heck of it, for the thrill and perhaps the notoriety it provides for the moment. They are not villains, true, but they take a delight in capering at the edge of criminality, stimulating the onlooker's sense of wonder—which, perhaps is their only pay-off. This category is, on this account, basically different from the one discussed earlier where real, deep-down perversity is involved. The people belonging to the present category possess an entirely different psychological set-up: they are essentially show-offs, they exude an insidious charm: these braggarts get themselves rather liked, though not many people will be inclined to take their claims seriously.

The earliest instance one can find in Sanskrit literature is Nārada, as portrayed by Bhāsa in his Bālacarita. We must remember that Nārada was a revered sage of the purāṇās, the favourite of the Gods, who was welcome not only in the counsel halls of the mightiest kings but equally without restriction in their closely guarded queen's quarters. He was the preceptor of Vālmīki and of Vyāsa, too and is counted among the foremost devotees of Lord Nārāyaṇa.

But Bhāsa has no hesitation in making Nārada declare that he is bored with the long-lasting peace in the heavens (an unusual phenomenon, to be sure) and that he has only two devices with him with which to lighten the leaden-footed day—his lyre on which he loves to play and the many misunderstandings among his friends which he likes to foment! The two verses on this are worth quoting:

क्षीणेषु देवासुरविग्रहेषु नित्यप्रशान्ते न रमेऽन्तरिक्षे ।
अहं हि वेदाध्ययनान्तरेषु तन्त्रीश्च वैराणि च घट्टयन्ति ॥

भक्तिः परा मम पितामह भाषितेषु सर्वाणि मे बहुमतानि तपोवनानि ।
सत्यं ब्रवीमि करजाग्रहता च वीणा वैराणि भीमकठिनाः कलहाः प्रिया मे ॥
[I/4 and 5]

This is not a wholly vain boast: the current story of Kṛṣṇa in the play as well as a large number of purānic episodes owe their pep and their structural strength to the machinations of this amiable and well-meaning trouble-maker.

In Duṣyanta, Kālidāsa has created just such a character. To state this is to fly in the face of all that *rājarṣi* image of his played up in the *Mahābhārata*: but a critical-minded student of the play can see that Kālidāsa has performed a grand salvaging operation in creating a highly interesting and credible character from out of the sadly unpromising epic material. In the first Act of Śākuntala he sees the heroine from a distance and falls precipitously in love with her. We must remember he is yet to meet her and talk to her; she is as yet wholly unaware of his existence (except, of course, impersonally as the king of the realm).

At this point a bee which has been disturbed from its perch by the girls watering the bushes starts annoying Śakuntalā. It brushes past her eyes, hums into her ears and sits on her lip. Now Duṣyanta would very much like to do these self-same things to her; but he desists from fulfilling himself on considerations of propriety and rectitude, while the bee, untroubled by such niceties has gone ahead and indulged its wishes. We can almost hear his sigh of envy whistling through the words of the last line of this remarkable stanza:

चलापाङ्गां दृष्टिं स्पृशसि बहुशो वेपथुमतीं
रहस्याख्यायीव स्वनसि मृदु कर्णान्तिकचरः ।
करं व्याधुन्वत्याः पिबसि रतिसर्वस्वमधरं
वयं तत्त्वान्वेषान्मधुकर हतास्त्वं खलु कृती ॥ [I : 21]

Then we have the heroes of Amaru—a thoroughly profligate, lecherous lot whose escapades are of absorbing interest precisely because of their cheerful lack of fine scruple. We shall quote two stanzas here: in one of them, the lover who was dismissed by his lady in anger at one of his many acts of faithlessness reappears at her side in the gloaming, dressed cunningly as her girl-friend. The poor girl immediately pours out her heart to him asking lamentingly whether she will ever be able to set her eyes on him after the way she has treated him. The fraudulent girl-friend says,

"It is very difficult indeed!" and bursts out laughing, giving himself away.

> कान्ते सागसि शापिते प्रियसखीवेषं विधायागते
> भ्रान्त्यालिङ्ग्य मया रहस्यमुदितं तत्संगमाकाङ्क्षया ।
> मुग्धे दुष्करमेतादित्यतितमामुद्दामहासं बला-
> दाश्लिष्य च्छलितास्मि तेन कितवेनाद्य प्रदोषागमे ॥

[Amaruśataka: 46]

In the other, the hero comes upon two girls with both of whom he is in love: with his catholic taste in feminine company he wants to enjoy some gesture of love with both, simultaneously, neither of them getting to know about the operation involving the other. As they are seated in the same bench, very near each other, this would take some doing but the cunning Lothario manages to solve the problem by covering with his palms the eyes of one as if in romantic play (with his body concealing the act from the other) and simultaneously kissing the other in the cheek, by extending his neck!

> दृष्टैवकासनसंस्थिते प्रियतमे पश्चादुपेत्यादरा-
> देकस्या नयने निमील्य विहितक्रीडानुबन्धच्छलः ।
> ईषद्वक्रितकंधरः सपुलकः प्रेमोल्लसन्मानसा-
> मन्तर्हसिलसत्कपोलफलकां धूर्तोऽपरां चुम्बति ॥

[Amaruśataka: 19]

2.14 *Mind-boggling, larger-than-life portraits*

Perhaps from being deeply religious in tone and having therefore to deal with acts of miracles and the deeds of divine beings, perhaps also from the proclivity of Indian poesy to paint tall and wide, Sanskrit literature abounds in mind-boggling, larger-than-life portraits: they cause surprise by the size and the boldness of design and the richness of the colours mixed: wonder soars when the barriers confining the mind are suddenly removed: if reality demands critical circumspection, then the removal of the hamstringing bonds permits the mind to soar above reality into the stratosphere of astonishment.

Playwrights seem to delight plying such free and bold brush strokes when they compose the initial, benedictory stanza, the *nāndi*. Bhāsa's *nāndi* verse at the start of his play the *Avimāraka* is a good instance: it is a neatly executed verse and simple as only Bhāsa can make it, in spite of its being set in the longest and the most complex metre in Sanskrit.

उत्क्षिप्तां सानुकम्पं सलिलविधिजलात् एकदंष्ट्राग्ररूढां
आक्रान्तामाजिमध्ये निहतदितिसुतां एकपादावधूताम् ।
संभुक्तां प्रीतिपूर्वं स्वभुजवशगतां एकचक्राभिगुप्तां
श्रीमन्नारायणस्ते प्रविशतु वसुधां उच्छ्रितैकातपत्राम् ।।

[Avimāraka-*Nāndi* verse]

The Earth pictured as a woman is so small in comparison with the Ancient Boar (an incarnation of Nārāyaṇa), it nestles comfortably at the tip of the Boar's protruding tooth. Such grand portrayals of the incarnation as the boar were very popular in Indian literature: Vedānta Deśika, no mean word-painter himself, has composed a stanza in the grand manner on this incarnation.

गोपायेदनिशं जगन्ति कुहना पोत्री पवित्रीकृत-
ब्रह्माण्डः प्रलयोर्मिघोषगुरुभिर्घोणा रवैर्घुर्घुरैः ।
यद्दंष्ट्राङ्कुरकोटिगाढघटनानिष्कम्पनित्यस्थितिः
ब्रह्मस्तम्बमसौवसौ भगवती मुस्तेन विश्वंभरा ।।

[Daśāvatārastotra-4]

The remarkable features of this verse going to illustrate this category are the very suggestive words used to describe the porcine grunts and the portrait of Earth appearing like a blade of grass in its mouth, thus emphasizing the difference in size.

This massive Boar was dirty as all proper pigs are expected in India to be and a devotee, intrepid and resourceful decides to bathe It. He somehow gathered the waters of all the seven seas in some vessels but, when he started bathing the animal, he found all this water could scarcely fill one hair follicle, and the project had to be abandoned. This picture is painted by a great minstrel-devotee who contrasts this with the Lord's subsequent incarnation as Kṛṣṇa whom His mother could bathe effortlessly by sprinkling water on Him with both the hands.

यद्रोमरन्ध्रपरिपूर्तिविधा ववक्षा
वाराहजन्मनि बभूवुरमी समुद्राः ।
तं नाम नाथभरविन्ददृशं यशोवा
पाणिद्वयान्तरजलैः स्नपयां बभूव ।।

[Kṛṣṇa Karṇāmṛta-II:27]

On the Ancient Boar, there is yet another verse (of unknown

authorship) quoted by Bhānudatta in the seventh taraṅga of his *Rasataraṅgini* as illustrative of the sentiment of wonder: the stanza is distinguished by a verbal felicity and by the use of unusual verbs.

भूयादेष सतां हिताय भगवान् कोलावतारो हरिः
सिन्धोः क्लेशमपास्य यस्य दशनप्रान्ते स्थितायाभुवः ।
तारा हारति वारिदस्तिलकति स्वर्वाहिनी मालयति
क्रीडादर्पणति क्षपापतिरहर्देवश्च ताटङ्कति ॥ [VII/22]

But more than the incarnation as the Boar, it is that as Narasimha, half-man, half-lion that has evoked the most colourful portraits from poets. Vedānta Deśika's verses on this incarnation are easily the most vivid; they are marked by appropriate sound effects in which the Dēśika is a master. One is from the *Daśāvatārastōtra*:

प्रत्यादिष्टपुरातनप्रहरणग्रामः क्षणं पाणिजैः
अव्यात् त्रीणि जगन्त्यकुण्ठमहिमा वैकुण्ठकण्ठीरवः ।
यत्प्रादुर्भवनादवन्ध्यजठरा यादृच्छिकाद् वेधसां
या काचित् सहसा महासुरगृहस्थूणा पितामह्यभूत् ॥

[*Daśāvatārastōtra*: 5]

The other, from the celebrated *Dayaśataka* (to which a reference was drawn earlier) offers the contrasting pictures of the awesome incarnation and of His compassion personified appropriately as a demure woman.

सटापटलभीषणे सरभसाट्टहासोद्भटे
स्फुरत्क्रुधि परिस्फुरद्भ्रुकुटिकेऽपि वक्त्रे कृते ।
दये वृषगिरीशितुर्दनुजडिम्भदत्तस्तना
सरोजसदृशा दृशा समुदिताकृतिर्दृश्यसे ॥

[*Dayaśataka*—84]

Coming back to the *nāndi* verses, those posited at the beginning of the Āścaryacūḍāmaṇi and the Mudrārākṣasa are most noteworthy from this viewpoint. The one shows the Lord recumbent on the serpent in the milk-ocean and the other captures the cosmic dance of Śiva. In the latter, the very attempts made by Lord Śiva to reduce the pace and tempo of His dance for fear of hurting the world suggest the fearsome power of the Dancer.

वीचीस्थाने सहस्रं भरतकपरिधस्पर्धि बिभ्रद्भुजानां
उत्फेनो हारजालैररुणरुचिरनन्ताहिरत्नप्रभाभिः ।

बिभ्राणः शङ्खमन्तश्चरमचरमनिवर्पिणीयं च तेजः
पायाद्वः शार्ङ्गधन्वा शयित इव समुद्रैकदेशे समुद्रः ॥

[Āścaryacūḍāmaṇi]

पादस्याविर्भवन्तीभवनतिमवने रक्षतः स्वैरपातैः
संकोचेनैव दोष्णां मुहुरभिनयतः सर्वलोकातिगानाम् ।
दृष्टिं लक्ष्येषु नोग्रज्वलनकणमुचं बध्नतो दाहभीतेः
इत्याधारानुरोधात् त्रिपुरविजयिनः पातु वो दुःखनृत्तम् ॥

[Mudrārakṣasa]

In order to dispel the notion that only physical entities can be painted up, a superb verse by Rājaśekhara from his play the *Bālarāmāyaṇa* is quoted here: this asserts the limitless range of a mighty intellect which, in accord with the philosophical principle that the subtle overcomes the gross, outreaches all physical things, even the sun in his heavenly orbit.

उदन्वच्छाया भूः स च निधिरपां योजनशतं
सदा पान्थः पूषा गगनपरिमाणं कलयति ।
इति प्रायो भावाः स्फुरदवधिमुद्रामुकुलिताः
सतां प्रज्ञोन्मेषः पुनरयमसीमा विजयते ॥

[प्रस्तावना]

Children are wonder-struck at outsize ogres and beanstalks climbing up to the heavens: grown-up man is not much different: and with the plentitude of oversize entities naturally available in the epic stories, Sanskrit poets find it easy enough to evoke the sense of wonder of their readers by slightly overpainting what is big by endowment.

2.15. *Superimposing human foibles on birds and animals*

Indians are justly celebrated for their fables which, collected under the headings, the *Pañcatantra* and the Hitōpadēśa have travelled all the world over and are retold in many languages: they please the childien and instruct the grown-ups: they possess an undying charm. When we find cats displaying cunning and dogs, servility, just like humans, there is an unusualness that evokes our sense of surprise.

Mama Mouse was teaching her offspring the ways of the world when a cat confronted them. Mama immediately began barking like a dog. The cat took off. Turning back to her young, mama announced: "That shows the importance of learning a second language."

Two men passing a fish shop in New York observed two drums full of live lobsters, one marked $3 and the other $6. Even as they were passing, they noticed a lobster in the $3 drum climbing the wall laboriously, teetering on the edge for a second and falling into the $6 drum, kept close. One remarked to the other, "This kind of thing can happen only in America, you know!"

The lower beings can have idiosyncracies, quirks of temperament and dislikes, prejudices and preferences, the same as we do. Listen to this. My young son and I spent much time in pet shops looking for just the right fish for his aquarium and for snails to keep the tank clean. One day he came home from a shopping trip, all excited, to tell me he had discovered some African frogs that really did a good job cleaning the aquarium. "Good" I said, "Then you won't have to buy any snails".

"Oh, yes" he said, "I have to buy them too. Those frogs don't do windows".

We have a nice comparison between the royal, disdainful behaviour of elephants and the mean servility of dogs in a verse in the *Hitōpadēśa*.

लांगूलचालनमधश्चरणावधातं
    भूमौ निपत्य वदनोदरदर्शनं च ।
श्वा पिण्डदस्य कुरुते गजपुङ्गवस्तु
    धीरं विलोकयति चाटुशतैश्च भुङ्क्ते ॥

[Suhrdbhēda—42]

While retailing the story of a lion called Piṅgalaka, the author makes a remark that has a surprising dignity and sweep.

नाभिषेको न संस्कारः सिंहस्य क्रियते मृगैः ।
    विक्रमार्जितराज्यस्य स्वयमेव मृगेन्द्रता ॥

[Suhrdbhēda—19]

The truth of this is apparent in these democratic times when leadership is acquired or seized, seldom conferred through formal rituals.

There is a pleasant verse occurring in the *Prasannarāghava* of Jayadēva where Rāma describes to Sītā the southern breeze, vesting it with human qualities. For a breeze to be pleasant, it has to possess three qualities—being cool, being scented and wafting slowly. While it has acquired the first two qualities on its way, Rāma ascribes its slow speed to its fear of the serpents in the Kailāsa mountain which are very partial to this light refreshment.

मलयशिखरादाकैलासं मनोभवशासना-
  द्रुलुवनवलयं जेतुं वाञ्छन्वसन्तसमीरणः ।
विहितवसतिकैलासाग्रे भुजङ्गधरं हरं
  मनसि विमृशन्भीतः शङ्के प्रयाति शनैः शनैः ॥ [II/4]

The cuckoo has several blemishes which would normally prejudice people against it: it is dark in complexion and is highly irresponsible in discharging its domestic obligations; still it is dearly loved by all the people: surely those with the gift of pleasant talk are forgiven their many shortcomings! This verse is from a hoard of *niti* aphorisms with which Sanskrit is replete.

पिकस्तावत्कृष्णः परमरुणया पश्यति दृशा
  परापत्यद्वेषी स्वसुतमपि नो पालयति यः ।
तथाप्येषोऽमीषां सकलजगतां वल्लभतमो
  न दोषा गण्यन्ते खलु मधुरवाचां क्वचिदपि ॥

[Subhāṣitaratnabhāṇḍāgāra 89/12]

We may end this section by reverting back to the Hitōpadēśa from which we started. The verses are self-explanatory and do not need any comments; everywhere the lower beings are portrayed as acting under typically human drives, as coloured by typically human foibles, fancies, whims.

मार्जारो महिषो मेषः काकः कापुरुषस्तथा ।
  विश्वासात्प्रभवन्त्येते विश्वासस्तत्र नोचितः ॥

[Mitralābha, 88]

नग्निस्तृप्यति काष्टानां नापगानां महोदधिः ।
  नान्तकः सर्व भूतानां न पुंसां वामलोचना ।

[Suhrdbhēda, 113]

2.16 *Presenting some sophisticated act requiring human skill, initiative and ingenuity as having been performed by other than human agency*

A kangaroo came to a soft-drink bar and ordered a lemonade. The clerk filled the order and placed the tumbler of drink before the animal. It did not drink it off but said to him, "What is this!

There is no red cherry in this!" The clerk apologised, placed a red cherry in the tumbler on which the kangaroo began to drink.

A customer said to the clerk, "Isn't this surprising?" The clerk said, "Yes! I have been working in this bar for five years and never once did I forget to add a red cherry to a lemonade".

The point of the joke, of course is that the clerk considers his failure to be the cause of surprise, not the kangaroo behaving like a human. There are many poets in Sanskrit making birds and beasts and even inanimate things behave like humans in displaying skill, initiative and ingenuity which are characteristic of humans. As lower grade beings are shown to display characteristics of the highest beings in the evolutionary scale, there is unexpectedness and hence wonder.

Kālidāsa makes nature a courtier to Dilīpa in the Raghuvamśa when the king visits the woods. When the king is around, the wind whistles through the bamboos producing music which lauds the achievements of Dilīpa as the songs of the bards in his palace do.

स कीचकैर्मारुतपूर्णरन्ध्रैः कूजद्भिरापादितवंशकृत्यम् ।
शुश्राव कुञ्जेषु यशस्स्वमुच्चैः उद्गीयमानं वनदेवताभिः ॥
पृक्तस्तुषारैः गिरिनिर्झराणामनोकहाकम्पितपुष्पगन्धिः ।
तमातपक्लान्तमनातपत्रमाचारपूतं पवनः सिषेवे ॥

[Raghuvamśa-II: 12 & 13]

The idea of the wind acting as a musician is more beautifully exploited by Viśākhadatta in a Rāma play of his which has been lost. In it Vibhīṣaṇa is shown remonstrating with Rāvaṇa sharply warning him of Rāma's prowess that is right out of this world—prowess that is panegyrised by the wind singing through the seven holes in the sal trees made by a single arrow from Rāma, the seven holes serving to produce the seven basic notes of the Indian musical scale.

रामोऽसौ भुवनेषु विक्रमगुणैर्यातः प्रसिद्धि परां
अस्मद्भाग्यविपर्ययाद्यदि परं देवो न जानाति तम् ।
बन्दीवैष यशांसि गायति मरुत् यस्यैकबाणाहति-
श्रेणीभूतविशालतालविवरोद्गीर्णैः स्वरैस्सप्तभिः ॥

This idea of the wind producing music is certainly not new, as we have seen: what is new is that the fact that seven sal trees were perforated has been exploited dexterously to yield the idea of music based on the seven musical notes: this is a fresh and novel turn to a worn idea and this is therefore unusual and evocative of wonder.

It is to be admitted that the element of surprise in such cases is not strongly marked. There can certainly be a range of intensity in the delineation of this sentiment, as there undoubtedly is in the case of the other sentiments like love, heroism and pathos. In stanzas coming under this category we feel a tickle of surprise and we are mildly puzzled, amused, diverted: all this has a certain aesthetic value, to liven up long epic narratives, among other things.

2.17 *Spurt of admiration for a character from another*

This category is intended to cover cases of excessive admiration for a character, as expressed by another and differs from a previous one encompassing cases of outstanding qualities in a character, on account of the personality of the speaker. In extreme cases, it is even possible for one to admire another without any outstanding qualities in the latter, owing only to some peculiar kink in the personality of the former or to the special nature of their relationship. A good example is the surprised reaction of Hanumān on arrival in Laṅkā, at the obvious power and pelf of Rāvaṇa: Vālmīki devotes as many as 25 verses to a description of the capital city as seen through Hanumān's eyes. The next two verses record Hanumān's words of despair about Rāma's prospects of defeating Rāvaṇa.

आगत्यापीह हरयो भविष्यन्ति निरर्थकाः ।
न हि युद्धेन वै लङ्का शक्या जेतुं सुरैरपि ॥
इमां तु विषमां दुर्गां लङ्कां रावणपालिताम् ।
प्राप्यापि स महाबाहुः किं करिष्यति राघवः ॥

[Sundarakāṇḍa-II: 27 and 28]

When we remember the worshipful reverence of Hanumān for Rāma, we register with surprise the former's evaluation of the invincible prowess of the foe. Such a description of Laṅkā by a rākṣasa or even by a less committed member of Rāma's camp will not occasion surprise. But coming from the mouth of Hanumān, this has the intended effect of shocking the reader into accepting the enemy as a very great warrior: and this naturally makes it possible for the gifted poet to create a transcendentally great image of the hero who laid low such a mighty foe. The surprise element in all the passages collected under this category is caused not so much by the qualities of the admired as by the personality of the admirer.

The statements of Duṣyanta in the first Act of Śākuntala representing his first reactions to the girl in the penance grounds come mostly under this category. He is amazed that an unsophisticated girl brought up in total innocence of coquetry in the penance-woods, replete with the atmosphere of austerity can outshine all the beauties of his capital city.

शुद्धान्तदुर्लभमिदं वपुराश्रमवासिनो यदि जनस्य ।
दूरीकृताः खलु गुणैः उद्यानलता वनलताभिः ॥

[Śākuntala-I:16]

Again and again the romantically inclined king with a nice eye for feminine beauty expresses amazement while applauding the beauty, his puzzlement arising from the years of intimacy with the urban belles whose natural endowment has been set off by the expert use of all the devices available to women for enhancing physical allure. The verse most expressive of this state of mind of the king is justly celebrated and extensively quoted:

सरसिजमनुविद्धं शैवलेनापि रम्यं
मलिनमपि हिमांशोर्लक्ष्म लक्ष्मीं तनोति ।
इयमधिकमनोज्ञा वल्कलेनापि तन्वी
किमिव हि मधुराणां मण्डनं नाकृतीनाम् ॥

[Śākuntala-I:18]

It is beyond doubt that Śakuntalā was a girl of matchless beauty: but here, the effusive remarks of the king are evocative of wonder leading on to the staple sentiment of love, mainly because of the personality of the king. To clinch the reasoning, the reader is invited to compare these passages with those uttered by Purūravas on being smitten by the charms of the highly sophisticated Urvaśi.

Duṣyanta has another facet to his personality—his deep frustration at his having to go through life without issue. So, when he sees his own son (without realising that he is his) in Kaśyapa's penance-grove, his love of children, generally, his long-felt frustration at his own childlessness and his admiration for the wonderfully alluring qualities of Sarvadamana gush out in the form of the well-known verse.

आलक्ष्य दन्तमुकुलाननिमित्तहासैः
अव्यक्तवर्णरमणीयवचःप्रवृत्तीन् ।
अङ्काश्रयप्रणयिनस्तनयान्वहन्तो
धन्यास्तदङ्गरजसा मलिनीभवन्ति ॥

[Śākuntala-VII:17]

Logically viewed, a child's laughter is often meaningless, it is not inspired by any humorous situation: nor does its talk have any significance, since it is made up of indistinct words, half-pronounced. Still a child captivates the onlooker, occasioning surprise on account of its illogical behaviour. There is yet another factor causing surprise in this verse: ordinarily poets are likely to present the matter in this way: "parents getting dirtied by their children at play eagerly coming and sitting in their laps are, indeed fortunate": Kālidāsa puts the emphasis on the process of getting dirtied as the most desirable end-result to be wished for, (the verb being the central word of a sentence) and he presents the idea in this manner: "Fortunate parents get dirtied by their children at play who eagerly rush to sit on their laps". This innovation designed by the master poet to create a greater poetic impact evokes surprise.

Srīharṣa is not particularly adept at portraying deep emotion: he skims the surface of life and his work is memorable for the mechanical skill with which he can manipulate the metres. But in *Nāgānanda* he has drawn a few emotional portraits, perhaps because of the nature of the story and also on account of the poet's own personal involvement in its religious appeal. One such is the stanza uttered in admiration of Jīmūtavāhana's decision to sacrifice himself in order that Saṅkhacūḍa may be saved: the stanza gets very much added value as it is uttered by the beneficiary himself.

विश्वामित्रः श्वमांसं श्वपच इव पुराभक्षयद यन्निमित्तं
नाडीजङ्घो निजघ्ने कृततदुपकृतिर्यत्कृते गौतमेन ।
पुत्रोऽयं काश्यपस्य प्रतिदिनमुरगानत्ति तार्क्ष्यो यदर्थं
प्राणांस्तानेव चित्रं तृणमिव कृपया यः परार्थे जहाति ॥

[Nāgānanda-IV:14]

Bhavabhūti was a great one for overpainting characters: his

characters seldom adopt positions of emotional equipoise, they are filled with overweening admiration or withering contempt or consuming anger or melting melancholy. Candrakētu reports to Rāma of Lava's flaring up on hearing Rāma's prowess being lauded by his army leaders: Rāma approvingly recites this verse paying warm tribute to the sure instincts of a proud *kṣatriya* displayed by the stripling: but the verse takes on an additional dimension on account of the suggestion conveyed, of Rāma's own twinge of jealousy at the vaulting fame acquired by the boy at his cost.

न तेजस्तेजस्वी प्रसृतमपरेषां विषहते
    स तस्य स्वो भावः प्रकृतिनियतत्वावकृतकः ।
मयूखैरश्रान्तं तपति यदि देवो दिनकरः
    किमाग्नेयग्रावा निकृत इव तेजांसि वमति ॥

[Uttararāmacarita: VI: 14]

While this verse has been singled out for its additional dimensions, one can refer to dozens of verses in Bhavabhūti's three works as illustrative of this category: stanzas I/35, I/38, IV/11, V/2 and 3, and VI/11 of *Uttararāmacarita* and a large number of verses recited by Mādhava and finding a place in the I and the III Act of *Mālatīmādhava* can be cited here.

If the nature of the speaker constitutes an important dimension of the poems coming under this category, then a lovely verse uttered by Rāvaṇa should fittingly be cited at the conclusion of this section. This occurs in the *Jānakīpariṇaya* of Rāmabhadra Dīkṣita: when Maṇḍodarī remonstrates with her husband for having brought on the ire of Rāma on himself, Rāvaṇa proudly talks of his sanguinary worship of Lord Śiva and how compassionate He is towards him. In a verse, Rāvaṇa lovingly describes His tender solicitude for himself at having got emaciated on account of his severe austerities: his great admiration for Śiva runs like a golden thread through the entire passage lending a special glow, a unique distinction to it, evoking surprise.

करकमलतलेन शैलकन्या-
    कुचतटसंगतकुंकुमारुणेन ।
सकरुणममृशन्ममापरांगम्
    त्वमसि कृशस्तपसेति चन्द्रमौलिः ॥

2.18 *Use of a device or measure designed for a purpose for a startlingly different purpose*

A book is written and published for entertainment or instruction: but books are often used as a paperweight or as a ruler to draw a line: a startlingly different use will be to hurl it as a missile, as Kay, a character in PG Wodehouse's Sam the Sudden does: the book hurled happened to be a heavy tome on theology entitled "Is there a hell?" The recipient, an amorous young man, the author observes, would have said there was.

The Most Reverend Geoffrey Francis Fisher, retired Archbishop of Canterbury maintains a healthy scepticism towards acts of excessive piety. "This scepticism," he explains, "goes back to the days when, as a young theologian I lived in the boarding house where the landlady always used to sing 'Nearer, my God, to Thee' while cooking our breakfast. One day I asked her, 'You like that hymn very much, don't you?'.

"'It's not so much that I like it' she replied, 'but I know that by the end of the third verse the eggs are soft-boiled and by the fifth verse, they are hard!' "

When asked about the ideal length of a film, director Mel Brooks suggested: "A comedy should never run over 90 minutes. By then the audience's sweets are all used up."

A young man and his fiancee visited a jewel store to select a diamond ring. He picked up a ring and wanted to know the price. When the shop owner mentioned a figure, the young man whistled in surprise and turned his attention to other rings in the display. When he came up with another choice and looked at the shop owner he replied, "That, sir, will be two whistles!"

The aptest verse from Sanskrit to quote under this category will be that recited by the *brahmin* thief Śarvilaka listing appreciatively the various uses (not mentioned in the ancient scriptural texts) to which a thief can put his sacred thread: this verse, a naughty one—and one that must have caused considerable astonishment and perhaps resentment too to the orthodox sections of the audience has been cited earlier.

Kālidāsa in his very first verse of the *Kumārasambhala* provides an instance of this in a verse of sweepingly gigantic proportions.

अस्त्युत्तरस्यां दिशि देवतात्मा
हिमालयो नाम नगाधिराजः।
पूर्वापरौ वारिनिधी वगाह्य
स्थितः पृथिव्या इव मानदण्डः॥

[Kumārasambhava—I:1]

In trying to provide to the reader an idea of the tremendous length of the Himālayan range, the poet suggests that it can provide a yardstick with which to measure the earth's circumference. This is quite a poetic way of suggesting the dimensions involved: but apart from this, Kālidāsa has succeeded, in the first stanza itself, in enlarging his reader's perceptions from everyday trivialities to reach out and absorb this overwhelming story where gods are characters and everything happens at a dizzyingly high level, physically as well as metaphorically.

2.19 *Underplaying a thing of value to make another appear more significant*

When characters indulge in self-denigration or running down others or other things (always making it look plausible and uncontrived) there is an element of unusualness that brings on surprise. This surprise may be caused by the extent of the underplaying done as well as by the contemplation of how gigantic the other appears in comparison.

Hanumān in Vālmīki's Rāmāyaṇa performs many wonderful feats (including a considerable amount of intelligent analysis) to reach Sītā in the pleasure-garden of Laṅkā. Sītā quite clearly realises how gifted this messenger of Rāma's is: this realisation raises in her mind the very reasonable doubt if Rāma and Lakṣmaṇa and the monkey army will be able to repeat his feats and cross the ocean to reach Laṅkā. Hanumān hastens to assure her in a remarkable passage where tact is enthroned at the cost of prosaic truth: this has the desired effect of bracing up the despondent Sītā.

मद्विशिष्टाश्च तुल्याश्च सन्ति तत्र वनौकसः।
मत्तः प्रत्यवरः कश्चित् नास्ति सुग्रीवसन्निधौ॥
अहं तावदिह प्राप्तः किं पुनस्ते महाबलाः।
न हि प्रकृष्टाः प्रेष्यन्ते प्रेष्यन्ते हीतरे जनाः॥

[Sundarakāṇḍa—39: 38 and 39]

Clearly this statement is untrue and it causes surprise to the reader on that account; but this piece of self-denigration by the mighty Hanumān, whose knowledge of psychology is as well developed as are his sinews, performs a vitally important function in boosting the flagging spirits of the heroine who, a few moments before, had decided to take her life, in a black mood of despair: truth has never been sacrificed in a better cause.

There are two verses appearing in Dāmōdara Miśra's Hanumannāṭaka which illustrate this category in two distinct ways. One is the reaction of Hanumān who, on return from Laṅkā after seeing Sītā, was given an affectionate bear-hug by the grateful Rāma: the deeply humble messenger feels he has done nothing of significance to merit so signal an honour from Rāma. The verse:

पीतो नाम्बुनिधिर्न कोणवपुरी निष्पिष्य चूर्णीकृता
नानीतानि शिरांसि राक्षसपतेर्नानायि सीता मया ।
आश्लेषार्पणपारितोषिकमहं नार्हामि वार्ताहरो
जलपन्नित्यनिलात्मजः स जयति व्रीडाजडो राघवे ॥

[Hanumānnāṭaka—VI:36]

The scope of the feats listed as not performed by Hanumān is so all-encompassing one feels a surge of surprise at it: they are not the things a messenger is expected to perform, by any reckoning: and if they had been done by Hanumān, then Rāma would be rendered redundant and the hero of the epic would be overwhelmingly outshone by a lesser character—which would have seriously flawed the epic.

The other is from a very different character, Rāvaṇa: when he sees the monkeys hordes led by a human camping in his territory, his towering self-confidence breaks down and a strange unwonted despondency takes over: the verse has been quoted under an earlier section.

Superficially this strange self-deprecation by Rāvaṇa will look unusual and will therefore evoke surprise. But to a deeper student of psychology, this despondency is another facet of arrogant confidence just as feelings of superiority are just another facet of an inferiority complex. For Rāvaṇa had been so drunk with his own exploits, he did not allow the possibility of an enemy appearing to challenge him: so, now, he is shocked into the nadir of self-denigration when he sees a human in the robes of an ascetic with a record of a number of astounding military exploits behind him, leading an expeditionary force across the seas right into his own bastion. Hence, while on its first impact it causes a surge of surprise, it does not strain the credulity of the reader beyond a point.

We have a stanza of unknown authorship which makes light of Hanumān's image—and this from the mouth, not of a rākṣasa but of Aṅgada; but Aṅgada indulges in this, not with a view to disparaging a fellow camp-follower but with a deeper purpose, of enhancing Rāvaṇa's distress. When Aṅgada reaches Rāvaṇa's court as an accredited messenger of Rāma, he, unfortunately for Rāvaṇa, reminds him of the other monkey, Hanumān who had worked havoc with the city's defences and set fire to the city. So Rāvaṇa demands to know what has happened to him—fully expecting that he would have been elevated to the pinnacle of glory. Aṅgada sizes up the situation and serves up a brilliant untruth that goes right to the heart of the rākṣasa king. For the messenger says that Hanumān's defeat at the hands of Rāvaṇa's son who took him prisoner so angered even the monkeys in-the-street, they started tormenting him badly: and unable to bear this, Hanumān fled the country leaving no address behind.

कस्त्वं वानर रामराजभवने लेखार्थसंवाहकः
यातः कुत्र पुरागतस्स हनुमान् निर्दग्धलङ्कापुरः ।
बद्धो राक्षससूनुनेति कपिभिः संताडितो भर्त्सितः
स व्रीडात्तपराभवो वनमृगः कुत्रेति न ज्ञायते ॥

[Kuvalayānanda, N.S. edition, page 92]

There is a type of under-valuation of a precious thing in order to laud another, carried on to excess in the field of bardic poetry: one example of this will represent this group. This is a panegyric on King Bhōja's munificence: the poem states that even maid-servants do not value highly the pearls strewn on the floor of the houses of scholars who enjoy the king's patronage: for they sweep them out along with the garbage for birds to pick. This is the well-executed verse.

मुक्ताः केलिविसूत्रहारगलिताः संमार्जनीभिर्हृताः
प्रातः प्राङ्गणसीम्नि मन्थरचलत्बालाङ्घ्रिलाक्षारुणाः ।
दूराद्दाडिमबीजशङ्कितधियः कर्षन्ति केलीशुकाः
यद्विद्वद्भवनेषु भोजनृपतेः तत् त्यागलीलायितम् ॥

[Kuvalayānanda, N.S. edition, page 186]

Such bards may not have been rich enough in reality, to disregard pearls on the floor: but from the volume of bardic poetry that has come down to us, one is tempted to conclude that the occupation was highly remunerative.

2.20 *The neat but unexpected way a problem gets solved*

A problem presents itself with no solution in sight—or there are only prosaic, drab solutions: but along comes a character with a neat and complete solution, surprising us with its unexpectedness and its nicely-rounded edges.

A stanza of contemporary English verse can be quoted as illustrative of this:

To every person comes his day,
So calmly wait your chance!
Pedestrians have the right of way
When in an ambulance.

A paper carried this advertisement in the Wanted column: "Reliable and hard-working clerk who is paid on Friday and broke on Tuesday would like to exchange small loans with another who gets paid on Wednesday and is broke on Saturday."

There was a bleak bridge on a river in a city which had gained considerable notoriety as the favourite spot for suicides to jump off and the municipal board had posted a policeman to discourage would-be suicides.

Sure enough, on the first day he found a man walking up, clearly intending to end it all. Now this man had been a very successful salesman whose persuasive abilities had carried him quickly to the top of the profession but he had a soured married life and had decided to jump off the bridge.

The policeman purposefully walked up to him and was seen engaged in earnest conversation with him, the other man doing most of the talking.

After a few minutes of this, both jumped.

Kālidāsa paints a beautiful picture of Pārvatī as a bashful bride on her first day in her husband's home on the Kailāsa mountain. Her bashfulness was very feminine and pretty upto a point but very soon, Lord Śiva found it irksome and decided to find a remedy for it. But it is not a very easy matter to accomplish—aggressive solutions would be counter-productive, driving her farther into her shell.

So the Lord merely ordered all the ghouls in his kingdom to march in a single file before the divine pair: no instructions were issued to them to put on an act. But their natural expressions were so weird, varied and funny, Umā smiled in amusement, her reserve was broken and her bashfulness banished. This is the nicely contrived verse in Kumārasambhava.

नवपरिणयलज्जाभूषणं तत्र गौरीं
वदनमपहरन्तीं तत्कृताक्षेपमीशः ।
अपि शयनसखीभ्यो दत्तवाचं कथंचित्
प्रमथमुखविकारैः हासयामास गुढम ।।

[Kumārasambhava—VII:95]

Amaru is a brilliantly innovative poet from whose collection of a hundred, a few cameo-pieces have been presented under various sections. One of these tells a naughty story with a surprise ending involving a neat, compact and ready solution to the problem on hand, though none of the readers could have anticipated it. A newly married couple had chatted away without restraint in the privacy of their bedroom. But with the dawn there is a big change in the bride (as everywhere in India, in the earlier epoch) for she now transforms herself into the responsible and highly restrained daughter-in-law of the house attending to her many chores under the watchful eyes of her in-laws.

Now the peace of the inner apartments is suddenly shattered by the pet parrot starting to mouth the endearments exchanged by the young people the night before: for the parrot had been there in the bedroom all through the night, with neither of the people in love noticing it.

Now the parrot has got to be silenced, this second, before the elders get wise to what goes on: but any overt step, anything aggressive done to stop the chatterbox would draw attention on to herself—which is no solution at all. What is the girl to do now—how is this delicate problem to be solved?

The girl unobtrusively takes off the ruby in her ear and just places it before the parrot: without a thought, the eager bird picks it under the impression it is a seed of the pomogranate. Now the gem is not soft and juicy as expected but the bird in its greed is unwilling to drop it. But the essential gain is that its beak is full, it cannot utter and its memory chain is disrupted: and the situation has been saved with grace and infinite tact and in an essentially poetic manner. Here is the exquisite stanza.

दम्पत्योर्निशि जलपतोर्गृहशुकेनाकर्णितं यद्वचः
तत्प्रातर्गुरुसन्निधौ निगदतः श्रुत्वैव तारं वधूः ।
कर्णालम्बितपद्मरागशकलं विन्यस्य चञ्च्वाः पुरो
व्रीडार्ता प्रकरोति दाडिमफलव्याजेन वाग्बन्धनम् ।।

[Amaruśataka : 16]

A similar neat solution to a problem that threatened to develop into menacing proportions is presented by an unknown poet. The very simplicity, compactness and poetic appropriateness of the solution evoke surprise even as they compel the reader's admiration. All the girls, even the married women of Ayōdhyā were deeply in love with Rāma. This is in conformity with Indian tradition involving no loss of the virgin image to the girls but a lot of repute to the hero concerned.

Now, a married woman of the capital city had regaled the long afternoon by painting a picture of Rāma: even while she was gazing on the picture and drinking in the beauty of the subject, her husband arrived unexpectedly early, as husbands would. No man can be expected to welcome this divided loyalty in his wife, even if the rival is Rāma himself. So the distracted woman, thinking quickly on her feet painted in, a bow of flowers in Rāma's hand: the situation had been saved as the husband took the painting to be Cupid's and it was customary for loving women to paint and worship the god of love.

The point of the poem, of course, is merely to say that Rāma was overwhelmingly beautiful, that he could be mistaken for Manmatha if he wielded a bow of flowers in place of his deadly kodanda: but the stanza serves as an admirable illustration of the category encompassing all neat and ingenious solutions.

गेहे गेहे सुभग भवतो रामभद्र क्षितीश
त्वामालिख्य स्वमपि सविधे सस्पृहं भावयन्त्यः ।
तस्मिन्नाकस्मिकमुपगते वल्लभे भीतिभाजः ।
पौष्पं चापं तव करतले वेपमाना लिखन्ति ।।

[Subhāṣitaratna-bhāṇḍāgāra 124/127]

2.21 *Instituting startlingly unusual comparisons*

Conventional comparisons between things of the same level or order of things may enlighten the reader or make clear an abstruse point but do not evoke surprise. Comparisons of an unconventional nature involving unlikely material may cause surprise: a good trencherman comparing the rising sun to a piece of ham or to a nicely fried puri soaked in red-coloured syrup will be an unusual experience (though quite appropriate to the character making it) and will cause amused surprise. Certain examples from contemporary life can be studied to get an idea of the general features of the cases coming under this category.

"She not only reads her husband like a book, she gives the neighbours reviews."

"A newspaper is a circulating library with high blood pressure".

"The search for a scapegoat is the easiest of all hunting expeditions."

"Money still talks but it has to catch its breath more often."

"Faith is the soul riding at anchor."

"When a woman falls, it is because, like a fruit, she was not picked in time."

"He who sacrifices his conscience to ambition burns a picture to obtain the ashes."

"Nostalgia is a file that removes the rough edges from the good old days."

In the Mṛcchakaṭika, Śakāra provides quite a few instances of such unusual analogy: in Act VIII he tells his amorous friend, "I am unable to forget Vasantasēna. Like the words of a wicked man, she does not leave my mind."

भाव, अद्यापि तां वसन्तसेनां स्मरामि । दुर्जनवचनमिव हृदयान्नापसरति ॥

And his description of noon is quite individual and unique.

नभोमध्यगतः सूर्यो दुष्प्रेक्ष्यः कुपितवानरसदृशः ।
भूमिर्दृढसंतप्ता हतपुत्रशतेव गान्धारी ॥

[Mṛcchakaṭika—VIII : 10]

Śakāra's analogies are uniquely different and they cause surprise: their uniqueness is mainly based on the fact that usually poets do not use bad things to compare with the good as the image will be warped but Śakāra rushes in where angels fear to tread. There are many examples of out-of-the-ordinary comparisons (not necessarily Śakāran in flavour) indulged in by writers of brilliant individual stanzas. The coquetry of women prods a poet to come out with a striking analogy.

भ्रूचापवल्लीं सुमुखी यावन्नयति वक्रताम् ।
तावत्कटाक्षविशिखैर्भिद्यते हृदयं मम ॥

[Kuvalayānanda, N.S. edition, page 103]

Serving the unwise is admittedly a frustrating experience: angered by perhaps a worse-than-average boss, a poet presents a series of comparisons, some of them unusual, even grotesque.

अरण्यरुदितं कृतं शवशरीरमुद्वर्तितम्
स्थलेऽब्जमवरोपितं सुचिरमूषरे वर्षितम् ।
श्वपुच्छमवनामितं बधिरकर्णजापः कृतो
धृतोऽन्धमुखदर्पणो यदबुधो जनः सेवितः ॥

[उद्वर्तितं = purgative administered]

[Kuvalayānanda, N.S. edition, page 56]

There is even a quasi-medical comparison sustained between phlegm and the wicked; both get worse with sweet things and are controlled by bitter things.

अहो प्रकृतिसादृश्यं श्लेष्मणो दुर्जनस्य च ।
मधुरैः कोपमायाति कटुकेनैव शाम्यति ॥

[Subhāṣitaratnabhāṇḍāgāra page 57, verse 63]

There are genuine poets, creative artists gifted with imagination: there are, on the other hand poetasters who grab words (from the dictionaries) with violence and force them into their banal verses. To talk of these two totally different types in equal terms—to refer to them all as poets is to equate the Creator and the potter who makes pots and pans.

हठादाकृष्टानां कतिपयपदानां रचयिता
जनस्स्पर्धालुश्चेदहह कविना वश्यवचसा ।
भवेदद्य श्वो वा किमिह बहुना पापिनि कलौ
घटानां निर्मातुस्त्रिभुवनविधातुश्च कलहः ॥

[Subhāṣitaratnabhāṇḍāgāra page 39, verse 24]

A poor man seeks to compare himself with a lotus for he blooms with hopeful expectation with the rise of the sun but wilts with sunset, in frustration.

विकसामि खावुदिते संकोचमुपैमि चास्तमुपयाते ।
दारिद्र्यसरसि मग्नः पङ्कजलीलामनुभवामि ॥

[Subhāṣitaratnabhāṇḍāgāra 69/38]

A *niti* verse makes adroit use of analogy to flash its teaching with a surprise element on to the reader: it is especially noteworthy on account of the unusual field from which the metaphor is drawn.

To most readers, if bad people and thorns are mentioned together, the only point connecting them will appear to be their proclivity to cause pain. But a certain *nīti* writer finds two more similarities one of which is downright naughty—for them he says there are only two ways of dealing with them: keeping them at a distance or (when this is not possible) impacting them with sandals.

खलानां कण्टकानां च द्विविधैव प्रतिक्रिया ।
उपानन्मुखभङ्गो वा दूरतो वा विसर्जनम् ॥

[Subhāṣitaratnabhāṇḍāgāra 56/6]

It may be borne in mind that in India getting beaten with sandals is the worst punishment one can conceive of, involving the total loss of social position.

2.22 *Stark contrasts too can occasion surprise*

Stark contrasts, puzzling emphases on differences, conclusions drawn from wrong premises which indicate the very opposite positions, all are natural excitants of the sentiment of wonder. The one condition here, as in all considerations of rasa is that the contrast etc. should not be wholly arbitrary but should have some reasonable basis, as otherwise no rasa can arise. A statement like, "It's remarkable that cold feet are often the result of burnt fingers" offers an exçellent example of this category. In a statement like, "True courage is not only a balloon for rising but also a parachute for falling" an important role is assumed by courage in two contrasting situations and an important lesson is taught that even a courageous man will not have continued success guaranteed to him but that, when he fails, he will not collapse totally like the coward but will be able to bear up and survive. This is a subtler case coming under this category, nonetheless: and it feeds our sense of wonder which lubricates the lesson that is taught by the statement, making it go smoothly through the resistant personality of the reader.

Consider, again, how basically true and wise is this statement, "Rumour is the one thing that gets thicker as you spread it";

it is true not in spite of its contradictoriness but precisely on account of it; its contradictory structure is an essential part of its unique truth and of its universal applicability; its contradictory structure arises from an implied comparison with jam or butter and this lends not only flavour to it but preserves it in human memory like salt and vinegar in a pickle. All these subtleties, however, strike the thoughtful reader as a result of sustained contemplation: but it is the initial surprise that has triggered on the process of thinking, and the surprise owes wholly to the contrast in the statement.

A fine example of this category is furnished by Kālidāsa in his Śākuntala where, in Act VII Duṣyanta observes certain ascetics performing strict austerities in the Hēmakuṭa region which is part of heaven. Men perform austerities in the earth so as to ascend to heaven: with what objective do these living in heaven perform austerities? The verse bristles with the contradictory behaviour of these exceptional people and is worth reproduction:

प्राणानामनिलेन वृत्तिरुचिता सत्कल्पवृक्षे वने
तोये काञ्चनपद्मरेणुकपिशे धर्माभिषेकक्रिया ।
ध्यानं रत्नशिलातलेषु विबुधस्त्रीसन्निधौ संयमः
यत् काङ्क्षन्ति तपोभिरन्यमुनयः तस्मिंस्तपस्यन्त्यमी ॥

[Śākuntala—VII: 12]

Though the poet has not provided the answer, we can infer that the objective of these hermits must surely be the highest that man can set up for himself—that is nothing less than the emancipation of the soul from the bondage of births and deaths, a state which leads to perennial beatitude unlike heaven where one's stay is only for a strictly limited period.

In the same play, earlier, in the V Act, in the course of the spirited, often acrimonious argument between the king and Śārṅgarava, the latter is stung by the imputation of fraudulent intentions and flashes a reply where he contrasts hermits like himself brought up from birth to value truth above everything else with mealy-mouthed royal personages who are taught the gentle art of lying (in the name of diplomacy) as part of their scholastic curriculum. It is a powerful indictment and is couched in appropriate language.

आजन्मनः शाठ्यमशिक्षितो यः
तस्याप्रमाणं वचनं जनस्य ।
परातिसंधानमधीयते यैः
विद्येति ते सन्तु किलाप्तवाचः ॥

[Śākuntala: V: 25]

We may also cite as illustrative of this category the verses (47 and 48 of II Canto of the *Raghuvaṃśa*) addressed by the lion to King Dilīpa contrasting his own exalted station in life, his matchless qualities, his achievements already notched up and the wonderful potential for further greatness he doubtless displayed, with the absurdly insignificant values represented by the cow to save which he was prepared to stake his life. So too are the verses in the V Canto of the *Kumārasambhava* where Pārvatī admits the contrast in the physical equipment and mental and spiritual calibre of Lord Śiva: but instead of seeing it as a dichotomy, Pārvatī argues fervently, it is an indication of His unequalled greatness that lies beyond the comprehension of mere mortals. We can quote two verses from this most interesting and poetically matchless passage in all Kālidāsa:

अकिंचनस्सन् प्रभवस्स सम्पदां
त्रिलोकनाथः पितृसद्मगोचरः ।
स भीमरूपः शिव इत्युदीर्यते
न सन्ति याथार्थ्यविदः पिनाकिनः ॥

विभूषणोद्भासि पिनद्धभोगि वा
गजाजिनालम्बि दुकूलधारि वा ।
कपालि वा स्यादथवेन्दुशेखरं
न विश्वमूर्तेरवधार्यते वपुः ॥

[Kumārasambhava—V: 77 & 78]

Similar in idea to these verses and doubtless influenced by them is the stanza occurring in Rājaśēkhara's *Bālarāmāyaṇa*, which is distinguished by the single quality he can claim to have, a capacity to compose smooth-flowing verses in long metres.

नग्नस्तिष्ठति तं नमन्ति विबुधाः संवीतदिव्यांशुकाः
प्रीतो याति वृषेण वारणगतः तं वासवस्सेवते ।
भूषा तस्य नृणां कपालशकलैः स्तोता धनेशस्स्वयं
दौर्गत्यस्य परं पदं स भगवान् शंभुर्विभुत्वस्य च ॥ [II/4]

This same apparent inner contradiction in the personality of Lord Śiva has inspired the hymnist Puṣpadanta to sing of it in his *Śivamahimnastōtra* celebrated for its fresh ideas (unusually for a devotional poem) and the well lubricated movement of the verses.

स्मशानेएवाक्रीडा स्मरहर पिशाचाः सहचराः
    चिताभस्मालेपः स्त्रगपि नृकरोटीपरिकरः ।
अमङ्गल्यं शीलं तव भवतु नामैवमखिलम्
    तथापि स्मर्तॄणां वरद परमं मङ्गलमसि ॥ [24]

There is a seeming dichotomy in the personality of the truly noble: they can be harder than adamantine and softer than flowers in their dealings. This dichotomy is only what a superficial observer notices and to him it causes a certain surprise: but a closer examination will reveal that their firmness is brought into play when they are faced with temptations, where principles are involved, where values are in danger; when they see suffering, however, they melt in pity, they get softer than flowers, they rush to succour the one in distress. The stanza is from Bhavabhūti's *Uttararāmacarita.*

वज्रादपि कठोराणि मृदूनि कुसुमादपि ।
लोकोत्तराणां चेतांसि को नु विज्ञातुमर्हति ॥

[Uttararāmacarita—II:7]

There is a naughty verse parodying doctors by contrasting them with the god of death: the latter takes away only the life of a person while a doctor first deprives him of his money and eventually takes away his life too!

वैद्यराज नमस्तुभ्यं
    यमराजसहोदर ।
यमस्तु हरति प्राणान्
    वैद्यः प्राणान् धनानि च ॥

[Subhāṣitaratnabhāṇḍāgāra 45/1]

2.23 *Normal, intelligent people acting absurdly under the urge of overpowering emotions*

When normal people who can be credited with a modicum of commonsense behave in an absurd way, doing preposterous things, while under the influence of overpowering emotions, the phenomenon can cause surprise without offending realism.

Rāvaṇa was clearly a man of high mental calibre who not only struck fear in the hearts of people and was regarded as the scourge of the three worlds but commanded fierce loyalties and administered a vast kingdom with great success. He must have been in the habit of taking decisions after due deliberation: impetuous, deluded and frankly foolish acts do not go well with such sustained suzerainty over so much of the world. But addressing the southern direction, Rāma taunts him from the woods with his folly pointing out how delusion drove him to plunge into a disastrously foolish act that goes ill with his great reputation. Murāri comes out with a fine stanza recording Rāma's observation in his *Anargharāghava.*

कुले वा शौर्ये वा भुजसमुदये वा तपसि वा
बभूवुर्न प्राञ्चस्त्वमिव भवितारो न चरमे ।
अहो धिङ्‌ मोहस्ते समजनि चिरादेष न खलु
प्रवीराणां पन्थाः दशवदन येनासि चलितः ॥ [V/13]

Purūravas, one of the great emperors of India's prehistory is presented as saying and doing absurd things under the stress of his love for Urvaśi in Act IV of Vikramōrvaśīya. Some of the poems and prose passages herein are well-written and they constitute good examples of this category: but they are very much tradition-bound and type-cast and they do not look invitingly fresh as most of the work of Kālidāsa manages to do: for this reason they are not being quoted here.

Most of the verses of the two one-Act plays entitled *Unmattarāghava* are similarly illsutrative of this category but are again very much in the traditional mould with little freshness to redeem them. One verse (from Virūpākṣadēva's play), however, merits quoting here on account of the happy diction employed and the facile manner in which the poet has handled the long metre.

गोत्रे चन्दनशीतले त्वमुदभूः सेव्यस्सदा भोगिना-
मुल्लासाय भवस्थलं सुमनसामामोदवान् वीजसि ।
मन्त्रित्वं भजसे च मन्मथमहाराजस्य दक्षिण्यवा-
नेवं त्वं गुणिनां वरः प्रणयिनीमेह्योहि मे दर्शय ॥ [45]

In the extensive *nīti* literature in Sanskrit we have several verses where man's surprising proclivity to fall a prey to sensory desires is held up to ridicule: two verses appearing in the

Vairāgyaśataka of the greatest moralist of them all, Bhartṛhari are quoted here: they register the shocked surprise of the author and his disgust at the pronounced weakness of man for sensory fulfilment despite factors like discernment and judgment and erudition.

भिक्षाशनं तदपि नीरसमेकवारं शय्या च भूः परिजनो निजदेहमात्रम् ।
वस्त्रं विशीर्णशतखण्डमयी च कन्था हा हा तथापि विषया न परित्यजन्ति ।।
अजानन् दाहात्म्यं पततु शलभस्तीव्रदहने
स मीनोऽप्यज्ञानाद्बडिशयुतमश्नातु पिशितम् ।
विजानन्तोऽप्येते वयमिह विपज्जालजटिलान्
न मुञ्चामः कामानहह गहनो मोहमहिमा ।।

[Bhartṛhari Vairāgyaśataka: 15 and 18]

The most interesting example of this category, however, occurs in the bhakti literature: in a verse in the Kṛṣṇa Karṇāmṛta, Līlāśuka presents Rādhā and Kṛṣṇa acting in a patently foolish manner under the influence of their limitless love for each other. Rādhā brings a vessel from inside the house and fitting a churn to it she churns hard for quite a time and is surprised that no butter has appeared, till she notices that she has all the time been operating on an empty vessel with no curds in it! Kṛṣṇa, for his part selects an animal in the shed and assiduously tries to milk it but with no success at all: he looks around in puzzlement till he notices he has been trying to milk a bull all the time! This is the felicitous verse from the great hymnist.

राधा पुनातु जगदच्युतदत्तचित्ता
मन्थानमाकलयती दधिरिक्तपात्रे ।
तस्याः स्तनस्तबकचञ्चललोलदृष्टि-
र्देवोऽपि दोहनधिया वृषभं निरुन्धन् ।।

[Kṛṣṇakarṇāmṛta—II : 25]

2.24 *When psychology is harnessed in a unique way to achieve a desired end*

A scheming mind can often put psychology to use, can harness it as it were to perform some useful function. Kings and leaders of men have often got a potentially inimical mob out of the way by throwing a bagful of coins, being sure that the lure of money will drive all other things from the minds of the people. A far subtler example will be the age-old strategy of tyrants of declaring war on a neighbouring country without any provocation, only to distract the minds of their subjects from a preoccupation with their condition.

A cinema theatre had a problem: women, sitting in the front rows, insisted on wearing their high hats shutting off the view from those sitting in the rear. Notices put up by the theatre staff appealing to their social sense had no effect, whatever. Finally a bright staffer put up a board saying, "All old ladies are requested to keep their hats on"—and promptly, off came all the hats.

Bhasa furnishes an excellent example of this in his Pratigñā—Yaugandharāyaṇa. The wily and devoted minister of King Udayana, Yaugandharāyaṇa by name, in sending a message to the queen mother that her son has been taken prisoner employs his expert knowledge of human psychology to soften the blow for her. He instructs the messenger to talk to her vaguely about the horrors of war: and when she begins to entertain fears of Udayana's death in the battlefield, she can be told he has been taken prisoner—which will be received by her almost as good news after the spell of tension and anxiety.

पूर्वं तावद् युद्धसंबद्धदोषा
प्रस्तोतव्याः भावनास्संशयानाम् ।
संदिग्धेऽर्थे चिन्त्यमाने विनाशे
रूढे शोके कार्यतत्त्वं निवेद्यम् ॥ [I/13]

Kālidāsa possessed a deep insight into the workings of the human mind: and in his plays and epic poems we have many instances of his putting this insight into use. Where Indra has to urge Manmatha, the god of love |to muster courge and aim an arrow at Lord Śiva, he makes expert use of psychology in flattering Manmatha, lowering his own image in the process: Indra observes that in the case of hermits, his own weapon, the deadly *vajra* is of no avail but Manmatha can freely function in such a forbidding field and can be effective too, everytime.

सर्वं सखे त्वय्युपपन्नमेतत्
उभे ममास्त्रे कुलिशं भवांश्च ।
वज्रं तपोवीर्यमहत्सु कुण्ठं
त्वं सर्वतोगामि च साधकं च ॥

[Kumārasambh ava—III:12]

The device proves effective: for, in the teeth of Lord Śiva's terrible reputation, the god of love now agrees to take Him on with disastrous consequences to himself.

Viśākhadatta's political play, the Mudrārākṣasa is replete with applications of this device: Rākṣasa, the minister of Malayakētu harnesses Candragupta's psychology dexterously to foment a quarrel between him and his most wily and effective minister Cāṇakya (In reality, Cāṇakya having scented his adversary's plans feigns a quarrel and leaves the emperor's presence). Cāṇakya, for his part, sets in motion an extremely complex stratagem involving secret, vaguely-worded documents and purloined seals to sow suspicion in the mind of Malayakētu regarding Rākṣasa's loyalty, as a result of which the minister is eventually dismissed.

Cāṇakya makes use of the same device to deliver Rākṣasa up to Candragupta, not by hunting far and wide for him but by making him come on his own: this, he accomplishes by letting him know that a loyal friend of Rākṣasa's, Candanadāsa by name was being executed for his friendship with him: the noble statesman now has no other thought than to rush to the place of execution where the triumphant Cāṇakya hands him over, with regard and affection to Candragupta for appointment as his principal minister.

2.25 *The sudden realization that the cause of all the trouble to which one is subject is oneself, no other*

The tendency of men to blame others for all their misfortunes is well-known: hence this is the expected thing: it is therefore a wholly unexpected thing if it suddenly flashes on us in a moment of honest appraisal that much of the blame must be laid at our own door: there is agonised surprise evoked by this unexpected diagnosis.

A scientist is reported to have embarked on a very delicate experiment involving the weighing of two objects to measure and verify the law regulating the force of attraction operating between things. To secure acceptable results, he systematically eliminated all heavy things around the balance which would warp the results but still found that there was some force operating to warp the measurements. He tried his best to locate it, failed and was resting in an unhappy mood when the solution flashed on him (as it often happens): the discovery was that he himself, weighing over 200 lbs was the object discommoding the experiment! He removed himself to a considerable distance and started observing the results through a telescope: he then found the results eminently satisfactory.

No one understood the subtle eider-down notions and fancies that float in a lover's mind better than Kālidāsa. Duṣyanta has been eagerly observing the reactions of Śakuntalā all through their first meeting to detect signs of affection for him, for like all lovers he is torn by the conflicting impressions—"she loves me, she loves me not." He now makes a series of observations, none of which is a clear pointer that she returns his love: for instance he says she looks at the things of the world with an affectionate gaze, her eyes shine with affection even when they are directed elsewhere than at him. She walks slowly as if under the urge of coquetry though this is surely on account of the heaviness of her hind portion. From such evidence he concludes that she must be in love with him.

Other poets, the best of them, may be able to conceive of this much, ending the passage with the conclusion that she loves him back indeed. But now comes the unique Kālidasian touch: for he makes the advocatus diaboli in Duṣyanta's mind come up with a sharp rejoinder: "This conclusion is surprising! There can be no certainty at all that all this is on account of her love for you. As a lover, in deep love, you are merely extending your subjective preferences into her personality, you think everything she does is on account of her love for you!" And it is on account of this tail-piece that this verse gets chosen as illustrative of this category.

स्निग्धं वीक्षितमन्यतोऽपि नयने यत्प्रेरयन्त्या तया
यातं यच्च नितम्बयोर्गुरुतया मन्दं विलासादिव ।
मा गा इत्युपरुद्धया यदपि सा सासूयमुक्ता सखी
सर्वं तत्किल मत्परायणमहो कामी स्वतां पश्यति ॥

[Śākuntala—II:2]

Rākṣasa in the political play, the Mudrārākṣasa makes a rueful observation with an edge of surprise (indicated by the word 'hanta') at the carefully-laid plans of his turning out to prove beneficial to Candragupta instead of hurting him, as intended. There is little artistry in Viśākhadatta's versification but this stanza is worth quoting for its honest reflection of the workings of a brilliant mind in a mood of bitter self-denigration.

कन्या तस्य वधाय या विषमयी गूढं प्रयुक्ता मया
दैवात्पर्वतकस्तया स निहतो यस्तस्य राज्यार्धहृत् ।
ये शस्त्रेषु रसेषु च प्रणिहितास्तैरेव ते घातिता
मौर्यस्यैव फलन्ति पश्य विविधश्रेयांसि मन्नीतयः ॥

[Mudrārākṣasa—II:16]

There is a beautiful verse in Amaru which illustrates this category: but there always is more in an Amaru stanza than in a comparable unit of writing from the other masters, which has given rise to the saying:

अमरुककवेरेकः श्लोकः प्रबन्धशतायते ।

A girl in love got annoyed by something her lover did or said and there was the usual tiff all married men are familiar with. The lover, distraught with grief at her anger so far forgot all questions of prestige that he fell prostrate at her feet begging her forgivance. But the girl, with his remissness still smarting, was disinclined to forgive him. This is the reaction of the coarser part of her personality: for, her nobler and subtler personality keeps reminding her that the ways in which lovers indicate their anger (and even their forgivance) are delicate, they are gentle gestures that suggest the feeling behind: love is not a battlefield nor even a melodrama where exaggerated gestures are the rule. It should not be necessary, she ruefully reflects, for the lover to roll in the dust pleading to be forgiven, with her anger still unquenched: it is all wrong, it is far too coarse and gross, she says to herself. It is a beautiful verse, rich with delicate shades, in the language only Amaru knows to wield:

कोपो यत्र भ्रुकुटिरचना निग्रहो यत्र मौनं
यत्रान्योन्यस्मितमनुनयो दृष्टिपातः प्रसाद : ।
तस्य प्रेम्णस्तदिदमधुना वैशसं पश्य जातं
त्वं पादान्ते लुठसि न च मे मन्युमोक्षः खलाया : ॥

[Amaruśataka : 38]

2.26 *Accomplishing mighty things with very unpromising implements*

Some gifted people do seem to accomplish mighty deeds using fragile, inadequate tools: this is certainly evocative of wonder, the emotion produced being directly proportional to the difference between the level of the accomplishment and the potential possessed by the tool.

There is a character in Wodehouse, a senior and highly respected gentleman of the underworld, by name Slattery, with the sobriquet Soup attached to it on account of his known proficiency in manufacturing and using a potent liquid called soup which can break the locks of safes. An amateur seeks his help in opening the safe in a chateau belonging to a lady: during the course of a highly diverting conversation, he asks the 'soup' artist anxiously if he has brought all his specialist tools for the job.

Mr. Slattery snorts in contempt, saying these safes owned by society ladies are so flimsy he does not need special tools to open them nor does he use his soup in such cases: what he does is to borrow a ladies' hairpin and use it to open the safe: if a hair-pin is not readily available, he is not going to get stymied, for he can open it by blowing on the hole after chewing a little garlic.

Rāma accomplished the most forbidding commission of killing Rāvaṇa and defeating his famed army but what were the tools he used and who were his allies in this mighty undertaking? There is a verse found in Hanumānnāṭaka which points to this feat of Rāma with wonder.

विजेतव्या लङ्का चरणतरणीयो जलनिधि-
विपक्षः पौलस्त्यो रणभुवि सहायाश्च कपयः ।
तथाप्येको रामः सकलमपि हन्ति प्रतिबलं
क्रियासिद्धिः सत्त्वे वसति महतां नोपकरणे ॥

[Hanumānnāṭaka—VII:7]

There is a similar verse relating to Manmatha, god of love, who, armed with fragile weapons like a bow of sugarcane, flowers for his arrows and a string of bees for his bowstring is able to subjugate the most austere and strongwilled of men.

There is a verse more or less in the same spirit as the above but giving credit to women and not to the god of love: women are termed weak (*abalā*) and the implements and weapons they wield are delicate but the world of men is at their mercy. This verse is from the Śṛṅgāraśataka of Bhartṛhari:

नूनं हि ते कविवरा विपरीतवाचो
ये नित्यमाहुरबला इति कामिनीस्ताः ।

यार्भिर्विलोलतरतारकदृष्टिपातैः
शक्रादयोऽपि विजितास्त्वबलाः कथं ताः ॥

[Bhartṛhari's Śṛṅgāraśataka :10]

2.27 *Things appear startlingly different when the angle of vision or point of focus changes*

If we are used to looking at a thing from one angle, then if the angle of vision is changed, we may be surprised at the change come over the once-familiar object. A magazine ran a contest in which an extremely complicated object with tube-like things criss-crossing was presented to the readers who were asked to guess what it is. Many readers turned in entries guessing the picture to be that of the engineroom of a big ocean-liner. The correct solution as announced by the magazine was that it was the underside of a cockroach photographed from below through a glasspane.

A variant of this is the change in the point of focus: if we are used to one of many objects being always the point of focus, then there may be great surprise in store for us when the focus shifts.

It was T.B. Macaulay who said, "Puritans disliked bear-baiting not because it gave pain to the bear but because it proffered pleasure to the onlookers." Here the focus of censure is turned, not on the expected thing, the bear getting tortured but on the onlookers enjoying the spectacle, this shift causing surprise.

When the teaching of the theory of evolution was sought to be barred through legislation in N. Carolina state, U.S. Senator Sam Ervin commented: "I don't see but one good feature in this proposal to bar the teaching of evolution and that is that it will gratify the monkeys to know that they are absolved from all responsibility for the conduct of the human race."

An elderly man was proposing to marry a young girl. "You are out of your mind" said his friend. "You are 60 and she is 20. In 20 years you will be 80 and she will be 40."

"I've thought about that", said the prospective bridegroom "But when that time comes I can get divorced and marry another 20 year-old."

The shift in emphasis may even be in regard to words: while the speaker may place the emphasis on one word or phrase, the listener may shift it to another, causing surprise. Robert

Benchley was taking the tea when a friend warned him, "You are drinking tea! It is a slow poison!" Benchley replied, "Well, I am in no hurry!" The friend naturally had wanted to emphasize the word "poison" but Benchley shifted the emphasis to the word "slow" with a startling, comic result.

There is an Indian story which, too, can be quoted as illustrative of this. A king woke up in the morning and just before getting up happened to look out of the window: he saw a man, who too noticed the king looking at him. The king withdrew his head from the window in a hurry and his head hit against the window-sill hurting him sharply. The king thought, "This man in the street must be a bad person: if my seeing him once can hurt me, the king of the realm, how much ordinary people will suffer if they look at him the first thing, every day of his life !" He ordered the man to be rounded up and beheaded, purely in the interests of the welfare of his subjects.

The hapless man was being led to the block when he expressed a desire to see the king once before he dies. The request was granted: he said to the king, "Your majesty, I gather I am getting beheaded as you saw me the first thing today morning and you hurt yourself slightly as a result. Well, your majesty, you were the first person I saw today and I am going to get beheaded as a result!..." The king was startled at the new picture laid open before him when the emphasis was shifted from the king to the man-in-the-street and, it is said, he ordered his release forthwith.

In the VII Act of the Śākuntala, Kālidāsa presents a startlingly new, unfamiliar, picture of the earth when seen from miles above, from an aerial vehicle. It is not clear how Kālidāsa was able to envisage this picture in those times when aeroplanes had not been discovered: it must be the fruit of his imagination helped by the pictures seen from atop high palaces projected liberally to cover much greater heights.

शैलानामवरोहतीव शिखरावुन्मज्जतां मेदिनी
कर्णाभ्यन्तरलीनतां विजहति स्कन्धोदयात्पादपाः ।
संतानैस्तनुभावनष्टसलिला व्यक्ति व्रजन्त्यापगाः
केनाप्युत्क्षिपतेव मर्त्यभुवनं मत्पार्श्वमानीयते ॥

[Śākuntala—VII : 8]

Similar is the picture of the Palk Strait separating India and

Śrīlaṅkā, seen from above, occurring in the *Raghuvaṃśa*, XIII Canto.

वैदेहि पश्यामलयाद्विभक्तं
मत्सेतुना फेनिलमम्बुराशिम् ।
छायापथेनेव शरत्प्रसन्नं
आकाशमाविष्कृतचारुतारम् ॥

[Raghuvaṃśa—III:2]

In fact, there are many such pictures of the earth and the sea looked at from above, in this beautiful canto, one of the best passages in all Kālidāsa: a memorable one is where the lord of the sea is presented as kissing the rivers in the mouth, as a *dakṣiṇanāyaka*.

There is a very unusual work by Nīlakaṇṭha Dīkṣita, the Śivalīlārṇava of which the original is a Tamil epic: it represents the playful activities of Lord Śiva in the city of Madurai in the South. Śiva's bride Taṭātakā, the Madurai princess of the *Pāṇḍya* clan is described as travelling in the *Puṣpaka* the aerial chariot to Madurai and her view of the earth below is graphically described in a stanza in the XI sargā.

ददर्श वल्मीकवदुन्नतान् गिरीन्
महान्त्यरण्यानपि शङ्कतानिव ।
सुरापगाद्याः सरितोऽपि तन्तुवत्
विदूरभावादवनौ नृपात्मजा ॥ [XI/2]

So far as we have discussed examples where there is a physical change of the angle of vision: there are examples available in Sanskrit where a change of viewpoint psychologically is involved. In fact there is a whole work devoted to the presentation of the startling differences brought up by two different onlookers of the same scene, the differences being the result of the very different psychological set-ups in the speakers. The work is called the *Viśvaguṇādarśa Campū* and is by one Vēnkatādhvarī who lived about 350 years ago. The poet presents the observations of two demigods one of whom is a perpetual critic inclined to see only the seamy side of things and the other, the very opposite in attitude, a fair observer and commentator of life and men. The attitude of the poet is very modern, his power of observation, excellent: and his considerable powers of versification and scholarship make his poems a pleasure to read.

We can cite a few examples that go to make this category better understood. The first demigod seeing the Ganga below begins to berate the river for its chequered career and its association with Śiva and the second corrects him, lauding the sacred and purifying qualities of the great river. The first one then enters into a broadside against the city of Benares citing the fact that it is full of corpses and burning ghats and Śaivite practices which last seem to irritate the sectarian Vaishnavite in this *gandharva*. The second one answers all of his criticisms, showing how the very things he had scored up as adverse are factors highly in its favour.

For instance, the first *gandharva* criticises the peculiar habits and dress of the people of Benares (or the absence of it) in the following manner:

दत्तं साधुमुदे यदेकमपि तत् क्षेत्रप्रभावाद्भवेत्
कामं कोटिगुणं भवान्तर इति ख्यातं त्वयि त्वास्थया ।
वासं प्राप्य मुहुर्बहूनि ददतो वासांसि जन्मान्तरे
लोका हन्त भजन्ति दिग्वसनतां हे काशि तुभ्यं नमः ।।

[Viśvaguṇādarśa Campū : 107]

The second, in his hot rejoinder points out that the residents of Benares, even if given over to enjoyment, achieve a similarity of appearance with Lord Śiva—a rarely-attained state of bliss. He then goes on to defend Kāśī as the home of the few brave men, steadfast in the observance of Vedic injunctions in the general context of indifference to religious precepts: he reminds the carper that in the *Kali* Age, if a few people are still devoted to right conduct and right living, they should be highly regarded as water-holes with a limited stock of water in a barren desert.

एतादृशे कलियुगेऽपि शतेषु कश्चित्
जातावरो जगति यः श्रुतिमार्ग एव ।
यत्किंचिदाचरति पात्रमसौ स्तुतीनां
श्लाघ्यं मितापमपि किं न मरौ सरश्चेत् ।।

[Viśvaguṇādarśa Campū: 122]

He says with a touch of finality that if even one man attempts to lead the people in the right Vedic path in an age when even God seems somnolent and foreigners rule the country, that man of heroic stature should be honoured.

आक्रान्तासु वसुन्धरासु यवनैरासेतुहैमाचलं
विद्राणे क्षितिभृद्गणे विकरुणे निद्राति नारायणे ।
निर्विघ्नप्रसरे कलावपि बलान्निष्कण्टकं वैदिकं
पन्थानं किल तत्र तत्र परिपात्येको हि लोकोत्तरः ॥

[Viśvaguṇādarśa Campū: 124]

Overcoming the temptation to quote many more stanzas from this excellent work, the present writer may be allowed the indulgence to cite one more episode selected for the poet's most unusual sense of fairness to a people regarded as exotic, unorthodox, unclean and cruel—to the English who came to trade and stayed to rule. To the stale and well-worn diatribes of the first *gandharva*, the second gives a reply underscoring the honesty of the whites in trade, their capacity to produce wonderful things (through machines) and their even-handed justice as administrators. The verse is nicely sculptored as most of Vēnkatādhvarī's are and evokes surprise at the radically different picture seen with the change in the viewpoint.

प्रसह्य न हरन्त्यमी परधनौघमन्यायतो
वदन्ति न मृषावचो विरचयन्ति वस्त्वद्भुतम् ।
यथाविधि कृतागसां विदधति स्वयं दण्डनं
गुणानवगुणाकरेष्वपि गृहाण हूणेष्वमून् ॥

[Viśvaguṇādarśa Campū: 370]

2.28 *Postulating surprising new causes for known phenomena of nature*

Man's fancy ranges wide, it is able to encompass even things beyond the earth: the black spot on the moon has attracted and held the attention of poets who have let their fancy dig up plausible explanations for the phenomenon. These attempts may not carry conviction but certainly stimulate a little surprised amusement—which is not without value in the aesthetic process.

One verse suggests, discounting the attempts of all the others, that the blackness is the result of all the darkness of the night drunk up by the moon and stored in his transparent stomach.

अङ्कं केऽपि शशङ्किरे जलनिधेः पङ्कं परे मेनिरे
सारङ्गं कतिचिच्च संजगदिरे भूच्छायमैच्छन्परे ।
इन्दौ यद्दलितेन्द्रनीलशकलश्यामं दरीदृश्यते
तत्सान्द्रं निशि पीतमन्धतमसं कुक्षिस्थमाचक्ष्महे ॥

[Kuvalayānanda, N.S. edition, page 26]

Another puts the blackness down to the scar produced on the body of the moon when, at the time of the churning of the milk ocean, the *manthara* mountain with its sharp rocks cut up its body causing nasty flesh wounds.

मन्थानभूमिधरमूलशिलासहस्र-
संघट्टनव्रणकिणः स्फुरदीन्दुमध्ये ।
छायामृगः शशक इत्यतिपामरोक्ति-
स्तेषां कथंचिदपि तत्र हि न प्रसक्तिः ॥

[Kuvalayānanda, N.S. edition, page 26]

Another fancy is presented in greater detail: the swarm of bees on lotuses, annoyed at their closing up with the setting of the sun, rises in a body and squats on the moon, misled, no doubt, by the surface similarities between a lotus and the moon: the black smudge is caused by this swarm of all the bees on the earth migrating to the moon at sun-down.

मधुव्रतौघः कुपितस्स्वकीय-
मधुप्रपापद्मनिमीलितेन ।
बिम्बं समाक्रम्य बलात्सुधांशोः
कलङ्कमङ्के ध्रुवमातनोति ॥

[Kuvalayānanda, N.S. edition, page 126]

A modern poet, Kaṇṭakārjuna has a very modern Indian explanation for the black spot. Everyone is aware that there is considerable black money (unaccounted money) with the people but no one, not even the omniscient government is able to locate it. The mystery is solved by the poet who points out that it is all hidden in the moon, smudging its surface.

नक्तं यो धवलेन्दुमण्डलगतः संलक्ष्यते कालिमा
तं पङ्कं शशकं घनान्धतमसं मूढाः समाचक्षते ।
एतन्मन्त्रिवणिक्जनैः सुकृतिभिश्चन्द्रस्य लोकं गतैः
साकं नीतमिहार्जितं भुवि पुरा कृष्णं धनं मन्महे ॥

[Kaṇṭakāñjali: चन्द्रस्य कालिमा]

The stanza is a good representative specimen of the social criticism rendered pungent with irony and sarcasm, found in many of Kaṇṭakārjuna's well-turned out verses. He is one of the latest but certainly not the last of the talented line of poets composing in Sanskrit, maintaining an unbroken tradition of creativity.

2.29 *Striking gradation through which are fashioned new techniques with which to measure intangibles*

Though everyone realises that there is no way of measuring intangible qualities like courage and prowess, certain characters find it necessary to set up a gradation showing that someone (newly being introduced or whose image is being drummed up for the first time) is braver, more valiant than others whose calibre is well-known. This gradation promotes surprise in proportion to the difference between the old and the newly drummed up image of the budding hero.

In Bhavabhūti's Mahāvīracarita, Rāma, an unknown stripling overcomes Paraśurāma, the world-conqueror. Rāma's preceptor Viśvāmitra proudly points up the achievement of Rāma by drawing up a graded list of famed heroes with Rāma reigning at the top:

मरुत्वन्तं देवं य इह भगवन्तं विजयते
विजिग्ये तं राजा युधि दशमुखं हैहयपति : ।
निहन्तारं तस्य प्रथितमहिमानं त्रिभुवने
महावीरं जित्वा किमिव हि न वत्सेन विजितम् ॥

[Mahāvīracarita—IV:40]

Indra, a no mean warrior himself suffered defeat at the hands of Kārtavīrya who, in turn, was worsted in battle by Paraśurāma: by defeating Paraśurāma, the young Rāma had clearly established himself at the top of the roll-call of heroes. One may note here, in passing, a little glimpse of character showing through: Viśvāmitra indulged in this bit of boasting as it was his own disciple that came out the champion: but in addition, there must have been an added incentive for him, a *ksatriya* feeling inwardly happy at the defeat of the sworn enemy of the whole clan of *kṣatriyas*.

Murāri offers a measure of Rāma's valour in precise arithmetical terms—a feat not considered possible by most. In the famous battle between the hero and the villain at the end of the play, the missiles hurled by one were destroyed by the other and for a long time, it was a battle equally poised: but Rāvaṇa brought into use all his twenty arms in hurling the missiles and defending himself while Rāma had but two arms to deploy. So, concludes the poet, Rāma must be at least ten times as great in the martial arts as his adversary.

यद्रावणो बहुभिरेष भुजैः करोति
तद्राघवः प्रतिकरोति भुजद्वयेन ।
कर्म द्वयोर्यदपि तुल्यफलं तथापि
रक्षोभटाद्दशगुणं नरवीरशिल्पम् ॥ [VI/63]

There is a slightly different context in which such a gradation may be explicitly presented or covertly suggested by one of the characters. In the Mahāvīracarita, Bhavabhūti brings in a hermit who tells Rāma of the misadventure Rāvaṇa had entered upon, taking on Vālin as adversary with very disastrous consequences to his own ego. The verse:

कैलासे तुलिते जिते त्रिभुवने वुष्यन्तमभ्युद्यतं
दोर्युद्धाय दशास्यमिन्द्रतनयः प्रक्षिप्य कक्षालये ।
सान्ध्यं कर्म समाप्य सप्तसु नदीनाथेष्वथो मुक्तवा-
नुन्मुक्ताय नताय याचितवते सख्यं च तस्मै ददौ ॥

[Mahāvīracarita—V:37]

The conflict between Rāma and Vālin is yet to be: but when it happens, the spectators will have the graded list of heroes fresh in their minds with Vālin above Rāvaṇa and now Rāma's name can be etched even above Vālin's: such a feat of valour, evoking the sentiment of heroism, the dominant rasa of the play is reinforced by a surge of surprise at this revision in the roll-call of martial prowess.

In the Hanumānnāṭaka, perhaps more than anywhere else, we find the most adroit use made of this device: for, by hernessing it, in the court of Rāvaṇa, Hanumān wins a great psychological victory over the Scourge of the Three Worlds by planting fear in his heart and the first seeds of diffidence.

The dialogue begins innocuously enough with Rāvaṇa demanding to know how Rāma was spending his time: "In conquering enemies" is the laconic reply and in answer to the next question, Hanumān breaks the news of Vālin's defeat and death at Rāma's hands. Rāvaṇa pretends not to have heard of monkey heroes like Vālin, with ill-assumed contempt: but the astute messenger of Rāma tells him, "Yes, we are aware that there has been a certain clouding of the mind that has overtaken you: but we did not realise the extent of the clouding. How can you forget your encounter with him where you suffered defeat and as a result got tied up ignominiously above the bed of child Aṅgada as a working toy for his amusement?" The verse is deliciously venomous and must be savoured.

रामः किं कुरुते प्रतीपविजयं कोऽसौ प्रतीपो जितः
वाली सोऽपि च को न वेत्सि किममुं को वेत्ति शाखामगम् ।
आस्तेऽद्यापि तवास्ति विस्मृतिरहो मोहो महानीदृशः
पर्यङ्के निजबालकेलिकृतये बद्धोऽसि येनोपरि ॥ [VIII/II]

We shall end this section with a verse where two products of the ocean are compared and graded for their lethal effect: the poison which emanated from the ocean and Lakṣmī the goddess who too came up out of the churning are rated wrongly by the people who regard the former as a terrible killer: in fact Śiva thrives on the poison while Hari who married Lakṣmī and has been living with her is in a comatose condition: this verse could fit in as illustrative of one or two other sections too, equally well.

हालाहलो नैव विषं विषं रमा
जनाः परं व्यत्ययमत्र मन्वते ।
निपीय जागर्ति सुखेन तं शिवः
स्पृशन्निमां मुह्यति निद्रया हरिः ॥

[Kuvalayānanda N.S. edition, page 27]

2.30 *Registering consternation at one's own great misfortune or cupidity*

Earlier we discussed a category where a character suddenly discovers itself to be the cause of a calamitous happening: here we shall discuss cases where a tragedy that befalls a character induces a wonderment laced with sorrow: the wonder is occasioned by the puzzlement, "Why am I chosen by unkind fate to suffer like this? Can man be visited by a greater calamity than this?" Admittedly sorrow is much the dominant partner here: but surprise nicely blends to set an edge on self-pity. The deeper implications of surprise blending with other sentiments will be examined more closely in the next chapter: in the meantime let us examine individual cases where the shrill note of wonder can be heard above the wail of sorrow if the ear is cocked for subtle notes.

Bhāsa in his Ūrubhaṅga presents the blind king Dhṛtarāṣṭra wailing over his singular tragedy of losing all his hundred sons at once: here we can hear the thin but high note of disbelief—"Why this cruellest of dispensations for me?" registering sorrow muted with wonder.

रिपुसमरविमर्दं मानवीर्यप्रदीप्तं
सुतशतमतिधीरं वीरमुत्पाद्यमानम् ।
धरणितलविकीर्णं किं स योग्यो न भोक्तुं
सकृदपि धृतराष्ट्रः पुत्रदत्तं निवापम् ॥ [39]

In Vikramōrvaśīya, Kālidāsa presents Purūravas shocked with sudden grief at the news that Urvaśi was to part forever from him: the shock was compounded by the manner in which the tidings came to him: for he had just savoured the delight of looking on the face of his son Āyus and she had to leave him for her heavenly abode as stipulated by Indra. So delight gets instantly metamorphosed into anguish with wonder exacerbating it—wonder caused by the fact that the sorrow issues from the same source from which he had derived all that delight. The whole thing is illuminated by a wonderful analogy as Kālidāsa alone knows how to fashion.

आश्वासितस्य मम नाम सुतोपलब्ध्या
सद्यस्त्वया सह कृशोदरि विप्रयोगः ।
व्यावर्तितातपरुजः प्रथमाभ्रवृष्ट्या
वृक्षस्य वैद्युत इवाग्निरुपस्थितोऽयम् ॥

[Vikramōrvaśiya—V:16]

A tree famished by drought is revived by rainfall: but the tree resurrected is struck by a thunderbolt—which issues from the same clouds that had sent down earlier the life-giving rain. Incidentally, the tragedy is averted in the last moment by the message of Indra who commands Urvaśi to continue to be with the king for some more time and the play comes to an end on this note.

We find many such cases in the Mṛcchakaṭika where sorrow is sharpened by surprise on account of some special factors connected with the nature of the source of sorrow. In the IV Act, Madanikā upbraids her lover Śarvilaka for having stolen the jewels of Vasantasēna kept as a trust with the penurious Cārudatta and suggests restoring them to him. Śarvilaka, shocked at this, speaks out in self-condemnation ruefully reflecting how even the all powerful kings find it difficult to deal with villains of his type. The thief's sense of horror comes out vividly in this verse, with an edge set by puzzlement.

न खलु मम विषादः साहसेऽस्मिन्भयं वा
कथयसि हि किमर्थं तस्य साधोर्गुणांस्त्वम् ।
जनयति मम वेदं कुत्सितं कर्म लज्जां
नृपतिरिह शठानां मादृशां किं नु कुर्यात् ॥

[Mṛcchakaṭika—IV: 20]

In the VI Act, Āryaka whose troubles started from the day astrologers predicted his ascending the throne, bewails his fate in rising self-pity laced with surprise at the fact that without having committed an offence he has suddenly become hateful in the eyes of the ruling king!

हित्वाहं नरपतिबन्धनापदेश-
व्यापत्तिव्यसनमहार्णवं महान्तम् ।
पादाग्रस्थितनिगडैकपाशकर्षी
प्रभ्रष्टो गज इव बन्धनाद्भ्रमामि ॥

[Mṛcchakaṭika—VI: 1]

भाग्यानि मे यदि तदा मम कोऽपराधो
यद्वन्यनाग इव संयमितो ऽस्मि तेन ।
दैवी च सिद्धिरपि लङ्घयितुं न शक्या
गम्यो नृपो बलवता सह को विरोधः ॥

[Mṛcchakaṭika—VI : 2]

One of the most touching scenes in Sanskrit is where Carudatta stands in the law court, charged with the murder of Vasantasena. Riding in tandem with his deep sorrow is his puzzled surprise that anyone could think him capable of killing a weeping woman —he who could not, for feelings of compassion, bring himself to pluck flowers from a living creeper !

योऽहं लतां कुसुमितामपि पुष्पहेतोः
आकृष्य नैव कुसुमावचयं करोमि ।
सोऽहं कथं भ्रमरपक्षरुचौ सुदीर्घे
केशे प्रगृह्य रुदतीं प्रमदां निहन्मि ॥

[Mṛcchakaṭika—XI:28]

In Harṣa's Nāgânanda the hero Jīmūtavāhana very nobly offers to become the day's victim of Garuḍa releasing the serpent Śaṅkhacūḍa from the obligation. The grateful Śaṅkhacūḍa is happy, at first, at his unlooked for release but when he sees the glory spectacle of his saviour badly mauled by the divine eagle a shock of self-deprecation overwhelms him for having involved the benevolent king in this horrible fate which should have been rightfully his own. In the passages before verse number 8 and in this verse there are a number of words that express his shock nicely blending with deep anguish. The verse is reproduced here:

नाहित्राणात् कीर्तिरेका मयाप्ता
नापि श्लाघ्या स्वामिनोऽनुष्ठिताज्ञा ।
दत्त्वात्मानं रक्षितोऽन्येन शोच्यो
हाधिक् कष्टं वञ्चितो वञ्चितोऽस्मि ॥

[Nāgânanda—V:8]

2.31 *Clever sophistry, specious arguments, cunning reasoning*

Usually a display of brash cleverness repels: we find our barriers of incredulity raised when we hear specious arguments, cunning reasoning: but, if the speaker manages to import a certain reasonableness, a certain inevitability into his arguments, our incredulity is momentarily suspended and we are taken in. However, when we come out of the ether, we are surprised we were taken in, even for the moment. This category can occasion only a mild surprise but the considerable artistry displayed by the speaker lends a certain charm eked out by the surprise.

David Ben Gurion, the Israel strongman, was known to be very undemocratic in his ways. When somebody made an accusation to this effect at a party meeting, he turned to a member of his cabinet whom he held to be unflinchingly honest. "Tell them, Naphthali" he asked, "do I really conduct party meetings undemocratically?"

Peretz Naphthali looked at Ben Gurion, turning on his most fetching smile. Then he answered reflectively, "I wouldn't say that. What I'd say is that the party always votes in the most scrupulously democratic fashion whichever way you want it to."

There is a well-composed one-Act play on the Rāma theme called Dūtāṅgada by Subhaṭa Kavi, where we find a specious argument from Rāvaṇa for not returning Sītā to Rāma as demanded by the messenger, Aṅgada: "I have committed my first mistake in abducting Sītā: my second mistake lies in the fact that even on deeper cogitation I failed to return her to her husband, on my own. Now, after the monkeys have built a bridge over the ocean and the enemy is in full cry, if I return Sītā to him, that would constitute my third mistake!" The speciousness, of course, consists in the fact that Rāma being well-known as a most fair-minded and chivalrous person, there will really be no insult coming from him or a loss of face happening to the arrogant Rāvaṇa if he returned Sītā to him, even at that late stage. Subhaṭa has an easy style of composition even when the longest metres are involved and the verse may be enjoyed for its lubricated mechanics:

एकं तावदकृत्यमेतदतुलं यन्मैथिलीयं हृता
द्वैतीयीकमिदं विमृश्य यदसौ तस्मै तदा नार्पिता ।
तार्तीयीकमिदं तु यत्कपिभटैर्बद्धेऽद्य वारां निधौ
संधानं दशकंधरो रचयति क्षमानन्दिनीमर्पयन् ॥ [18]

In another Rāma play, Sītārāghava by Rāmapāṇivāda of Kērala, Rāvaṇa expostulates with the god of love who is torturing him with love darts. Rāvaṇa's peculiar sophistry runs thus: "You were once burnt to ashes by Śiva and I shook up His abode Kailāsa and caused Him some annoyance. I have benefitted you by annoying your mortal enemy, O Manmatha and is this the gratitude you show me for all that?" This is the verse, smoothly turned out and easy on the tongue:

दग्धं येन पुरा वपुस्तव पुरां जेत्रा स्वनेत्रानले
तस्यावासमहाचलोऽपि हि मया दोर्भिः समुन्मूलितः ।
इत्युच्चैरुपकारि मित्रमपि मामस्त्रानले निस्त्रपो
निर्धक्ष्यन्निव लक्ष्यसे कथमहो भिन्नक्रमो विक्रमः ॥ [IV/15]

Rāvaṇa's arguments addressed in the main to his intrepid minister and in part to Sītā herself (as presented in the Āścarya-cūdāmaṇi) offer excellent examples of sophistry but are not quoted here as they have been shown under other categories. Rāvaṇa had the necessary intelligence, self-confidence and the lack of scruples to qualify as the primemost dispenser of sophistry: he has the Satanic quality of "making the worse appear the better reason".

Nīlakaṇṭha Dīkṣita is a writer of considerable sophistication which runs to cynicism, particularly in his Kaliviḍambana. In one of the verses he offers professional advice to doctors which is clearly intended in their, not the patients' interest. "When you are consulted on behalf of a patient", he counsels, "you need not be fussy about the medicine you prescribe, as almost anything would do: but you will be well advised to lay down extremely stiff do's and dont's—particularly in the matter of diet. If the patient recovers, it will be put down to the efficacy of your prescription: if otherwise, the relations of the deceased would put it down to some transgression of one of the many conditions imposed (which is certain to have happened)." This the verse:

भैषज्यं तु यथाकामं पथ्यं तु कठिनं वदेत् ।
आरोग्यं वैद्यमाहात्म्यात् अन्यथात्वमपथ्यतः ॥

[Kaliviḍambana:25]

Such tongue-in-the-cheek advice is proffered to astrologers and to polemicians also in this interesting work where we find that rare quality of genuine "modern" humour.

2.32 *Deriving a general principle from an all-too-inadequate number of cases and applying it universally with amusing results*

Scientists take good care to study a sufficiently large number of individual cases distributed over a wide range before they venture to generalise and derive a law which they then proceed to prove (in the sense of testing) by applying it to other cases. But in life, outside of laboratories and in literature, a person in a hurry or under the urge of a powerful emotion may derive a general principle from a limited number of cases (sometimes it may be as low as one) and then hasten to apply it to other cases with very unlooked—for results, evoking the sense of wonder of the onlooker or the reader.

After a long night in the maternity ward, the doctor emerged exhausted. A sympathetic nurse who had assisted him asked him, "Why is it babies always arrive at night?"

"What begins at night ends at night" the doctor replied, reflectively.

A short time later he became a father. The hospital staff has never let him forget that his baby arrived at high noon.

In the eighth canto of the Raghuvaṃśa, Kālidāsa narrates

the sad story of Aja's young wife dying of the contact with divine flowers—the result of a *ṛṣi*'s curse and its termination. The sorrowing husband laments wondering if flowers can kill a human: and as finds he cannot continue to live after his wife's death, he places them on his own chest, expecting to die: but flowers cannot kill, one cannot draw a general conclusion that flowers are lethal from this single instance. Aja notes with anguish the truth of this: he laments with wonder lending an edge to his melancholy. The verse has been quoted to illustrate an earlier category.

Rāma, by the mere act of touching her with his foot had restored Ahalyā back to human status from the state of being congealed into a rock: this happened purely in accord with the terms of her hermit-husband's curse and reprieve. Now, deriving a general, all-encompassing principle from this, true everywhere, in all cases, a forest-dweller wonders how many more hermits are going to be united with their wives in the Vindhya country where Rāma is destined to walk—there are so many, many boulders strewn there! While this is one of the characteristic poetic conceits of Sanskritists, it causes a certain surprise because this foot-and-boulder sequence has not been worked before. The verse, occurring in the Hanumānnāṭaka has been elegantly executed in the musical *mālini* metre:

पदकमलरजोभिर्मुक्तपाषाणदेहां
अलभत यदहल्यां गौतमो धर्मपत्नीम् ।
त्वयि चरति विशीर्णग्रावविन्ध्याद्रिपादे
कति कति भवितारस्तापसा दारवन्तः ॥ [III/19]

There is another verse of uncertain authorship which merely extends the idea to another situation. When Rāma is about to step into one of Guha's boats which would ferry him across the Gaṅgā, the boatsman stops him politely with the request to wash his feet clean of dust before setting foot on the boat. Rāma looks up in surprise and Guha adds by way of explanation: "There is little difference, your majesty, between wood and stone. You have the reputation of converting stones into women with the dust of your feet." Clearly the canny boatman did not want the boats, his working assets, to be converted into so many liabilities. This is the stanza:

क्षालयामि तव पादपङ्कजम्
पश्य दारुदृषदोः किमन्तरम् ।
मानुषीकरणचूर्णमस्ति ते
पादयोरिति कथा प्रथीयसी ।।

2.33 *A quick and smart retort, paying the offender in the same coin: Clever saucy dialogue*

Often our surprise nerve is tickled by a smart retort: a saucy, impish remark surprises us by its suddenness and its unlooked-for cutting edge. This device is much prized by politicians debating in the parliament or addressing election meetings: they use it adroitly to turn the tables on the opposition or silence the lone heckler. A candidate was talking about the improvements his party, if elected to office would bring about in different parts of the country: when he was listing the areas he was frequently heckled by a member of the audience who kept shouting, "What about hell?" The candidate calmly turned to him and said, "Sir, I shall come to your constituency, presently."

There are possibilities in courtrooms, too. When a witness was answering all the questions of the defence attorney sensibly, the latter, becoming desperate sneered at him: "You seem to have plenty of intelligence for a man in your position."

"Thank you", answered the witness. "If I weren't under oath I'd return the compliment."

A small boy leading a donkey passed by an army camp. A couple of soldiers wanted to have some fun with the lad. "What are you holding on to your brother so tight for, sonny?" asked one of them.

"So he won't join the army" the youngster replied without blinking an eye.

There was a tradition in the Heroic Age of heroes hurling challenges at each other when they met in the battlefield: some of these exchanges are interesting and one from Murāri's play can be cited as a good illustration of this category. Rāvaṇa hurls an insult at Rāma, boastfully pointing out his having worsted and killed in battle Anaraṇya an ancestor of Rāma. Rāma retorts with spirit telling him that victory and death are the two honorable conclusions for a hero engaging himself in war. But to Rāma what is painful to recall is that Rāvaṇa was defeated and taken prinsoner by Kārtavīrya and Pulastya, Rāvaṇa's grandfather had to beg the legendary hero to release his grandson from his prison. This is an extremely sharp rejoinder indeed as the haughty Rāvaṇa did not care to be reminded of these few instances in his career when he had been humbled. The verse:

न ब्रूये नः पूर्वं नृपतिमनरण्यं यदवधीः
जयो वा मृत्युर्वा युधि भुजभृतां कः परिभवः ।
जितं तु त्वां कारागृहविनिहितं हैहयपतेः
पुलस्त्यो यद्भिक्षां अकृत कृपणस्तद् व्यथयति ॥ [VI/58]

There is an acrimonious, long drawn-out verbal duel between Aśvatthāman and Karṇa (both belonging to the same side) in *Vēnisamhāra*. Among the many retorts which are more spirited than intelligent there is one from Karṇa which has the polemical force in it to quell the adversary and at the same time that universally applicable wisdom which makes it memorable. Stung by the reference of Aśvatthāman to his low beginnings (Karṇa was brought up by a charioteer) Karṇa says: "Let me be a (low-born) son of a charioteer: what does that matter? The caste I belong to was determined by destiny: but my skill and prowess I have acquired, on my own!"

All old societies had set considerable store by the circumstances of one's birth: if it was caste in India, it has been aristocracy versus the masses in England and elsewhere. In such an age and tradition, for a character to proclaim that the achievements of a man are the only criteria to be examined, not the circumstances of his birth over which he has no control, that, in effect.

"The rank is but the guinea stamp.

And man's a man for a 'that'—must have caused more than passing wonder: it must have made men think, it must have caused the more thoughtful leaders of society to question traditional ideas. The sentiment of wonder, specifically and literature itself in general cannot expect to have a more dramatic vindication than this, of its role as a fashioner of men's attitudes of mind.

2.34 *Relating, in a startling manner, present experience of individuals to a tradition, a myth, a classical concept*

There is a marked tendency among people to relate their experience to some well-accepted old concept, myth or tradition, on the basis of some comparable feature, however tenuous the comparability. This may be due to the innate desire of everyone to raise his own banal triviality to classical levels: but, in many cases the eagerness they display in so relating may in greater part reflect their expectation that their problem would be solved in the manner it was resolved in the myth. A good example of the former is provided by the observation of the man living across the way, quite an ordinary citizen going unnoticed: "Mahātma Gāndhi is dead, Nēhru is dead and I am not feeling too well, either."

There is a passage in the *Prasannarāghava* where Janaka who had taken an instant liking to Rāma ruefully contemplates the heavy bow of Śiva which must be broken by the suitor for Śitā's hand. He addresses Earth regarded as Śītā's mother and says, "Rāma is like Manmatha, the god of love and your daughter Sītā is like Rati, his spouse. Now, I would regard this pattern of similarity with Manmatha and Rati complete only if the bow of Śiva, on being taken up by Rāma becomes light like the bow of flowers wielded by the god." The verse has been rendered in the highly musical *mālini* metre and is smooth-flowing.

रतिरिव जननेत्रानन्दिनी नन्दिनी ते
कुसुमशर इवायं रूपसारः कुमारः ।
धनुरपि च यदीदं प्राप्तमेतस्य हस्तम्
कुसुमचयमिव स्यात् संभृतः संप्रदायः ॥ [III/56]

Handsome humans have always been compared to Manmatha and Rati in popular patois as much as in literature in India and this part of the poem is not at all new. What raises it above the level of everydayness is the similarity prayed for between Śiva's bow and that of Manmatha and this evokes the spectator's sense of surprise and simultaneously creates for his satisfaction on artistically complete pattern.

A verse from Kālidāsa's Raghuvamśa can be cited here, which, though it does not present a startling relationship as the above is still suggestive and is executed in way only Kālidāsa can. King

Dilīpa and his queen serve the divine cow who releases them from a curse: in due time the queen becomes pregnant. The verse anticipates the delivery of a boy (to be called Raghu), sustaining analogies with two divine events: the birth of the moon from the eyes of Atri the sage and the river Gangā nursing the foetus of Skanda. The suggestion clearly is that Raghu shall be as pleasing to the people as the moon and as valiant in war as Skanda, the commander of the gods.

अथ नयनसमुत्थं ज्योतिरत्रेरिव द्यौः
सुरसरिदिव तेजो वह्निनिष्ठ्यूतमैशम् ।
नरपतिकुलभूत्यै गर्भमाधत्त राज्ञी
गुरुभिरभिनिविष्टं लोकपालानुभावैः ॥ [II/75]

There is a stanza of unknown authorship where women's prowess in the field of love is praised by relating it to the well-known myth of Śiva reducing the god of love to ashes. Women, through their coquetry displayed through the medium of the eyes are able to bring back to life the god of love who was reduced to ashes by the fire issuing from Lord Siva's eye: thus women have proved that they are more powerful than the Lord Himself and this proving has been carried out neatly through the same medium used by Him, the power of the eyes. In the first two verses cited, only equality is suggested through relating present situation to a myth: here, by the same means, superiority is suggested, over the Lord Himself, a no mean feat.

दृशा दग्धं मनसिजम्
जीवयन्ति दृशैव याः ।
विरूपाक्षस्य जयिनीः
ताः स्तुवे वामलोचनाः ॥

[Kuvalayānanda, N.S. edition, page 116]

The tradition of poets exaggerating a great deal while panegyrising their patrons is well established in Sanskrit, indeed in all the literatures in India. A poet praising his king describes the trepidations of the lord of the ocean when the king camps at the shore. The ocean regards the king as another Lord Nārāyaṇa: now the Lord has done two things to the ocean in the past—both mighty feats impossible to others—the churning of it producing many wonderful and valuable things, the best of all of them being

Lakṣmī, goddess of wealth, and the bridging of it, as Rāma, to go to Laṅkā and kill his enemy. The unease felt by the ocean, the poet points out, is quite unnecessary for the king is having the goddess of wealth at his side always and he has no enemies left to conquer, in any corner of the globe. The verse certainly involves a complex conceit but the basic idea is very clever and it illustrates the category to a nicety.

त्वय्यागते किमिति वेपत एष सिन्धुः
त्वं सेतुमन्थकृदतः किमसौ बिभेति ।
द्वीपान्तरेऽपि न हि ते ऽस्त्यवशंवदोऽथ
त्वां राजपुङ्गव निषेक्त एव लक्ष्मीः ॥

[Kuvalayānanda, N.S. edition, page 18]

The identity of neither the poet nor the king has been traced: this is not unusual in India as authors here appear to have been singularly self-effacing: they only wanted their work to live on.

2.35 *Neighbouring pastures greener, in some cases, startlingly so*

This is a phenomenon common to all living things and not confined to the homo sapiens (as the words pastures and greener would certainly indicate): the psychology behind this is not far to seek: the situation one lives in or with is all too familiar to one with all its drawbacks while the other situation looked at from a distance appears more attractive as the greenery effectively conceals the dry patches. While this attitude of mind is all too common, in some cases it is carried to excess with startling results.

A fellow confessed to a friend, "I got married because I was tired of going to the launderette, eating in restaurants and wearing socks with holes."

"Funny", the friend replied. "I got divorced for that reason."

Māgha has a verse in his *Śiśupālavadha* in the long passage devoted to a description of the Raivataka mountain, which can serve as an excellent example of this category. The different groups of gods who inhabit the slopes of the mountain have different bodybuild; for instance, the *Kinnaras* have horse-like bodies and human faces and the *Kimpurushas* have human bodies and the face of a horse. One group envies the other for what it does not have and is envied back by the other for the same reason. For the beings with human faces can kiss while those with human bodies can embrace as a couple but the one cannot do the other thing and derive fulfilment. The verse has been nicely turned out and for a passage from the recondite Māgha it is quite simple.

बिम्बोष्ठं बहु मनुते तुरङ्गवक्त्रः
चुम्बन्तं मुखमिह किंनरं प्रियायाः ।
श्लिष्यन्तं मुहुरितरोऽपि तं निजस्त्रीम्
उत्तुङ्गस्तनभरभङ्गभीरुमध्याम् ॥ [IV/38]

Bhartṛhari has a *niti* verse which too can serve as an example of this human perversity. "I love a girl", says the poet, "but she does not love me back: in fact, she is very much in love with another who, however, is much taken up with a different girl: in the meantime this girl is in love with me though I do not return her love" and in fine disgust curses the whole lot, including himself, for their perseverence in misery.

यां चिन्तयामि मनसा मयि सा विरक्ता
साप्यन्यमिच्छति जनं स जनोऽन्यसक्तः ।
अस्मत्कृते च परिशुष्यति काचिदन्या
धिक् तां च तं च मदनं च इमां च मां च ॥

[Attributed to Bhartṛhari]

2.36 *Unbelievable, inexcusable bungling evoking startled surprise*

To err may be human but it is given to few humans to err on a Himālayan scale, surprising even those who are familiar with his fallibility.

Some overnight flights from Los Angeles to New York have a single stop enroute, Dallas. A passenger on this flight told the flight attendant at the start to make sure he woke him in time to get off at Dallas. He awoke as the plane was landing in New York. Furious, he called the attendant and demanded an explanation. The fellow mumbled an apology and in a range the passenger stamped off the plane.

"Boy, was he ever mad!" another crew member observed to her colleague. "If you think he was mad," replied the flight attendant, "You should have seen the guy I put off the plane in Dallas!"

Such a rounded and aesthetically perfect piece of bungling

is fortunately rare in real life and that is why it comes to possess considerable wonderogenic propensity when it happens.

Śakāra, in the Mṛcchakaṭika is a consummate villain who has the cunning to foist a fairly convincing case on the innocent Cārudatta, forcing the fair-minded judge to convict him of the murder of Vasantasēna. But at the incipient stages, probably on account of excitement and fear, he almost gives the whole game away, when, after stating in the court that Vasantasēna had been killed in the garden, strangled with the arm by someone for the sake of filthy lucre, he impulsively adds the words "na mayā" (not by me). The judge who had him nicely sized up now seizes on this piece of bungling and instructs his assistants to note down these tell-tale words carefully as part of the plaint—making the villain bitterly rue his monumental mistake at this critical moment. The passage occurs in the IX Act, after verse 7.

An interesting illustration is provided by Amaru. He describes the case of a lover whose faithlessness had been found out by his girl: he is frightfully worried that he may blurt out the name of his latest flame if he talks: so he decides to keep silent: and in order to keep himself engaged, starts to draw a figure.

But Fate was clearly against him that day: for he realises with a shock that he has inadvertently drawn the portrait of the very girl he was secretly in love with. The wronged lady-love, looking on, goes red in the face with the shock of dismay and exclaiming, "*aho, citram, citram*" (lo ! what a shocking thing this is !) kicks him with her foot. The two stanzas describing this are reproduced here for enjoyment.

पुरस्तन्व्या गोत्रस्खलनचकितोऽहं नतमुखः
　　प्रवृत्तो वैलक्ष्यात्किमपि लिखितुं दैवहतकः ।
स्फुटो रेखान्यासः कथमपि स तादृक्परिणतः
　　गता येन व्यक्तिं पुनरवयवैः सैव तरुणी ॥
ततश्चाभिज्ञाय स्फुरदरुणगण्डस्थलरुचा
　　मनस्विन्या रूढप्रणयसहसोद्गद्गदगिरा ।
अहो चित्रं चित्रं स्फुटमिति निगद्याश्रुकलुषम्
　　रुषा ब्रह्मास्त्रं मे शिरसि निहितो वामचरणः ॥ [51, 52]

2.37 *In a world given over to diplomatic euphemism, a blunt piece of straight-talking, a bland mouthing of the brutal truth may cause surprise*

If, as we all realise, diplomatic euphemism is what is universally bandied about, then the mouthing of the blunt, unvarnished truth is totally unexpected and therefore evokes surprise. We can see a lot of contemporary illustrations around. Aide to election campaigner: "According to this latest poll, 52 per cent of the voters think you are the lesser of the two evils."

In a case before Vienna traffic court, the judge interrupted the accused who was volubly describing the accident from his own point of view: "If I understand you correctly, the tree you hit suddenly veered to the left without giving the proper signal."

Few of us can be as brutally candid as Mark Twain was when he wrote on the envelope of a letter addressed to his wife: "Opened by mistake to see what was inside."

James Langley, Governor of Maine received this advice from his mother after graduation ceremony: "Jim, I am very proud of you today and I think you will win many honours in your life. But keep this in mind! Despite the honours, there is one circumstance more than any other that will determine the turn-out at your funeral. And that will be the weather."

A reporter told Churchill, "Sir, you must feel proud that whenever you speak, the hall gets filled to overflowing." Churchill said, "Yes, I feel proud. But I also realise that if I am to be hanged, the turn-out will be thrice as big."

Cāṇakya, the dominant prime-mover of Mudrārākṣasa who could coo like a dove when it suited him, could be brutally frank too when circumstances called for such a response. In the episode of the feigned quarrel, where he wants the (non-existent) differences between him and the king to be displayed, he tells him why he countermanded his instructions about celebrating the Kaumudi festival. The verse:

अम्भोधीनां तमालप्रभवकिसलयश्यामवेलावनानाम्
आपारेभ्यश्चतुर्णां चटुलतिमिकुलक्षोभितान्तर्जलानाम् ।
मालेवाज्ञा सपुष्पा तव नृपतिशतैरुह्यते या शिरोभिः
सा मय्येव स्खलन्ती प्रथयति विनयालंकृतं ते प्रभुत्वम् ॥ [III/24]

Cāṇakya's emphatic assertion that he countermanded the king's orders only so that the latter may be seen to practise humility, that though his writ runs everywhere in the kingdom, it stops before Cāṇakya is refreshingly (though brutally) frank and will always evoke surprise. Of course, no king can tolerate this kind of recalcitrancy of the most open self-assured type and the world naturally concludes that all is over between the celebrated preceptor and his royal disciple—which is exactly the impression the wily Cāṇakya planned to create.

The Mṛcchakaṭika is a play marked by a wonderful sense of realism rarely to be met with among the works of the Romantic Age. Śakāra, the brother-in-law of the king (a relationship he never allows us to forget) makes many realistic statements, some of which border on the brutal: as, for example, his description of Vasantasēna whom he loves after his own fashion. In this he calls her ten names, some of which are hardly complimentary, like 'a flat-nosed maiden' and 'a destroyer of families' and complains at the end of these endearments that she still does not love him back!

एषा नाणकमोषिकामकशिका मत्स्याशिका लासिका
निर्नासा कुलनाशिका अवशिका कामस्य मंजूषिका।
एषा वेशवधूः सुवेशनिलया वेशाङ्गना वेशिका
एतान्यस्या दश नामिकानि मया कृतान्यद्यापि मां नेच्छति ॥ [I/23]

In verses 29 and 30 of the same Act he proceeds from this kind of endearments to regular threats uttered in a wholly callous manner without any consideration for her feelings, so that when, after this, he suddenly tries to be courteous, Vasantasēna states truthfully that even his courtesy strikes terror.

2.38 *Confusion worse confounded*

Confusion worse confounded can cause surprise at the point when things get beyond comprehension and again at the point when clarity begins to dawn. In this category we plan to include only cases of contrived confusion: the other type which arises naturally is likely to be so much beyond anyone's control that it will not fall within the confines of conscious art. There are at least three plays in Sanskrit where this kind of confusion, artistically contrived to evoke surprise (and also to delineate character) gets considerably confounded before it is resolved: let us examine them briefly here.

The Mudrārākṣasa is a sternly political play with no passages given over to the tender passion, where there is no heroine and in fact, no woman characters with the exception of a female factotum. The dominant activity on which the play turns is political intrigue and it is everywhere Cāṇakya versus Rākṣasa pitting their brains against each other. The fabric of intrigue woven by Cāṇakya is so complex, so involved that quite a few of the commentators of the play have got confused and have misinterpreted the play. The apparently loyal advisers and minions of Rākṣasa turning out to be Cāṇakya's men planted in the enemy's camp, the letter with the jewels carried by Siddhārtaka seemingly from Rākṣasa to Candragupta constituting an act of betrayal in the eyes of Malayakētu, the very tricky wording of the letter itself are things which would confuse most of the spectators causing surprise at the extent of the confusion and, again at the point of elucidation of the mystery. Indeed it would seem that this play, when produced must have attracted only the brighter men, the truly dedicated lovers of the theatre who could unravel this complex plot as the play unfolded itself before them and who could enjoy sitting through long sessions where there is no love sequence at all. And it is a tribute to a society which can generate such a play-one that offers no concessions to the gallery by way of glamorous scenes, of love duets, of handsome, accomplished women, of miraculous deeds—a play solely sustained by the intrigues of a master plotter, where battles are fought with the grey cells and not with lances and bows and muscular power, where things are not what they seem, where the whole interest lies in the interplay of political sophistication, subtlely and finesse: such a work is rarely met with in the annals of the ancient civilizations of the world.

The confusions that arise in the Ācaryacūḍāmaṇi are on account of the magic of the *rākṣasas*: Mārīca and Rāvaṇa appear as Rāma and Śūrpaṇakhā impersonates Sītā. The resolution of these frauds is on account of the magic effect of the ring and the head ornament worn respectively by Rāma and Sītā. But till it is all resolved there is much confusion in the III and IV Acts of the play causing no end of surprise with a second wave of wonder at the points of elucidation.

But the art of fabricating confusion rises to dizzy heights in Rāmabhadra Dīkṣita's *Jānakipariṇaya*: in fact the mix-ups in it are so thoroughgoing, all but the most astute of the spectators will find themselves wholly in the dark about what is going on. Groups of rākṣasas appear as Rāma, Lakṣmaṇa and Sītā and Virādha impersonates Rāma and Śūrpaṇakhā comes in the disguise of Sītā: these last two worthies fall into the net they had cast for the real Rāma and Sītā, for they fall in love, each taking the other for the genuine article and there is blood and thunder when they attempt to carry away each other, till mercifully for them and more for the hapless spectators, Lakṣmaṇa puts an end to the whole shoddy affair by quickly killing Virādha and inflicting injuries on Śūrpaṇakhā. There is an impersonation at the very end, the indefatiguable Śūrpaṇakhā appearing as a nun and spreading false stories of the death of Rāma and Sītā and almost succeeding in securing the self-immolation of the distracted Bharata.

In fact there is too much of confusion generated by impersonation in the play and one who reads it has the distinct feeling that Dīkṣita has overdone what, within limits would have turned out to be a good dramatic device. It must be remembered that, in the written play when read, we get hints about who is appearing in what disguise, but on the stage, when the play unfolds itself, no such hints are available and the spurious article may be taken by most of the spectators for the genuine. However in a consideration of the confusion-creating potential of various devices, these impersonations portrayed by Dīkṣita must rank very high indeed.

2.39 *Presenting a thing of significance in deprecatory terms*

We examined earlier a category where a big thing is underplayed in order to boost another. Without such an objective, it sometimes becomes necessary to present a thing of significance in deprecatory terms, playing it down: it does not certainly mean the speaker thinks light of the thing: it merely signifies that it pays the speaker to speak in such terms of it, in some manner. The category includes the presentation of a thing in an innocuous manner thereby enhancing its ominously significant clout. This category evokes surprise sometimes at the earlier stage of underplaying but more often at the later stage when the listener realises the true magnitude of the thing underplayed.

Comedian Woody Allen said, on the termination of a six year marriage: "We pondered whether to take a holiday or get a divorce and we decided that a trip to Bermuda is over in two weeks but a divorce is something you always have."

There is a fine verse in Subhaṭa Kavi's one-Act play, the *Dūtāṅgada* where Aṅgada replies to Rāvaṇa's question "What is Rāma doing now?" by stating that Rāma is relaxing in a recumbent posture: this would suggest an ease-loving "softie" and it is presented this way on purpose for the objects and the people referred to as surrounding Rāma in the rest of the verse all indicate a former act of unique valour: among the objects we can mention the skin of the golden deer and among the people, Hanumān for whom Rāvaṇa has come have a healthy respect and Vibhīṣaṇa, the brother who has left him to join hands with Rāma. The verse, put in the longest metre has, withal, been very smoothly constructed.

अङ्के कृत्वोत्तमाङ्गं प्लवगबलपतेः पादमक्षस्य हन्तुः
कृत्वोत्सङ्गे सलीलं त्वचि कनकमृगस्याङ्गमाधाय शेषम् ।
बाणंरक्षःकुलघ्नं प्रगुणितमनुजेनादरात्तीक्ष्णमक्ष्यः
कोणेनोद्वी क्षमाणस्त्वदनुजवचने दत्तकर्णोऽयमास्ते ॥ [27]

Bhallaṭa, the Kashmiri poet has composed a verse in which all institutions held in respect by the people are undervalued systematically in the most cynical manner, as an example of a distinct mode of composition. The verse is interesting.

ग्रावाणो मणयो हरिर्जलचरो लक्ष्मीः पयोमानुषी
मुक्तौकाः सिकताः प्रवाललतिकाः शैवालमम्भः सुधा ।
तीरे कल्पमहीरुहाः किमपरं नाम्नापि रत्नाकरम्
दूरे कर्णरसायनं निकटतस्तृष्णापि नो शाम्यति ॥

[Anyāpadeśaśataka anthologised in Subhāṣita ratnābhāṇḍāgāra 226/26]

In a society where reverence was the prevailing spirit and even the ladle and the stones used to crush the soma stems in a sacrifice were raised to the level of gods and hymns composed in their praise, this apparent belittling of highly regarded institutions is certainly rare and will cause surprise and shock to the reader on account of its unexpectedness.

Such an underplaying may in some cases merely be the manifestation of an innate quality and not the result of purposeful design. Calvin Coolidge, a famous President of U.S.A. was a man known to be laconic in his speech. He once attended a very long Sunday service in the White House Chapel and on his return Mrs. Coolidge said, "I presume the sermon was long. What did the pastor speak on?" "Sin" replied the President. "What did he say about it?" asked the first lady. "He was against it" replied the Chief Executive.

Bhāsa with his penchant for abbreviated statements and avoidance of theatrical exhibitionism provides several good examples of this category. In the Pratimānāṭaka we have two excellent examples. One is the simple, unemotional account by Rāma to Sītā of the early stages of the ceremony of coronation which came to an abrupt end on the machinations of Manthara: as a result he, the rightful person is cheated out of the most splendid throne in the world. But Rāma plays it down from his own innate nobility, making the whole nefarious conspiracy look a simple routine transaction of no great import. The result is what a dozen verses highly charged with Bhavabhūtian pathos could not have achieved: the very bland, unemotional, unstressed statement goes to the heart of the reader.

शत्रुघ्नलक्ष्मणगृहीतघटेऽभिषेके
छत्रे स्वयं नृपतिना रुदता गृहीते ।
संभ्रान्तया किमपि मन्थरया च कर्णे
राज्ञः शनैरभिहितं च न चास्मि राजा ॥ [I/7]

Sumantra the charioteer of Daśaratha returns to report to the dying king that Rāma, Sītā and Lakṣmana had been left at the edge of the woods. The old king pathetically asks, "Did they send any message to me?". The faithful charioteer replies they did not, that they kept silent for a moment in a contemplative manner and then left without a word. The spectator would feel that this "leaving without a word" is far more moving than a thousand wordy messages.

कमप्यर्थं चिरं ध्यात्वा वक्तुं प्रस्फुरिताधराः ।
बाष्पस्तम्भितकण्ठत्वात् अनुक्तैव्व वनं गताः ॥ [II/17]

2.40 *Consciously saying the opposite just to secure a better effect through surprise*

Poets sometimes use this device effectively to secure greater emphasis through the medium of surprise: they say "there is" when there isn't and "there isn't" when there is, so that this contradiction, flying in the face of other facts available to the reader may shock him and thereby secure his attention.

A girl in an ancient Tamil Sangam lyric in fling a secret tryst for her lover refers to a bower frequented by cranes which come to fish in the river running by: the very reference to the presence of cranes is eloquently indicative of the total freedom from humans in the bower. In another lyric a girl who has had secret union with her lover sits worrying if he would deny all connection with her: for, in the bower by the river where they met, there was a lone crane looking for fish in the shallow water: the crane was witness to all the goings on.

In Sanskrit we may quote two verses of unknown authorship as illustrative of this category: both happen to be panegyrical in content. One of them seemingly contests the general claim that the king's fame (which, in Sanskrit tradition, is white in colour) has spread to all the far corners of the universe, whitening everything there is: the poem is devoted to a list of several things that still remain black, uninfluenced by the whitening effect of the king's renown: but it is the nature (and perhaps the stature) of these things listed that reveals the poet's intention. For in the poet's list are the black spot in the moon, Lord Śiva's dusky neck, Lord Nārāyaṇa's complexion and the cheeks of the elephants guarding the eight quarters which have been rendered black by the flow of inklike must: these still remain black, they have not been whitened by the king's renown:

इन्दोर्लक्ष्म त्रिपुरजयिनः कण्ठमूलं मुरारेः
दिङ्नागानां मदजलमषीभाञ्जि गण्डस्थलानि ।
अद्याप्युर्वीवलयतिलक श्यामलिम्नानुलिप्तान्या-
भासन्ते वद धवलितं किं यशोभिस्त्वदीयैः ॥

[Kuvalayānanda, N.S. edition, page 146]

The other poem extols the great philanthropical propensity of a king: but instead of directly praising the quality, the poet says, "It is quite wrong to claim that you offer everything to everyone at all times, O King! For, you do not offer (show) your back to your enemies nor do you offer your chest to other women." The first, of course is a tribute to his valour and grit, the second to his marital faithfulness. The verse is in the simple *anuṣṭubh* metre:

सर्वदा सर्वदोऽसीति
मिथ्या संस्तूयसे बुधैः ।

नारयो लेभिरे पृष्ठं
न वक्षः परयोषितः ॥

[Kuvalayānanda, N.S. edition, page 146]

2.41 *Bizarre fancies, grand delusions, singular self-deception*

There is usually a limit operating to curtail the height to which delusions and fancies can soar in real life: when, in the random case the limit is passed in life or in art, wonder is turned on. A reported conversation between two inmates of a mental institution.

First inmate: Betcha, you can't climb up the beam of light from my torchlight. Second inmate: Do you think I'm crazy? I'd get half way up and you would turn it off.

The next example is to illustrate the self-deception part of the category. A fellow goes into a bar at noon and orders two drinks in separate glasses, downs them in alternating gulps and departs. After several days of this, the bartender enquires "What goes on?" The man explains, "My best friend and I always had a drink together at noon but he has been transferred to another city, so we made a vow to still drink together—me here—him there".

A few days later, the fellow comes in and orders only one drink. After he downs it the bartender asks, "What happened?"

"Oh, I am on the wagon" the man explains.

Lovers in Indian literature are shown to suffer from bizarre fancies and when separated from each other, they get delusions many of which run true to tradition but some of which can startle the reader with their unexpectedness. There are men and women who love in vain, persuading themselves through an exercise of self-delusion that their love is being returned. Examples of the first type can be seen in most of the major epic poems and plays, chief among them being Vālmīki's *Rāmāyaṇa*, Kālidāsa's *Vikramōrvaśiya*, Bhavabhūti's *Uttararāmacarita* and the two one-Act plays both called *Unmattarāghava*.

Examples of the latter type (nurtured by self-delusion) are Rāvaṇa in all the Rāma plays and Virādha and Sūrpaṇakhā in the *Jānaki-pariṇaya*. One verse only need be quoted here, this from the *Āścaryacūḍāmaṇi* showing Rāvaṇa under the grip of his grand self-delusion.

मरतकतटे मन्दाकिन्या मदङ्कनिषादिनी
कनकनलिनोद्गन्धीन् स्वर्गानिलान् प्रतिगृह्णती।
भयपरवशे दत्तापाङ्गा महेन्द्रपरिग्रहे
मनुजमवधूयैषा कामं मया सह रंस्यते ॥ [III/26]

2.42 *Giving eloquent, unambiguous expression to one's innermost thoughts without the aid of words*

The ability to talk is a great gift given to man: it places him at the top of the evolutionary ladder: it aids the process of thought (thought is regarded as silent talk), it lubricates communication, it enables preservation of thought for posterity, too. But, on the negative side, this gift has put man out of practice in the use of gestures, in facial expression, even in body postures. When, therefore, we find occasionally effective use of these latter modes in literature we are apt to be surprised. Not that we see instances of such effective silent communication only in literature: life offers far more examples of this and men and women manage to communicate a great deal without the agency of words: in fact characters in literature are more inclined to be verbose, wordy: and surprise is occasioned when, in rare instances, characters communicate their inner thoughts through other media than words.

In Hanumannāṭaka there is a delicious passage where the wives of co-travellers lovingly ask Sītā, "Lady, is the youth of blue complexion over there your husband?" and she replies, not in bland language, but as befits a Hindu girl, through a smile lighting up her cheeks and through fluttering eyelids that spoke out her bashfulness. The poem has been rendered well in the highly musical *mālinī* metre.

पथि पथिकवधूभिः सादरं पृच्छ्यमाना
कुवलयदलनीलः कोऽयमार्ये तवेति ।
स्मितविकसितगण्डं व्रीडविभ्रान्तनेत्रम्
मुखमवनमयन्ती स्पष्टमाचष्ट सीता ॥ [III/15]

In the *Prasannarāghava*, Jayadeva makes a character exclaim with wonder and admiration, nicely blended, how Sītā taught all her relatives the proper course of conduct of a wife, not through long homilies but by her act of following her lord to the forests voluntarily, though it was not part of the king's stipulation: this lovely verse also happens to be cast in the *mālinī* metre.

गहनविपिनवासोत्कण्ठया संप्रयातम्
प्रियतममनुयान्त्या तत्क्षणं राजपुत्र्या ।
चरणकमलगुञ्जन्मञ्जुमञ्जीरशब्दैः
स्फुटतरमुपदिष्टाः बान्धवाः साधुवृत्तम् ॥ [V/13]

In both the cases the poets make it clear (through the words "*spaṣṭam*" and "*sphuṭam*") that the message had been conveyed expertly beyond the shadow of a doubt: the fact that words were not used in the communication did not affect the effectiveness of the message: it could even be that this non-verbal mode of communication was more effective than the verbal could have been. Indeed, the use of the comparative degree in the second verse could only mean that this was undoubtedly the more efficient means of communication. There is, too the question of decorum involved in the first case, of delicacy and rectitude in a young wife referring to hẹr husband in talking to strangers—quite an important matter in old societies like the Indian: in the second case, long sermons will not be received well by older relatives from this slip of a girl and generally such sermons excite the spirit of contradiction from them: setting an example by one's conduct is always far the more effective means of passing on a message.

2.43 *Something happens that should not have happened and it is contemplated with disbelief, surprise and sorrow*

With our experience we budget for certain unpleasant things to happen: but when things happen for which we have not provided we are assailed by disbelief, surprise and sorrow, generally in that order. Both the examples selected for this category are from Bhāsa's *Pratigñāyaugandharāyaṇa.*

In Act I of the play, Hamsaka the guard describes in detail for the benefit of Yaugandharāyaṇa how Udayana had been tricked and captured prisoner by Pradyōta's men. The loyal minister listens with alternating pride and anguish as the guard details the heroic responses of the master and the thrusts of the enemy. But, when the guard tells him how at the end of the encounter Pradyōta's henchmen, adopting trickery, bound him hand and foot with wild creepers—callously, without regard to the quality and the status of the prisoner, the minister bursts out with a verse registering his surprised dismay.

पीनांसस्य विकृष्टपर्वमहतो नागेन्द्रहस्ताकृतेः
चापास्फालिकरस्य दूरहरणाद् बाणाधिकारोपिणः
विप्राभ्यर्चयितुः श्रमेषु सुहृदां सत्कर्तुरालिङ्गनैः
न्यस्तं तस्य भुजद्वयस्य वलयस्थानान्तरे बन्धनम् ॥ [I/8]

The last line brings out in a spontaneous uncontrived manner the grief of the good man laced with surprised disbelief when he learns that the king's hands, used to wearing bracelets were bound with thongs of prickly creepers.

The guard, in order to provide some relief to the suffering minister hastens to add how Pradyōta's minister more conscious of the calibre of the prisoner relieved him of the thongs, spoke courteously to him and took him in a litter to Pradyōta's capital city, seeing how badly wounded he was. This provides the loyal minister some measure of temporary relief. But again reflecting on what has happened he gets sad at the thought that despite these courtesies, the basic fact is that the king is now a prisoner in the hands of Pradyōta. Physical torments loom large but are superficial; to proud men like Udayana mental torture is far more harrowing, difficult to bear. The verse suggests that even the courtesies of the victor are patronising, they pierce the ego of the proud victim like a rapier.

कथमगणितपूर्वं द्रक्ष्यते तं नरेन्द्रः
कथमपुरुषवाक्यं श्रोष्यते सिद्धवाक्यः ।
कथमविषयवन्ध्यं धारयिष्यत्यमर्षम्
प्रणिपतति निरुद्धः सत्कृतो धर्षितो वा ॥ [I/11]

2.44 *Raising a thing to a high level only to drop it to the ground, blowing up a thing to outsize to burst it to smithereens*

This category can cause surprise at two stages: once when the thing is raised or blown up excessively and again, more emphatically when it is debunked to nothing. This double harvest is not guaranteed, of course, in every case.

There was a football match at Athens between the Greeks and the Chinese. Just before the match started, a strange music was heard: Greek spectators stood up in respectful silence, taking it to be the Chinese national anthem; the Chinese players thought it was the Greek national anthem and stood still in a respectful pose. Then a lilting female voice rose above the unfamiliar music to extol the virtues of a local toothpaste. Possibly for the first time since the game was invented, a football match was delayed by laughter ensuing when the mistake was realised.

A lady reports: being alone after children had married, my husband and I spent most of our time watching T.V. Husband said one day, "Let's do something exciting tonight." All agog at the prospect of a night on the town, I said, "Good! What shall we do?" "Well", he replied, "let's swop chairs".

In the last Act of the *Vēṇisamhāra* when a happy ending is sensed to be very near and those of the spectators that live in distant suburbs are reaching for their impediment there is suddenly stark tragedy unravelling itself—or so it seems. For Duryōdhana, all smeared with the red blood of Bhīma and Arjuna is sighted entering the *Pāṇḍava* camp, clearly to destroy the last remaining survivors among them. The *Pāṇḍava* camp is thrown into utter confusion: the women prepare to enter the fire and the luckless Yudhiṣṭhira lamenting on the fate of his two worthy brothers determines to fight the villain to the bitter end. The spectators must be really taken aback at this radical turn taken by the play. After a lot of tension is allowed to build up, the intruder reveals himself as Bhīma, all bloody after his successful duel with the villain, coming to report to his king and get congratulated. After the buildup, the relief to the characters on the stage and the spectators must have been terrific.

In a similar way Rāmabhadra Dīkṣita in the VII Act of his play brings Śūrpaṇakhā to Ayodhyā as referred to earlier, in the guise of a hermit of Kiṣkindhā, after Rāvaṇa is killed. The ogress, determined to wreak vengeance on the Raghu clan, pretends she does not recognise Bharata and Śatrughna and taking them to be ordinary citizens she tells them of the holocaust that had destroyed Rāma and Lakṣmaṇa. Bharata and his brother are in extreme grief and they prepare to immolate themselves in a fire. Even the spectators who all must know the Rāma legend backwards might sit tensed, await for a surprise twist in the hoary story. The timely arrival of Hanumān carrying good tidings harbingering the imminent return of a triumphant Rāma with his wife and brother and his monkey and rākṣasa allies destroys the spell and saves Bharata and Śatrughna from a fiery end. Tension is built up in minutes to a high crescendo only to be quenched in even less time, surprising the spectator on the way up as well as on the way down.

These two innovations obviously designed in fulfilment of the dictum

कुर्यान्निर्वहणेऽद्भुतम् ।

[Daśarūpaka III/33]

do certainly add to the dramatic value of the plays by raising the spectre of a tragic turn to an ancient story that eventually does not come off.

2.45 *Adroit verbal tricks*

Poetry of the early epochs in all countries provided an excellent opportunity to poets to indulge in verbal tricks and play on words: much of it repels the modern reader. But here and there we do come across passages which provoke amused surprise on account of the unexpected adroitness of their manipulation.

Let us see some western examples before we take up Sanskrit illustrations. "When a child asks difficult questions, invention is the necessity of mother." Employee noting the newest tax deducted from his salary: "This must be part of a continuing programme to handicap the hired."

My friend who had been invited to give a lecture on birds was introduced as "Miss Thompson who is going to talk on Orthography." After the talk, the introducer approached her hesitantly. "I hope that was allright", she asked. "Orthography is bird-watching, isn't it?" "No" my friend replied gently, "That's word-botching."

A plump old lady struggled on to a bus without her husband making any attempt to help her. "Eh, Henry", she said as she sank into a seat. "You ain't as gallant as you was when I was a gal."

"No luv" he replied, "And you ain't as buoyant as you was when I were a boy".

There is a verse in Sanskrit which can be consistently interpreted to refer to Rāma or to Kṛṣṇa, the words employed being capable of yielding ambivalent meanings. The verse is :

प्रातः काकोदरो येन द्रोग्धापि करुणात्मना ।
पूतनामारणाख्यातः स मे ऽस्तु शरणं प्रभुः ।।

[Kuvalayānanda, N. S. edition, page 75]

The word '*kāka*' in the poem refers to Jayanta, son of Indra who, though he perpetrated an unpardonable crime was rendered fearless (*adara*) and given succour by Rāma: His name is sacred (*Pūtanāma*): may He be our sanctuary! Referring to Kṛṣṇa, *Kākōdara* would mean an serpent: Kāliya the terrible serpent was given protection by Kṛṣṇa, after some punishment. He was the killer of Pūtanā, the ogress: may He be our sanctuary! To accomplish a sustained double meaning referring to two different incarnations of the Lord in this manner is a surprising feat even in Sanskrit.

A conversation between the lustful Rāvaṇa and the chaste Sītā is presented with the aid of an unusual verbal effect. The first three lines of the stanza are uttered by Rāvaṇa presaging disaster for the monkey army, defeat for Rāma and disappointment for the devas. Sītā gives a very short rejoinder directing Rāvaṇa to reread the three lines omitting the sixth letter from the beginning of each: the result is, of course, all unfavourable to Rāvaṇa. The verse has been cleverly composed.

भवित्री रम्भोरु त्रिदशवदनग्लानिरधुना
स ते रामः स्थाता न युधि पुरतोलक्ष्मणसखः ।
इयं यास्यत्युच्चैर्विपदमधुना वानरचमूः
लघिष्ठेदं षष्ठाक्षरपरविलोपात्पठ पुनः ॥

[Kuvalayānanda, N.S. edition, page 162]

Sanskrit literature is replete with such verbal gymnastics: we may see two examples of such verbal feats just to judge the range of their reach. One is a sum in arithmetic but resolvable only through knowledge of grammar. On first reading we would think nineteen women went to the Sarayū river to bathe and one (gentleman) having been eaten by a tiger, twenty women returned home. Despite the tragedy, the ranks of the women appear to have been reinforced by the addition of one. The solution is that the word ēkōna should be dissolved as ekaḥ and nā, the second word meaning a male. So now the arithmetic is right: twenty women and a male went to the river, the male formed the tiger's lunch and the rest, the twenty of them returned home. The verse:

एकोना विंशतिःस्त्रीणां स्नानार्थं सरयूं गता ।
विंशतिः पुनरायाता एको व्याघ्रेण भक्षितः ॥

[Subhāṣitaratnabhāṇḍāgāra, 194/19]

There is a whole class of verses where the verb is concealed causing a certain puzzlement. In the following verse, after *sarve*, by *sandhi*, we get the verb *aduḥ* (they gave): so Duryōdhana disappears and the word gets broken into three words, adu: yo and dhanasamihayā. The meaning of the verse now is: the *Pāṇḍavas* gave gold and different kinds of gems to the one who came to them with the desire for wealth.

आगतः पाण्डवाः सर्वे दुर्योधनसमीहया ।
तस्मै गां च सुवर्णं च रत्नानि विविधानि च ॥

[Subhāṣitaratnabhāṇḍāgāra, 201/1]

In a similar manner different parts of speech may be concealed causing puzzlement and the challenge is to discover the fugitive word. There are other, more complicated riddles which are quite tiresome to unravel, though one is left with a deep sense of wonder at the cleverness and the dexterity and the intricate scholarship that have been expertly harnessed in their composition. Clearly such versification was the popular pastime of scholars over hundreds of years: even today setting such riddles is a pastime popular in villages where sophisticated means of entertainment have not yet penetrated: the language of such riddles is however not Sanskrit but the regional tongue.

2.46 *The same thing being different things to people in diverse situations*

Things in the physical world act in a predictable way in all situations, in obedience to inexorable laws. But when sentient beings enter the field, unpredictability begins to rule: temperament is the factor behind all the mischief, everywhere, inclusive, of course, of all literature and all art. And unpredictability breeds surprise, being a synonym for unexpectedness.

In the case of lovers when they are together, everything works out finely for them: but when they are separated, factors which were in their favour now work adversely causing them pain and anguish. King Purūravas is separated from Ūrvaśī whom he loves to distraction when at last they are united, the king says that the rays of the moon and the arrows of Love which were extremely unpleasant to him have now become pleasant: they themselves are basically the same, of course, but their impact on the lover changes radically in nature after union. The passage:

अहो विरुद्धसंवर्धन ईप्सितलाभो नाम ।
पादास्त एव शशिनः सुखयन्ति गात्रम्
बाणास्त एव मदनस्य ममानुकूलाः ।
संरम्भरूक्षमिव सुन्दरि यद्यदासीत्
त्वत्संगमेन मम तत्तदिवानुनीतम् ॥ [III/20]

In two verses in Śṛṅgāraśataka, Bhartṛhari portrays opposite results from the impact of a girl on a young man, ambrosial when she is with you, a bitter poison when she is away.

नामृतं न विषं किंचिदेकां मुक्त्वा नितम्बिनीम् ।
सैवामृतलता रक्ता विरक्ता विषवल्लरी ॥ [44]
मधुरयं मधुरैरपि कोकिला-
कलरवैर्मलयस्य च वायुभिः ।
विरहिणः प्रहिणस्ति शरीरिणो
विपदि हन्त सुधापि विषायते ॥ [82]

In another, author unknown, a long list of cooling agents like the stalks of lotus and chandan paste is recounted as so much fuel for the fire of love: what is by nature very cooling acts radically differently on lovers-in-separation.

हारो जलार्द्रवसनं नलिनीदलानि
प्रालेयसीकरमुचस्तुहिनांशुभासः ।
यस्येन्धनानि सरसानि च चन्दनानि
निर्वाणमेष्यति कथं स मनोभवाग्निः ॥
[Subhāṣitaratnabhāṇḍāgāra, 262/15]

2.47 *Applying double standards*

Without being notably wicked, most of us do apply double standards in our transactions in life. This fact was dramatically demonstrated by the response to a contest in an English periodical inspired by an idea of Bertrand Russell, termed the New Conjugation. It goes like this, "I like to use a little perfume: you rather overdo it, dear: she stinks." Another example: "I have firm views: you are rather inflexible; he is pig-headed."

That normally level-headed, reasonable folk with some objectivity could be so swayed by egotism on the one side and by dislike and intolerance on the other that they can indulge in this kind of statements is a matter of surprise to the onlooker (but seldom to the sufferer). Here, the greater the deviation from the truthful position, the sharper the gush of surprise.

Gōvardhanācārya has a stanza illustrating this.

अन्यमुखे दुर्वादो यः प्रियवदने स एव परिहासः ।
इतरेन्धनजन्मा यो धूमः सोऽगुरुसमुद्भवो धूपः ॥

[Quoted by the commentator of Amaruśataka under verse 8]

We are prepared to put up with a good deal of badinage from those we like while a remark with much less of a barb from others will be regarded as offensive. The smoke from the *aguru* is not termed mere smoke, it is glorified by the special term *dhūpa* (incense).

2.48 *Display of accurate knowledge in a background of widespread popular misconceptions*

It is generally assumed that our forebears were labouring under a whole lot of supersitions and misconceptions about the physical world around them and that it is only after the advent of modern science that they have been set right. While in many cases this is true, it is a matter of great surprise that ancient India had acquired accurate knowledge in some fields like astronomy: it would be more correct to say that some of the wisest men in the ancient Indian society had the key to some of the secrets of the universe on which the populace had deeply grounded misconceptions. Varāhamihira of the 5th century AD (approx.) knew clearly that the earth rotates round the sun and not the other way about though till the advent of Copernicus and Galileo, the western world did not possess this knowledge and these brilliant scientists ran a terrible risk in propagating such dangerous truths.

In literature we have occasional gleams of accurate conceptions in the writings of great masters, in fields where ignorance is widespread. We have seen, under an earlier category, the fanciful interpretations of the origin of the black spot in the moon: they are interesting but they stem from a basic ignorance of the scientific reason for the phenomenon. Kālidāsa refers to this popular misconception and provides the correct scientific reason for the spot: and all this is brought in to illustrate a profound psychological principle, denoting great insight on the part of the poet.

This occurs in the XIV canto of the Raghuvamśa: Rāma has just been told of the scandal concerning Sītā and in the nadir of anguish he cries out against the injustice of it all. His lament does not merely portray the depth of his sorrow: it probes the psychology of scandal-mongers and comes out with a brilliant piece of insight and it illustrates all this by an astonishingly scientific and wholly apt metaphor. For Rāma says: "I know she is pure but I also know, as a king, I cannot ignore the feelings of the people. There is, however, this to be said about the calumny: it is the people who have moral dirt in their mind that cast doubts about the morality of others. The stain on the moon is merely the shadow cast on it by the earth: but the denizens of the earth stigmatise the moon for wearing the spot." The stanza is quoted here.

अवैमि चैनामनघेति किं तु
लोकापवादो बलवान्मतो मे ।
छाया हि भूमेः शशिनो मलत्वे-
नारोपिता शुद्धिमतः प्रजाभिः ॥ [XIV/40]

Shrewd observers would all agree that it is the oversexed woman (for it is a woman more often than a man) who has strayed from the moral path or would have, if she had had the courage, that is given to scandalizing other women for lapses from the moral law. The Mrs. Grundies of the world who insinuate moral dirt in others are contaminated by it themselves. In the same way, experience tells us, it is the corrupt people who talk incessantly of corruption in others. Kālidāsa's poetic insight has been able to penetrate the murk of pretensions like a search-light and come out with a basic failing of man. While this is most creditable, the analogy which is the relevant part here displays an admirably accurate knowledge of physical entities, at a very early stage of civilization: the reader is surprised at the gleam of scientific perspicacity in a work, not of scientific knowledge but of creative literature of a bygone epoch.

2.49 *Unique relationships, unusual bargains with God*

Relationship with God for puny, mortal man can only be one of a suppliant towards the giver and is marked by condescension on His part and by a proper attitude of submission on the part of man. We see this relationship generally maintained and referred to in all hymnal literature in all religions. But here and there, when we see a notable exception, where the attitude of submission is clearly absent and God is not allowed to condescend, where God's gifts to man are even shown as man's helping hand extended to solve His problems, the reader is bound to suffer a shock. We shall show four verses here from the bhakti (or devotional) literature in Sanskrit, two of one kind and two of the other, but all of them exuding a uniquely different spirit from what is commonly met with.

One from the Śivānandalaharī of Śaṅkarācārya runs thus: "Lord, you are the greatest patron of the poor and I am the foremost among the indigent. What a wonderful relationship subsists between us! You are bound to succour me for this is an inherent implication of this relationship: you cannot get out of the obligation !" The suggestion is that even as man in his condition needs God, God in His condition as the one Saviour needs man in order to confirm and fulfil His role as the Saviour.

प्रभुस्त्वं दीनानां खलु परमबन्धुः पशुपते
    प्रमुख्योऽहं तेषामपि किमुत बन्धुत्वमनयोः ।
त्वयैव क्षन्तव्याः शिव मदपराधाश्च सकलाः
    प्रयत्नात् कर्तव्यं मदवनमियं बन्धुसरणिः ॥ [14]

This idea finds a clearer, more direct expression in Ālavandār's *Stōtraratna*: just as the poet will be left friendless, without a protector if God does not extend a helping hand to him, God too will miss the opportunity to succour the most wretched of all objects of pity and vindicate His position as the one Saviour if He fails to help the poet. Just as man finds fulfilment in worship, God finds it in succouring: there is a great new religious doctrine embedded in these two verses and the reader takes it in with a dose of surprise at the daring innovation.

तवहं त्वदृते न नाथवान्
    मदृते त्वं दयनीयवान्न च ।
विधिनिर्मितमेतमन्वयम्
    भगवन् पालय मा स्म जहिपः ॥

In a different mood, Śaṅkara tries to entice God to accept something from him as a gift: the devotee becomes the giver and the Lord the grateful suppliant ! This is the relationship that is openly referred to in the two verses quoted below but the reader cannot miss the point of the saint-minstrel who is eagerly seeking the Lord's grace, in refreshingly different language.

In the first of them, he notices the Lord engaged in the job of begging for alms and suggests that He may take his mind with Him: for, his mind is a restless monkey jumping from desire to desire: He can tie it with a string called devotion and take it with him to the houses of men where the monkey with its antics will attract patrons to Him, rendering His work easier. Lord Śiva is portrayed as a beggar in the Puranas and the mind-monkey analogy is not unknown in Indian literature. Śaṅkara's genius combined these two concepts and presented them in a unique lyric full of musical charm.

सदा मोहाटव्यां चरति युवतीनां कुचगिरौ
नटत्याशाशाखास्वटति झटिति स्वैरमभितः ।
कपालिन् भिक्षो मे हृदयकपिमत्यन्तचपलम्
दृढ़ं भक्त्या बध्वा शिव भवद धीनं कुरु विभो ॥

[Śivānandalaharī 20]

In the other, Lord Śiva is addressed as the Ancient Hunter (which He is, according to the Vēdas) and He is advised to shift His venue of operations to the mind of the poet which is an uncharted forest teeming with wild animals like desire, anger, greed, animus: He can have greater fulfilment as a hunter by making the devotee's mind His permanent abode. Thousands of devotees have prayed to God to come down and reside in their hearts but none else has had the temerity to invite Him for His good, as a favour to Him !

मा गच्छ त्वमितस्ततो गिरिश भो मय्येव वासं कुरु
स्वामिन्नादिकिरात मामकमनःकान्तारसीमान्तरे ।
वर्तन्ते बहुशो मृगा मदजुषो मात्सर्यमोहादयः
तान्हत्वा मृगयाविनोदरुचिता-लाभं च संप्राप्स्यसि ॥

[Śivānandalaharī 43]

2.50 *Relative notions of time*

Time marches on inexorably, unhurried, at the same specified speed: but it seems to highly subjective man to move at very different speeds at different points and its objective in so varying its speed appears solely to torment him. A striking instance is furnished by Kālidāsa in his play the Vikramōrvaśīya: the king gets united with Ūrvaśī whom he loves passionately: this reunion comes after a prolonged period of anguished waiting: now he tells Ūrvaśī he has a prayer and that is that nights which seemed to move on leaden feet when they were separated should not fly fast but move at the same slow pace, now when they are together. The stanza:

अनुपनतमनोरथस्य पूर्वं
शतगुणितेव गता मम त्रियामा ।
यदि तु तव समागमे तथैव
प्रसरति सुभ्रु ततः कृती भवेयम् ॥ [III/22]

Examples like this where time is felt to race past a happy person and is held to crawl for an unhappy one are scattered all over Sanskrit literature: these are relative notions of time. Examples of relative time are found in the philosophical and religious literature of India too. While for one person only a few moments have passed by, for another it is a whole lifetime during which he marries, begets a number of children and becomes the king of the realm having a long reign. Such illustrations of an interesting kind are to be found in a work of philosophy called *Tripurā-rahasya*. They are all evocative of wonder in the reader.

2.51 *Getting badly trounced by the very thing that was expected to save*

Occasionally fate seems to get extra nasty and take sadistic delight in doing down a person with the aid of the very agency he relied upon to save him. The person gets more sharply aggrieved if this happens than if his troubles are caused by something that looks, not inviting but obviously forbidding.

Śrīharṣa has a verse in his Naiṣadha which aptly illustrates this. The *aśoka* tree looks very benevolent to the weary traveller long separated from his beloved: they expect the grief (*śōka*) caused by the separation to be dissipated by the *aśoka* tree, even on the basis of pure semantics. But when they approach it, they are shocked to find their troubles multiplied manifold: the red flowers of the *aśoka* are the arrows of the god of love ! This is the verse:

अशोकमर्थान्वितनामताशया गतान् शरण्यं गृहशोचिनोऽध्वगान् ।
अमन्यतावन्तमिवैष पल्लवैः प्रतीष्टकामज्ज्वलदस्त्रजालकम् ॥

[I/101]

2.52 *One man's meat turns out to be another's poison, startlingly in some cases*

Likes and dislikes are strictly individual and subjective; there can never be one rule regulating this matter. Garlic is today widely popular as a seasoning in the Arab and European cuisine but with what Victorian prudery Mrs. Beeton screws her patrician nose in fine disgust at this spice which had just crossed the channel!

Śrīharṣa has a fine stanza in his Naiṣadha giving a classical imprimatur to the popular saying: Damayanti, in giving a no for a reply to Indra, her suitor, through his messenger cites this in a diplomatic explanation of her preference for Nala over the lord of the gods. An animal fond of soft food criticizes the taste of a camel for thorny fodder while a camel makes no attempt to hide her disgust at the soft food of the other. It is, however, true that the satisfaction derived by both is the same, though the means by which it is brought about varies so sharply. Hence the attitude of a wise man should be one of tolerance and not of supercilious contempt at the (to him) peculiar tastes of others. The verse, for a composition of Śrīharṣa is engagingly simple.

क्रमेलकं निन्दति कोमलेच्छुः क्रमेलकः कण्टकलम्पटस्तम् ।
प्रीतौ तयोरिष्टभुजोः समायाम् मध्यस्थता नैकतरोपहासः ॥

[VI/104]

It may be recalled that Kālidāsa steps in to offer a generalisation in explaining Indumatī's rejection of a king in the *svayamvara*, in the Raghuvaṃśa:

अथाङ्गराजादवतार्य चक्षुः याहीति जन्यामवदत्कुमारी ।
नासौ न काम्यो न च वेद सम्यक् द्रष्टुं न सा भिन्नरुचिर्हि लोकः ॥

[VI/30]

Clearly Śrīharṣa took up this idea of the master and enlarged on it to good purpose, harnessing an apt simile.

2.53 *The damming up of strong emotions and the bursting of the dam*

When there is a strong passion raging in the heart and it

clamours to burst out, it becomes often necessary to dam it up and pass off the occasion with talk that gives the lie to it. When characters known to have raging emotions in them succeed in shoring them up their will power compels our admiration and wonder: when, instead, the truth comes out bursting the dam (as it happens on occasions) surprise is again caused at the sudden break up of restraint and by the realisation of its consequences.

For the former, we have examples in Mudrārākṣasa where diplomacy is displayed by many characters whose strong loyalties have to be kept bottled up on occasions. A good example will be Emperor Candragupta himself, who, after the feigned quarrel with Cāṇakya feels the need to flout his preceptor's advice most distasteful: he, however, bottles it up successfully and acts the part of a disenchanted king convincingly. In this mood he utters a verse (III/26 praising Rākṣasa before Caṇakya, clearly chastising the latter as a braggart when he says

विश्वास्येष्वपि विश्वसन्ति मतयो न स्वेषु वर्गेषु न:।

[III / 26]

Provoking Cāṇakya to simulated anger which he acts out so convincingly the king anxiously observes in an aside, "Is he truly angry at me?" And finally, the decisive words of command: "Chamberlain, let the people be told clearly that I shall ignore the words of Cāṇakya and rule the kingdom according to my own bent."

How much grief all this causes him is made clear through the verse recited in an aside by the emperor.

आर्याज्ञयैव मम लङ्घितगौरवस्य बुद्धिः प्रवेष्टुमिव भूविवरं प्रवृत्ता।
ये सत्यमेव हि गुरूनतिपातयन्ति तेषां कथं नु हृदयं न भिनत्ति लज्जा॥

[III/33]

Such a dichotomy will certainly cause surprise to the spectators who have seen on the stage earlier the adulation in which the king holds his preceptor and the present acrimonious contention.

Equally surprising is the case where the character, unable to dissemble, bursts out with the truth, causing astonishment and consternation in diverse quarters. Urvaśī playing the role of Lakṣmī in the play staged in heaven is deeply in love with Purūravas. When, as Lakṣmi on emerging from the ocean she is asked "On whom are your affections centred?" she is expected to reply "On Puruṣōttama". Unfortunately for her, the word begins with the (Sanskrit) letter Pu and this lets loose the pent-up flood in her heart making her flash the reply on the stage "On Purūravas".

This enrages the producer of the play Bharatamuni who curses her to a life on earth in fulfilment of her secret desire; this slip, indeed, becomes the cornerstone of the plot of the play the Vikramōrvaśīya, with the *muni*'s curse and its reprieve so graciously pronounced by Indra as the chief motive forces. The consequences of the Freudian slip of the tongue are truly catastrophic and this total collapse of restraint in Urvaśī must have caused startled consternation in many hearts on that fateful day.

2.54 *Drawing a conclusion from material which seemingly suggests the very opposite*

From certain parameters listed one feels that a certain conclusion is inevitable; but if a different, even radically opposite conclusion is arrived at (and it can be reasonably sustained) it will cause wonder. Mrs. John and Mrs. James are engaged in neighbourly conversation across the fence. Mrs. James: You were worrying a lot about Mr. John being unemployed, but I saw him going out dressed on a few mornings. Has he got a job?

Mrs. John: Yes, he has. It's hard work and it's killing him: but thanks be! It's permanent.

Poets of a philosophical bent—a tribe more numerous in India of earlier epochs—present certain observations which seemingly lead the reader on to a certain conclusion and proceed to draw a startlingly different conclusion, taking good care to make this not unreasonable: this can induce an aesthetically enjoyable sensation of wonder and at the same time drive home the lesson better.

Nīlakaṇṭha Dīkṣita in his Śāntivilāsa lists a series of materially favourable conditions like good health, a satisfactory financial position, youthfulness and the total absence of sad happenings; if these things happen all together for one, well, that one clearly is a lucky mortal who can be expected to go ahead and enjoy all these blessings in a frenzy of hedonism. But, Dīkṣita has quite another pattern of life in mind for such a lucky person if, in the midst of these things he is able to turn his mind inward to a contemplation of the divinity within, then and then only is he to be classed as supremely fortunate. The verse has been nicely rendered.

भव्ये देहे पटुषु करणेष्वालये श्रीसमृद्धे
कौमारान्ते वयसि कथमप्यप्रवृत्ते च दुःखे ।
प्रत्यक्पुष्पीप्रसवविधया यस्य पुंसो निसर्गात्
प्रत्यग्वक्त्रं भवति हृदयं कस्ततोऽप्यस्ति धन्यः ॥ [48]

There is a story related in the Hitōpadeśa where a brahmin laments over the death of his son and one Kapila reasons with him, with a long passage of deep philosophical import. During the course of it he says; "Man establishes affection in his heart for many people, many things. These things which he loves, these people he likes—all turn out to be so many pointed arrows that pierce the heart."

यावतः कुरुते जन्तुः संबन्धान् मनसः प्रियान् ।
तावन्तोऽपि निखन्यन्ते हृदये शोकशङ्कवः ॥

[Sandhi—Story II]

From the early reference to love and affection, one may be led to expect something good, something favourable to be said about the objects of love; but no ! the poet says the very opposite, he regards them as arrows that pierce the heart ! The objects of love, far from generating happiness behave like pegs driven painfully into the living flesh of the heart ! On account of the way it is all presented, on account of the unexpectedness, it evokes a certain surprise, even in a society dominated by compulsive moralists.

2.55 *Steps taken against deeply held preferences fail, leading to joy unbounded*

Sometimes people are forced to act against their own predilections: the ostentations zeal shown by them in thus acting against their preferences causes surprise; when the step taken fails of its purpose there is joy laced with a mild surprise at the failure. Many a young lover has incurred the wrath of his girl by following implicitly what she asked him to do in a mood of mild irritation. There are many heroes in Wodehouse who need to be told that if their girl says she does not want to see him again in this world or the next, it means that love still lingers, that she is only mildly annoyed at something he has done or failed to do. The language of love is very different from what Pāṇini or the Fowler brothers ordained and things are not what they seem, they are often the very opposite.

A girl having a tiff with her lover and deeply desiring the restoration of amicable relations is advised by the hawks among her friends to maintain a belligerent attitude. When the lover comes, in keeping with this advice she looks down and not at him, ears closed with the hands to prevent her hearing what he was saying (though burning with eagerness to hear his words): the exciting horripilation and sweating in the cheeks are ignored. But all this proves useless—her dress gets loose in a hundred places signalling impending union with him (according to the texts of sexology). The stanza from Amaru can be savoured now.

तद्वक्त्राभिमुखं मुखं विनमितं दृष्टिः कृता पादयोः
तस्यालापकुतूहलाकुलतरे श्रोत्रे निरुद्धे मया ।
पाणिभ्यां च तिरस्कृतः सपुलकः स्वेदोद्गमो गण्डयोः
सख्यः किं करवाणि यान्ति शतधा यत्कञ्चुके सन्धयः ॥ [II]

Mild surprise is occasioned by the determined steps taken by the girl in opposition to the dearest wish of her heart: there is likely again to be a charge of surprise shooting through the reader's mind when he reads of the sudden and total collapse of all such endeavours: a little surprise may lace amusement at the unmitigated joy that results from such a collapse. There are quite a few examples of this category in Sanskrit and generally in Indian literature but none that has the high distinction of Amaru's artistry.

2.56 *Making much of a thing, unbridled exaggeration*

Some characters blow up a fact of ordinary significance, make a big fuss over something that is really not worth that much attention; this is done with a purpose in view in many cases; in others it is revelatory of deeper attachments under the surface, not to the thing blown up but surprisingly to the other that gets belittled, underplayed. In the last aspect mentioned above, this has similar psychological motivation to what has been discussed earlier; but, while in the earlier category the undervaluation has been stressed, here the exaggeration receives emphasis and in some examples no undervaluation may be involved at all.

In the first two examples both factors are clearly illustrated. Rāma sees Lakṣmaṇa fallen in the field cut down by the enemy's arrows and taking him to be dead, laments, belittling everything including the reunion with Sītā in the gush of anguish at the tragedy. These are his words in Vālmīki's great epic:

किं नु मे सीतया कार्यं लब्ध्या जीवितेन वा ।
शयानं योऽद्य पश्यामि भ्रातरं युधि निर्जितम् ॥
शक्या सीतासमा नारी मर्त्यलोके विचिन्वता ।
न लक्ष्मणसमो भ्राता सचिवः सांपरायिकः ॥

[Yuddha Kāṇḍa 49/5&6]

Lakṣmaṇa is his own brother who had elected to go with him to the woods in order to be in a position to serve Rāma: so these words do not constitute much of an exaggeration, perhaps. But, surely, his observation addressed to Sugrīva when he returns from a duel with Rāvaṇa (the monkey chief had impetuously leapt on to the terrace where Rāvaṇa was airing himself and engaged him in a short duel where he is almost killed by a blow from the *rākṣasa* is most unwarranted: for he says, "If something untoward had happened to you, then, of what use will the reunion with Sītā be?"

इदानीं मा कृथा वीर एवंविधमचिन्तितम् ।
त्वयि किंचिद् समापन्ने किं कार्यं सीतया मम ॥
भरतेन महाबाहो लक्ष्मणेन यवयिसा ।
शत्रुघ्नेन च शत्रुघ्न स्वशरीरेण वा पुनः ॥

[Yuddha kāṇḍa 41/4&5]

How can this be? Devoted readers of the *Rāmāyaṇa* through the centuries have been roused to indignation, wonder and sorrow at this observation of the hero: they have protested in the commentaries and disquisitions asking "Is the monkey of yesterday more important than Sītā, the Mother of the world, his own inseparable consort?" One explanation is that he has to motivate his allies, keep them in good humour, with the terrible war looming before them. But a better explanation may be found in the psychological set up of Rāma. For Rāma, the most beloved object in the world is Sītā; and, as a consequence, she constitutes the measuring tape of love in Rāma's hands: and when Rāma has to laud the value of his brother or his ally, he applies this measuring tape to declare that they are dearer to him than Śitā herself. This psychological peculiarity is often met with in the world of men: those who value money most highly are the very men who declare that other things are more valuable to them than money. These statements of Rāma portray his great love for Lakṣmaṇa and Sugrīva: they indicate his preoccupation, his being wrapped up in love with Sītā, at a deeper level.

In the next example, we find an exaggerated emphasis placed on something without anything else being specifically undervalued. And what a fall in the calibre of the character now to be discussed from the moral heights of Rāma ! For it is Śakāra, the unmitigated villain of the Mṛcchakaṭika that we propose to quote from. In Act IX of the play when called up on by the judge to swear to his identity, he presents his relationship with the king of the realm in four different ways, underscoring his impregnable social position to impress the judge and the others assembled. This remarkable, indeed unique, statement is bound to draw amused or derisive laughter reinforced by surprise from the spectators of all epochs, as this is a clear demonstration of a man claiming immunity from the law of the land on the basis of his relationship wiih the king; no age and no country has been totally free from such moral quirk, even our contemporary democratic societies being no exceptions.

राजश्वशुरो मम पिता राजा तातस्य भवति जामाता ।
राजश्यालोऽहम् ममापि भगिनीपती राजा ॥ [IX/6]

Bardic poetry has been the happy hunting ground for the poor panegyrist who expects to find rich harvests from an unbridled exaggeration of the qualities of egotistical potentates: truth naturally becomes the first casualty in this and there is no atmosphere for critical, balanced statements where eveiy word is weighed before use. Nīlakaṇṭha Dikṣita pokes fun at this tendency in a verse in his Sabhārañjana-śataka.

काणाः कमलपत्राक्षाः कदर्याः कल्पशाखिनः ।
कातरा विक्रमादित्याः कविवृक्गोचरं गताः ॥ [21]

So, when confronted by bardic poetry the cautious reader is not likely to be surprised by the commonly-met-with levels of exaggeration: his threshold of surprise in this field gets quite broadened through experience. But even to him the level of exaggeration reached in the following verses may cause a double-take, may overwhelm him with an incredulous surprise. Here are the verses:

मार्तंडमण्डलसमं भवतः प्रतापं ये वर्णयन्ति न हि ते कवयः प्रवीणाः ।
अम्भोनिधौ विलयमेति परं पतङ्गः पारं प्रयाति जलधेस्तु तव प्रतापः ॥
[Subhāṣitaratnabhāṇḍāgāra, 139/9]

कतिपयदिवसैः क्षयं प्रयायात् कनकगिरिः कृतवासरावसानः ।
इति मुदमुपयाति चक्रवाकी वितरणशालिनि वीररुद्रदेवे ॥
[Kuvalayānanda, N.S. edition, page 42]

2.57 *The surprising perseverence of a character in an illusion*

It is surprising how many of us who regard ourselves as normal people and (what is more important) are regarded as normal by other people harbour illusions at some stage of our lives. The greater our ambition and the stronger our attachments, the more powerful is the hold of illusions over us. This perseverance in illusions often holds out against the attack of reality and this is seen in life and literature: the cases cause surprise in proportion to the weight of the evidence of reality and to the strength and duration of the illusion persevered in.

There are many cases in Sangam Tamil literature (one of the oldest specimens of love poetry in India) where such persistence of illusions which constitutes the core of the poem is able to hold out against irrefutable evidence to the contrary. The lover promises to return to her with the first rains but fails to live up to his promise: the first rains come down and the *mullai* begins to blossom: there is unmistakable ocular evidence that the lover has failed her: but no, she does not believe all that, she allows herself to be persuaded that the monsoon rains have not yet come down, that these are mere passing showers, that these may be the arrears of the previous year!

In a poem by Amaru the rich emotional potential of this device is fully exploited. A (girl) friend of the girl in love advises her to develop a belligerent attitude towards her lover who has not been true to the love: angrily the devoted friend counsels her to adopt a militant posture and give up her sweet conciliatory ways. The girl in love gets worried at this counsel: she tells her friend, "Not so loud! For he reigns in my heart and may hear all your loveless words of advice!" Far from being annoyed at his devious ways, at the many glib promises he has broken to shreds, she perseveres in her illusion that he still loves her, that he may get upset at the harsh counsel of the friend, listening in from his vantage seat in her heart. In the higher reaches of love, physical union, even physical presence, counts for much less: the most significant transactions take place in the mental field. Her lover's availability so near to her (seated in her heart, enthroned) may look a ridiculous illusion in the eyes of the pragmatic friend and the rest of the world: but it is a glowing reality to the girl in love. Through the effective medium of incredulous surprise, her deep and lasting love that transgresses physical parameters comes out strongly in the stanza, not in spite of the fragile illusion but precisely on account of it.

मुग्धे मुग्धतयैव नेतुमखिलं कालं किमारभ्यते
  मानं धत्स्व धृतिबधान ऋजुतां दूरे कुरु प्रेयसि ।
सख्यैवं प्रतिबोधिता प्रतिवचस्तामाह भीतानना
  नीचैः शंस हृदि स्थितो हि ननु मे प्राणेश्वरः श्रोष्यति ॥ [70]

2.58 *With vaulting ambition goes a frailty of heart, causing surprise twice over*

Ordinary men and women sometimes pitch their goal very high—so high in relation to their resources and talents that it causes eyebrows to rise in surprised consoriousness. But if, along with such soaring ambitions and lofty goals goes such a pusillanimity, such a poor spirit, such a weakness of heart that there is sensational failure registered, then again a certain surprise is caused. Surprise is generated by and is proportional to the height to which the goal is raised and the difference between the goal and the achievement.

Girl tells boy to go and raise a fortune on which they can marry and live happily ever after. Ten days later girl asks him,

"How much have you got?" "Fifty-six rupees" says he. "That is enough!" says the girl, "let us get married immediately".

There is a fine stanza in Śāntivilāsa which serves this idea with a sauce of puckish humour. A man got disgusted with worldly life and decided to take *sannyāsa*: he wonders whether he should consult an almanac to fix an auspicious time for leaving home, then decides in a true spirit of renunciation that for one who is giving up everything, no auspicious time is needed. When he is stepping out of the house on his austere mission, the sound of his youngest children crying in the house assails his ears: "Who looks after the children in the house but me?" he mutters to himself as he returns home to his old mode of life.

जातं जातं गतमपि गतं बाल्यतो लौल्यतो वा
नेतः स्थेयं क्षणमपि गृहे मुञ्चतः को मुहुर्तः ।
इत्यत्यन्तव्यवसितधियो निःसरन्तोऽपि गेहात्
आवर्तन्ते झटिति रुदतां सान्त्वहेतोः शिशुनां ॥ [22]

There are stanzas in Bhartṛhari which too can be quoted at least as partially illustrative of this category: the surprise they serve up may be of the mildest. Verses 74 and 77 of Śṛṅgāraśataka describe how even intelligent persons who have set up for themselves high goals in life—even the highest goal of total emancipation, who assiduously carry on spiritual practices, study the scriptures and control the senses, utterly collapse when beautiful women start working their coquetry on them. Verse 74 is nicely composed in the majestic *sragdharā* metre and would bear being quoted.

सन्मार्गे तावदास्ते प्रभवति च नरस्तावदेवेन्द्रियाणाम्
लज्जां तावद्विधत्ते विनयमपि समालम्बते तावदेव ।
भ्रूचापाकृष्टमुक्ताः श्रवणपथगता नीलपक्ष्माण एते
यावल्लीलावतीनां हृदि न धृतिमुषो दृष्टिबाणाः पतन्ति ॥

2.59 *Small factors used to create a smokescreen to conceal a significant fault*

Clever, unscrupulous men raise a number of small difficulties, plead small excuses in the hope that the other party will be put off: they have something big, some serious transgression to conceal and they make use of these insignificant things as a smokescreen to hide it. When the other party proves tenacious and persistent and the transgression comes to light, surprise is evoked partly on account of the efforts at concealment and partly by the size of the thing uncovered.

A young man standing near the gate of an exhibition appeared a most devoted factotum of the organisation. The sun was beating down mercilessly on his head, there were shady spots nearby but he would not move so much as an inch: he kept on saying, "This is where my boss asked me to stand and regulate the entry of people and this is where I shall stand." Everyone was highly appreciative of the stand of this modern Casabianca, till the mystery was cleared (later) that some visitor had inadvertently dropped a ten-rupee currency note at that point and he had been standing with his foot covering it, hoping to pocket it when no one was looking.

Bhāsa introduces in his Pratigñāyaugandharāyaṇa an elephant-tender Gātrasevaka looking after Bhadravatī the famed elephant belonging to King Pradyōta. One day, when princess Vāsavadatta wanted to go to the river to bathe and sport in the water, her mount and its tender were found missing: a search is instituted and a guard discovers Gātrasevaka drunkenly walking down a street not far from a wine-shop.

The guard accosts him with the instruction to hurry to the palace with the elephant. The elephant man replies evasively, "Alas ! I have pledged the goad of Bhadravatī:" The guard counters this saying the elephant is gentle and needs no goad. The drunk pleads saying he has pledged various appurtenances of the elephant, successively, one after the other; but the guard is persistent and is getting increasingly annoyed. So Gātrasēvaka comes out with the truth, eventually: "I have pledged Bhadravatī herself with the vintner !"

The spectators must have been registering amused surprise at this when there is great commotion in the street and the startling news is heard that Udayana has eloped with the princess and the elephant tender now reveals himself as Yaugandharāyaṇa's man planted in the enemy's camp: more surprises follow.

2.60 *People unknowingly working at cross purposes with surprisingly hilarious consequences*

People do work at cross purposes, unknowingly, cancelling

out the efforts of each other: when besides being amusing, it has startling elements in it, it can qualify as a distinct category in our study.

Two moving men were struggling with a big crate in a doorway. They pushed and tugged until they were exhausted but it wouldn't move. Finally the fellow on the outside said, "We'd better give up—we will never get this crate in".

"What do you mean get it in?" screeched the man on the inside. "I thought we were trying to get it out!"

A good example of this category is provided by Rāmabhadra Dīkṣita in his play. This has been briefly referred to, earlier. During the stay of Rāma and Sītā and Lakṣmaṇa in the woods, Virādha, a rākṣasa conceives a hopeless passion for Sitā: learning of her great attachment to Rāma, he appears on the stage impersonating him so that he can trick Sītā and carry her off: at the same time, Śūrpaṇakhā who is infatuated with Rāma comes in the guise of Sītā so as to ensnare Rāma. Now this fraudulent Rāma and Sītā mistake each other for the genuine article and make ardent advances to each other—a transaction that would stage very well indeed. Śūrpaṇakhā pretends, in an exhibition of coyness, to be interested in gathering flowers and Virādha losing patience at this impulsively takes her up and rises in the air through the aid of *rākṣasa* magic.

Lakṣmana notices this and jumps to the conclusion that the genuine Sītā is being abducted: with him, to think is but to act: he leaps at the pair and kills Virādha with one stroke; Śūrpaṇakhā now reveals herself and Lakṣmaṇa cuts off her nose and drives her away.

Dīkṣita has contrived four distinct sets of impersonation in his complex play, but of them all, this is the most hilarious and also most naturally evocative of the sense of wonder. The denizens of the night appearing as Rāma and Sītā, their trying to talk like the genuine couple they impersonate, their strong-arm tactics at a later stage and the glory end to their antics all have a strong element of surprise in them.

2.61 *Startling mental state on waking up from illusions*

The evocation of wonder through the presentation of the perseverance of characters in illusions has been discussed earlier: now the startling mental state with fancies in smithereens all around and realism starkly dominant can be discussed as a distinct category: for the sudden onrush of reality and the tumbling of enthroned illusions can be distinctly unsettling, evocative of surprise.

After an American college dance where the dates were arranged by a computer, I asked a friend what it was like. "It's a frightening experience" she answered, "finding out just what you deserve". James Thurber says that the brief moments of lucidity his grandfather had were somehow more embarrassing than his normal state.

In Bhāsa's play, the *Svapnavāsavadatta*, the king, in actuality sees his queen, supposed dead: but as he is in a stupor induced by sleep he thinks it is a dream. He is rudely awakened when he gets up to rush in pursuit of her rapidly vanishing form and gets a knock on the head against the doorpost. The king now sadly ruminates over the significant difference between the waking state and the state of dreaming: how in the state of sleep he can at least dream of her but brutish reality denies him even this satisfaction. Naturally he prefers to persevere in a state of dream or illusion rather than wake up to face the shock of disenchantment. The verse:

यदि तावदयं स्वप्नः धन्यमप्रतिबोधनम् ।
यदयं विभ्रमो वा स्याद् विभ्रमो ह्यस्तु मे चिरम् ॥ [v/9]

Sharper surprise is evoked by two epigrams presented in a stanza from Bhartṛhari: and a valuable lesson is taught more effectively through the sense of wonder. The poet ruminates: "During the (long) period I was almost ignorant, knowing but little, I was proud, I went about as if I knew everything. When, as a result of my contact with the wise, a little wisdom was acquired by me, I began to realise how ignorant I was, in truth and my pride departed from me as a fever is cured."

यदा किंचिज्ज्ञोऽहं गज इव मदान्धः समभवम्
तदा सर्वज्ञोस्मीत्यभवदवलिप्तं मम मनः ।
यदा किंचित्किंचिद्बुधजनसकाशादवगतम्
तदा मूर्खोऽस्मीति ज्वर इव मदो मे व्यपगतः ॥

[Nīti 8]

This awakening from a state of illusion is succinctly portrayed in the statement: "If you realise you aren't as wise today as you thought yesterday, you are wiser today." The awakening comes as a shock with considerable anguish but accompanied by wisdom too which redeems the whole process.

2.62 *When road-blocks startlingly turn out to be stepping stones*

Certain factors which look very much like obstacles (and indeed, intrinsically are) can sometimes be harnessed by a resourceful wayfarer to serve him as accessories to help him along in his journey. Perhaps, in a deeply philosophical sense all difficulties encountered by man are intended to help him in some way. It is said that the northwind made the vikings, meaning that the icy wind toughened these Nordics and fitted them for their sanguinary career. Almost every hardship, obstacle or disability can be converted into an advantage by a person of inflexible will. But there are some cases out of them where this metamorphosis of roadblocks into stepping stones is startling: for it to evoke surprise there must be a strong element of unexpectedness. For instance, I read somewhere that in these days of rising prices, one good thing about the rise of Christmas tree prices is it's a lot easier to reach the top of the tree.

The most classical example of this is provided by Kālidāsa in his play the Vikramōrvaśīya.

The verse (II/16) has been quoted earlier as an example for a different category but this profound statement can equally well illustrate this. The verse is uttered by the king in reply to the report of Ūrvaśī's maid that Ūrvaśī is suffering acute pangs of love disease. The king says ruefully: "You have eyes only for her suffering; you do not realise how much I suffer on her account. Such agony is the common lot of all the lovers, both the man and the woman being subjected to such travail. Indeed this agony is necessary to bring them together as heat is needed to solder two pieces of iron."

Under the earlier category itself we have discussed the implications of this wonderful stanza. Suffering is the lot of lovers and it has to be undergone, not merely because it is fated but more significantly as it is the one means of bringing them together. What looked like a massive roadblock turns out to be a most convenient stepping-stone that leads the lovers on to beatitude.

We may also cite the many philosophical texts which eloquently proclaim all the evil wrought by the mind which distracts man from his onward march to emancipation. But, they all unanimously point to the mind as the only means available to man to secure emancipation. To give just one example of the latter, we have in the Muṇḍakōpaniṣad.

एषोऽणुरात्मा चेतसा वेदितव्यः ।

[III/1/9

A popular line of verse

मन एव मनुष्याणां कारणं बन्धमोक्षयोः ॥

Cryptically brings into focus both the propensities of the mind—its well-known tendency to push man into bondage and its less known potential to help him to emancipate himself. Summing up both the aspects nicely is a verse in Śaṅkara's philosophical text Vivekacūḍāmaṇi.

वायुना नीयते मेघः: पुनस्तेनैव नीयते ।
मनसा कल्प्यते बन्धः मोक्षस्तेनैव कल्प्यते ॥ [174]

The next two verses of the same work get into details and confirm the same conclusion. So, indubitably the mind acts as a great road-block for the spiritual seeker till it is controlled and firmly harnessed when it becomes a stepping-stone through which he can elevate himself.

2.63 *The simultaneous advocacy of two radically opposed concepts*

Life is infinitely more complex than the one dozen copy book maxims we are taught in our childhood. It sometimes demands the holding of two opposite concepts ourselves or the advocacy of such a feat to be performed by the listener. Normally, such a basically contradictory situation will not arise: when such arises and the contradiction has not been artificially contrived, then it evokes a certain amount of surprise.

It has been said: "The art of living successfully consists of being able to hold two opposite ideas in tension at the same time: first to make long-term plans as if we were going to live for ever: and second, to conduct ourselves daily as if we were going to die tomorrow." This, of course, is an ideal example illustrating this category: about the reasonableness of the proposition there can be no doubt at all: for though, statistically, for large populations death has definitely been put off, individuals may die any moment, despite all this progress in the medical science.

Surprisingly there is an old Sanskrit verse quoted in the Hitōpadeśa advocating this same set of opposite concepts; this short verse in *anuṣṭubh* metre actually manages to pack more detail than the statement in English.

अजरामरवत् प्राज्ञो विद्यामर्थं च साधयेत् ।
गृहीत इव केशेषु मृत्युना धर्ममाचरेत् ।।

[Introduction-3]

This law will be found, on reflection, to apply to all life situations. Bureaucrats and politicians should learn to keep their seats free of arrears, treating each day as a self-sufficient unit, as they may be transferred (in the case of the former) or unseated (in the case of the latter). At the same time, they are expected to process long-term projects the completion of which they will not be able to witness from the seat of power.

2.64 *Cause operating at a point and effect appearing at another*

This phenomenon appears to defy the law of causation and it is this that causes surprise. It is, of course, always necessary to make the phenomenon plausible and not arbitrary, this being a basic condition in aesthetics. A somewhat superficial example of this category will be: back from an economic conference in Paris, a banker was asked if he had had any difficulty with his French. "No" he asserted. "But the French did".

A lover in Amaru's century of verses complains of precisely this inconsistent situation in his case: for, the girl he loves is very young—was a child but yesterday: but it is he who suffers from a juvenile lack of confidence: she, as a girl should be timorous, afraid of things: but no, it is he that is timorous. She carries a pair of very well-developed breasts all the time: but it is he that gets fatigued, spent out with the slightest exertion. Her lower hip is big, ponderously heavy: but it is the lover that finds it increasingly difficult to move about. The causating factors all doubtless lie in her but the effects all are to be noticed in the lover!

सा बाला वयमप्रगल्भमनसः सा स्त्री वयं कातराः
सा पीनोन्नतिमत्पयोधरयुगं धत्ते सखेदा वयम् ।
साक्रान्ता जघनस्थलेन गुरुणा गन्तुं न शक्ता वयम्
दोषैरन्यजनाश्रयैरपटवो जाताः स्म इत्यद्भुतम ॥ [34]

Love accomplishes many strange things. Lovers deeply wrapped up in each other are observed by poets of greater insight, actually to have imbibed some aspects of each other's personality. What Amaru observes as a metamorphosis in the lover alone is seen to have happened to both of them: thus Tamil Sangam poets paint the lover as anxiety-ridden, prone to fears that the worst might come to pass, unsure of himself, hesitant: the girl herself may develop courage and initiative to elope with him, in defiance of parental disapproval.

There is a poem in the famed Pañcatantra which serves up a similar kind of exception to the rule of causation. It says a wicked man is often compared to a serpent but he functions very differently from the reptile: for, when a serpent bites a person, it is that person that dies: but the wicked person bites the ear of A and it is B (who is the subject of the calumny) that dies as a result.

अहो खलभुजङ्गस्य विपरीतो वधक्रमः ।
अन्यस्य दशति श्रोत्रं अन्यः प्राणैर्वियुज्यते ॥ [I/329]

2.65 *Cause judged as inadequate for the scale of the effect*

It is a law in Indian logic, much later confirmed by science that the effect is proportional to the cause, that the effect cannot exceed the limitations set up by the cause. So when we see an effect big in scale or rich with unusual qualities and we find the cause to be obviously inadequate we are naturally surprised. A great wit said: the hardest thing to believe about the Bible is that there were only two jackasses in the Ark. The present density of population of jackasses in the world of men would lead us to expect a much larger number of initial progenitors.

Purūravas in Kālidāsa's Vikramōrvaśīya, deeply in love with Ūrvaśī contemplates her form, when alone and observes with wonder that the creator of this bewitching beauty after all was the hoary old sage, dullened with years of rote repetition of the *vēdas*, the austere hermit who as part of his spiritual practice had systematically destroyed all sense of appreciation of aesthetic excellence.

वेदाभ्यासजडः कथं नु विषयव्यावृत्तकौतूहलः
निर्मातुं प्रभवेत् मनोहरमिदं रूपं पुराणो मुनिः ॥ [I/8]

Only the Indians, very familiar with priests who know only the words of the *vēdas* to recite and whose daily chore is the rote repetition of *vēdic mantras* can judge how deadeningly dull a lifetime of such practices can make them. It must be conceded that it is an amazing feat that the *Vēdas* have been preserved over this vast country intact over millennia but it is a sad fact that the agents responsible for this feat do not prove to be exactly interesting company. The surprise in these two lines of poetry is augmented by the reflection that the poet had mustered the courage to poke gentle fun at these practitioners, in that distant epoch when the sacerdotal class was at the zenith of its influence.

2.66 *The discovery of complexities in things regarded as simple and straight-forward*

In our hurried, superficial view of things, many of them appear simple enough: and since we do not investigate deeply into anything unless there is need for it, we go through life persevering in such a view. When the need arises to investigate (or quite accidentally too, in some cases) we realise that some of them are far from simple, that they display ramifications and complexities we did not dream of and we are naturally surprised.

For instance, we all tend to dismiss the common housefly as a no-account creature, a nuisance at best and a killer at worst which is liable to be crushed by a wave of the swatter. When we are told it has as many as 4000 lenses in each eye (we, at the top of the evolutionary ladder have just one) we are surprised: again, when we read that the geyser, the Old Faithful spurts after exactly the same interval of time with clocklike precision we get wonderstruck, as we tend to think of nature as unprecise, arbitrary.

There is a glow-worm show in Thailand which attracts many thousands of tourists: the show takes place in a jungle many miles north of Bangkok where, in the night many hundred thousands of glow-worms show up, the incredible thing being that they all glow precisely at the same time and wink out at the same time, this cycle alternating many times during the night. As a result of this meticulous timing the woods are dark one moment and brilliantly illumined, the next. This accurate co-ordination taking place among such large numbers of lowly insects without external leadership (no whistles blown, no signals shown) is an amazing fact of nature and it never fails to draw gasps of wonderment from the tourists.

The next time you go to bed, dear reader, please contemplate the awful step you are about to take—for statistics show that of all the various points at which death may take place like highly mechanised factories, high-rise buildings at the stage of construction and highways with high-density traffic, the most lethal is the bed where 98% of all deaths occur. This causes a twinge of consternation laced with surprise: with what sense of total trust have we been going to bed all these days, unaware that we are walking into a sure-fire death-trap! This morbid contemplation goes on till we realise (or we are told) that even those who are fatally injured elsewhere are brought to hospitals where they eventually die-in bed.

A housewife was attracted by an advertisement about a new and very favourable class of insurance and applied in the form prescribed, identifying her occupation as housewife in the space provided. She received a reply from the insurance firm regretting their inability to cover her case under these specially favourable terms as she was following a particularly risky and dangerous occupation.

There are instances in the Mudrārākṣasa where King Candragupta, as a novice in diplomacy thinks lightly of certain things till the wily Cāṇakya points out to him the ramifications. We get two of them in the III Act: one is where Cāṇakya shows two ways of silencing disloyal people neither of them guessed at by the young king earlier.

The other is where the king asks, if all this were so, why these disloyal people were allowed to get away: in reply follows an extra-ordinarily clever and closely argued series of steps with their potential consequences, not a tenth of which the neophyte in diplomacy was able to anticipate. In a fitting tribute to his masterly powers, Candragupta praises his preceptor in these words at the end of the play:

विगुणीकृतकार्मुकोऽपि जेतुम भुवि जेतव्यमसौ समर्थ एव ।
स्वपतोऽपि ममेव यस्य तन्त्रे गुरवो जाग्रति कार्यजागरूकाः ॥

[VII/11]

But the point of the illustration, of course, is that while the logic of all this after the guru's explanation is quite convincing, one marvels at the extra-ordinary mental processes which can identify, analyse and describe these complex ramifications of political action where none is suspected.

2.67 *A complex medley of emotions, some running counter to others, rarely found subsisting in a single human breast together*

At the base is great love between the boy and the girl. But something happens (as it will between young lovers) and a misunderstanding arises lighting up a blazing fire of anger in her heart. At this point of time, despite the obvious contrition shown by him, the girl is not disposed to forgive him: she now feels and acts under the influence of contradictory emotions—undoubted love for him which still waxes powerful in her and anger which prompts her to punish him, make him suffer and a lingering contrition at her own heartlessness in repudiating the overtures of the penitent lover.

Kālidāsa has an instinctive grasp of the complex inner workings of the human mind, particularly of the lovers' mind: he makes Purūravas guess at the thought processes of his queen (whom he has wronged), when she suggests that they spend sometime in the terrace of the palace enjoying the moonlight. He ruefully reflects how she had ruthlessly refused to forgive him despite all his attempts at mollification: now, he concludes, her heart is taking her to task for this and hence this conciliatory gesture. Here is the verse:

अवधूतप्रणिपाताः पश्चात्संतप्यमानमनसोऽपि ।
निभृतैर्व्यपत्रपन्ते दयितानुनयैर्मनस्विन्यः ॥ [III/5]

Amaru, a specialist in the affairs of the heart reports a similar medley of mutually opposed emotions. A lady ruefully recalls, in a conversation with a friend, how she asked her lover to go away, in playful anger and was much put out when the heartless man carried out her expressed wish: when he left her presence in obedience to her command, she quickly realised how much she needed him and started to blame her own petulance and his lack of real affection for her: but obviously she could not call him back, her pride standing solidly in the way.

कथमपि सखि क्रीडाकोपाद्व्रजेति मयोदिते
    कठिनहृदयः शय्यां त्यक्त्वा बलाद्गत एव सः ।
इति सरभसं ध्वस्तप्रेम्णि व्यपेतघृणे स्पृहाम्
    पुनरपि हतव्रीडं चेतः करोति करोमि किम् ॥ [15]

A similar situation is reported by an unknown poet, where a girl laments how everything dear to her had been forsaken for the sake of her lover but now she has insulted him, perhaps driven him away from her presence: love and anger and pride and penitence are fighting a battle for supremacy in her heart: here is the verse, anthologised in the Subhāṣitaratnabhāṇḍāgāra.

भर्तुर्यस्य कृते गुरुर्लघुरभूद् गोष्ठी कनिष्ठीकृता
    धैर्यं कोषधनं गतं सहचरी नीतिः कृता दूरत :।.
निर्मुक्ता तृणवत्त्रपा परिचिता स्रोतस्विनी बिन्दुवत्
    स क्रोधादवधीरितो हतधिया मातर्बलीयान्विधिः ॥

[323/14]

2.68 *Solid reliance on sandy foundations, on vague, shadowy insubstantials*

Much solid reliance may be placed on non-existent things, shadowy insubstantials, misty emptiness, gossamer webs, causing a certain surprise. Such a transaction may be entered into out of hallucination or, with the eyes open, for a certain definite purpose or for pure fun.

A young couple were both doing part-time university courses. When household chores and university work become exacting, the wife feels depressed: just then she is typing her husband's papers and he is cleaning the floor. Husband replies consolingly, "Things can't be that bad as long as I have a secretary and you have a maid".

Two families which were shipwrecked landed in a lonely island where they lived for two years till they were spotted and brought back home to civilization. To the correspondent who asked one of them "How did you manage, these two years?" the reply given was: "We made a living by taking out each other's washing".

There is a poem included in the anthology the Subhāṣitaratnabhāṇḍāgāra which flippantly wreathes together four concepts that have no basis in truth.

एष वन्ध्यासुतो याति खपुष्पकृतशेखरः ।
मृगतृष्णाम्भसि स्नातः शशशृङ्गधनुर्धरः ॥ [379/5]

In another piece in the same compilation we have a number of negative statements but the verse itself ends on a positive note: the negatives actually are not really so, they are presented that way through a play on words.

स्थाणुः स्वयं मूलविहीन एव पुत्रो विशाखो रमणी त्वपर्णा ।
परोपनीतैः कुसुमैरजस्रम् फलत्यभीष्टं किमिदं विचित्रम् ॥ [379/13]

A third stanza in the same compilation also wreathes together a number of impossibles with no other purpose than pleasing the reader with a piece of whimsical nonsense.

मूकारब्धं कमपि बधिराः श्लोकमाकर्णयन्ति
श्रद्धालुस्तं विलिखति कुणिः श्लाघया वीक्षतेऽन्धः ।
अभ्यारोहत्यहह सहसा पंगुरप्याद्रिशृङ्गम्
सान्द्रालस्याः शिशुभरणतो मन्दमायन्ति वन्ध्याः ॥ [379/20]

2.69 *What looked bad initially proves good and what looked good proves bad in the sequel, evoking surprise through misappraised values*

Our dreams are not fulfilled, our hopes are belied and we feel frustrated: but time shows how it was better that our dreams were not fulfilled and our hopes belied: we do not in reality, know what is good for us and a compassionate God turns down our prayers but shapes our ends to our ultimate advantage. And our sense of wonder is evoked in proportion to the difference between our expectations and the sequel.

A striking instance of this forms the basic foundation of the plot of the Vikramōrvaśīya; this was used as illustration for another category, earlier. Ūrvaśī, wholly wrapped up in love makes a slip in the play produced by Sage Bharata for the entertainment of Indra: Ūrvaśī in the role of Lakṣmī, on emerging from the ocean was expected to say she was in love with Puruṣottama (Lord Nārāyaṇa) but, perhaps confused on account of the fact that the first letter was the same in both the cases, she blurted out on the stage that she was in love with Purūravas. Bharata, after the well-trodden practice of all Hindu sages pronounces a curse on her that she should go down from heaven to the earth to live with the king, to work off her passion for him. Ūrvaśī is most unhappy at this as the effect of the curse is to down-grade her from a denizen of heaven to a mere earthling. Now Indra takes pity on her and says she can come back to the heaven the moment the issue of their union is seen by the king: Ūrvaśī is distinctly relieved at this. These, then, are her reactions to the curse and to the reprieve, while still in heaven.

But, after she goes down to live with the king, the curse appears to her the best thing that could have happened to her. And when a child is born, the terms of the reprieve so considerately pronounced by Indra loom as a catastrophe to be circumvented. So she hands over the baby to a hermit to be brought up. When the boy is suddenly and, without a warning returned to the palace to account of what the hermit considered to be a misdemeanour, there is consternation at the sequel: Ūrvaśī says tearfully,

मामपि मन्द भागिनीं कृतविनयस्य
पुत्रस्य लाभानन्तरं स्वर्गारोहणेन
अवसितकार्यां महाराजः समर्थयते ।

[V Act]

The king too feels deeply auguished at the impending separation from Ūrvaśī and he makes up his mind to abdicate the throne so that he may live out the rest of his life in the woods. Eventually, however, Ūrvaśī finds she can stay on as Nārada brings Indra's message permitting her to continue to live with the king for some more time and there is joy everywhere. This is a vivid illustration of things appearing in a radically different light in the heaven and in the earth.

There is a story in a puranic work of a venerable sage who has to live in the earth as a pig for a limited period: he wallows in the mire with a large family of piglets and seems not to mind it at all: in fact when the time comes for his ascending to the glories of heaven he resents it and tries his hardest to escape his killer. There is a similar story about Nārada too: all this is intended to teach the lesson that man's tragedy lies in the fact that he loves, not hates the tethers that bind him to a dismal worldly life. However, from the viewpoint of aesthetic experience it is a strange thing—but true nevertheless—that he hates the banishment to an earthly life while in heaven but hates its termination while living that life here.

2.70 *Where misunderstanding is mutual and total*

Misunderstandings in life are often one-sided: they are amusing and they may cause a little surprise even: on occasions they may cause serious friction and even a permanent break of relations. For an amusing, one-sided misunderstanding we can cite an example: an old man greets a youth with, "Rāmu, how you have changed! you are so much taller now and so much fairer!" The youth replies, "I am not Rāmu. I am Kiṭṭu"! on which the old man says, "O you have gone and changed your name, too!"

But then, there are occasions when misunderstanding is not confined to one party but is mutual, total and decisive: other emotions may follow but surprise must surely be the first sensation one feels when confronted by such a situation.

Two persons both hard of hearing met in the street and the following conversation ensued:

"Are you going to the theatre"?

"No, I am going to the theatre".

"O, I thought you were going to the theatre".

My grandfather came home from his daily walk rather agitated. "I met Śrīnivāsan" he told me, "and I said, 'How have you been, Śrīnivāsan?' And Śrīnivāsan replied, 'Fair to middling, thank you. How have you been, Raghavan?' 'Rāghavan!' I said, 'That is not my name!' 'Nor is my name Śrīnivāsan' said the other fellow. Then we looked each other over, and true! It was neither of us!"

There is a stanza by an unknown poet describing a similar situation happening lower down in the evolutionary scale. A bee, eager to garner honey mistakes the red beak of a parrot to be the blossom of the palasa tree and hovers over it: the parrot mistakes the bee to be the glossy black fruit of the *jāmun* tree and grabs it with the beak.

पलाशमुकुल भ्रान्त्या शुकतुण्डे पतत्यलिः ।
सोऽपि जम्बूफल भ्रान्त्या तमलिं धर्तुमिच्छति ॥

[Kuvalayānanda, N.S. edition, page 24]

2.71 *A thing paraded as something much bigger or better, causing surprise by the clever presentation*

There was a lot of discontent in the grease pit of a major repair shop and thousands of manhours continued to be lost despite better perks being offered till one day a person in the personnel department came up with an inexpensive idea which was implemented: all trouble vanished overnight and total peace began to reign in the Lubricarium—for that was the new name given to the greasepit by the ideasman.

There is a poem by an unknown poet where there are two such exercises—at parading a lesser as a greater thing. With his tongue in the cheek he advises a crow to shift to a mango tree and stop making any noise: for, he then will be taken for a cuckoo which, too, is dark and prefers a mango branch for his habitat. As confirmation of his theory that the place where one is placed is all important, he points to the fact that the spot of dirt on the forehead of the king of Nepāl (whose court-poet he must have been) will be universally mistaken to be kasturi, the expensive perfume worn by aristocrats. The verse has been smoothly written and races off the tongue and the cynicism is quite deliberate.

कर्णारुन्तुदमन्तरेण रणितं गाहस्व काक स्वयम्
माकन्दं मकरन्दशालिनमिह त्वां मन्महे कोकिलम् ।
धन्यानि स्थलवैभवेन कतिचिद्वस्तूनि कस्तूरिकाम्
नेपालक्षितिपालभालपतिते पङ्के न शङ्केत कः ॥

[Kuvalayānanda, N.S. edition, page 134]

2.72 *Pride expressed at things not regarded as worthy of it*

While justifiable pride is quite reasonable and even a little excessive pride at small achievements may be allowed to pass as a common human foible, pride expressed at deficiencies, at positively evil tendencies will evoke surprise. Jimmy Durante, the famous American comedian, while walking along a New York street in 1930 met a bum who asked for a dime. Jimmy said, "I suppose you were well off before and, on account of this Depression became a bum?" The bum reared up in pride and said, "No, sir! I was a bum in the boom".

Rowdies everywhere usually are proud of the fact that the

residents of their area go in fear of them. But, if the claim strikes one as extraordinary on account of the fact that credit is claimed for excessive wickedness, it can cause surprise: this is on account of our experience testifying to the effect that even bad characters are secretly ashamed to their wickedness and would like to be taken as good citizens by society. As the braggart's claims to excessive sinfulness go against normal experience, they do evoke a certain surprise.

Talking with mournful pride, Rāvaṇa tells Mārīca how Khara and his henchmen on his orders went about in peace, striking terror into the hearts of ascetics who wanted to follow dharma. Instead of being allowed to pursue this rightful path of terrorising the hermits, a kill-joy called Rāma comes along and slaughters all of them—and stark tragedy! The Daṇḍaka forests have been rendered fearless! This interesting passage occurs in the 36th sarga of Āraṇya Kāṇḍa of Vālmīki's Rāmāyaṇa and has been quoted earlier.

He then secures the half-hearted assent of Maricha to help him in his nefarious scheme and he goes to the hermitage disguised as a suppliant when Sītā is alone. He tries to tempt Sītā to accept his advances and is spurned by her. He forsakes all finesse and threatens her with serious consequences if she does not accept him: this is accompanied by much bragging of what extremes of evil he can encompass: this is contained in verses 2 to 19 in the 48th sarga of Āraṇya Kāṇḍa.

There is considerable arrant bragging in the Naishadha charita of Śrīharṣa done by Kali, the personification of all evil, in the XVII canto when he is provoked by the gods with the assertion that Kali cannot harm Nala on account of his unassailable virtues, Kali says in anger and pride:

सा वव्रे यं तमुत्सृज्य मह्यमीर्ष्याजुषः स्थ किं ।
कृतागः सद्मनस्तस्माच्छद्मनाद्याच्छिनद्मि ताम् ।।

[XVII-130]

This drives Indra to close his ears in horror and exclaim, "You seem to have a mind (for all) to wonder at!" Such a sadism as Kali gave expression to must cause pained wonder to normal people, seeing that Nala was blameless and Kali had absolutely no reason to hate him.

Śakāra is yet another character so thoroughly rotted at the core that he can derive prideful pleasure at the contemplation of actual harm done or the potential for it. Throughout the play, the Mṛcchakaṭika, he goes about his boastful way, mouthing with pleasure the harm he will cause to the noblest of his contemporaries, Cārudatta and Vasantasena. After the incident in the pleasure garden when he is convinced that he has murdered Vasantasena, he feels no pity nor any contrition but observes boastfully how proud his family will be at the horrible deed perpetrated by a scion of their line.

सेवावञ्चितो भ्राता मम पिता मातेव सा द्रौपदी
योऽसौ पश्यति नेदृशं व्यवसितं पुत्रस्य शूरत्वम् ॥ [VII/37]

We have not quoted yet from Ananta Bhaṭṭa's Bhāratacampū which enjoys a certain degree of popularity among speakers on religious topics, particularly in South India. He is a difficult writer and verbal gymnastics is his forte: but he comes up with a new and fresh concept now and then and has some gifts of fluent poesy. After the splendid *rājasūya* sacrifice performed by Yudhiṣṭhira, Duryōdhana begins to work up the greenest envy at the glory garnered by his cousin and is despondent when Śakuni points out that he cannot defeat the Pāṇḍavas in battle. But the resourceful Śakuni, wishing to revive his confidence in himself, claims that he can defeat them in a game of dice, deprive them of their kingdom and their pelf and drive them to their death or banish them to distant lands. Untroubled by any scruples, this arch-plotter carries out his boast to the letter and thus sows the seeds of the armageddon later which was to engulf all of the known world. Śakuni's boast is partly in prose and partly in verse.

तथाप्यहं तु तव च तेषां परस्परं विभवे
परिपणनपदाधिरोहिणी क्षणाद क्षममाणेन
जगत्सामान्यताम क्षसंप्रदायेन तं
पराजयघण्टापथे संचारयिष्यामि ।
वित्ते हृते दरिद्रास्ते विसृष्टा बन्धुभिः स्वयम् ।
विनाशं वा शुचा यायुः विदेशं वाथ लज्जया ॥ [IV/24]

2.73 *Excess is in such abundance, it can over-fulfil want, creating an excess wherever it operates*

Occasionally we come across instances where a thing is in such excess that it overfulfills points of want so that they too have an excess of it and can fulfill other points of want. Electricity has a magnetic effect which an ordinary piece of iron does not have: but if electricity is passed into a piece of iron, that too acquires magnetism and can magnetise other pieces of iron.

In bardic poetry potentates are praised, using this technique. Vedānta Dēśika praises the munificence of King Yadu in the following manner, in his epic poem the Yādavābhyudaya.

अपुनःप्रार्थनीयस्य प्रार्थिताधिकदायिनः ।
अर्थिनः प्रथमे तस्य चरमान् पर्यपूरयन् ॥ [I/23]

Śrīharṣa lauds the philanthropic propensities of his hero Nala in a similar vein, in his Naiṣadhacarita.

तथा पथि त्यागमयं वितीर्णवान् यथाऽतिभाराधिगमेन मागधैः ।
तृणीकृतं रत्ननिकायमुच्चकैः चिकाय लोकश्चिरमुच्छमुत्सकः ॥ [XV/2]

The impoverished suppliants were showered with so much wealth in both the cases that they were roused to munificence, themselves and were in a position to fulfil others down the line.

CHAPTER 3

THE LITERARY BENEFITS ACCRUING FROM WONDER

While some lesser writers may portray sensations just for a whim or only to show off their powers, it can be assumed for our purposes that worthwhile poets never bring in anything unless it has a certain literary utility. Now we have seen how, even though aestheticians have neglected this sense of wonder, poets have made rich use of it, invoking it again and again in their works. Admittedly it can serve only as an ancillary and not a main sentiment: but having conceded this much, the present writer wants to state emphatically that all the major poets have made intense use of this device and the patient student will come across numerous passages evocative of wonder in the vast panorama of Sanskrit literature. It is certainly more prolifically used than most other ancillary sentiments—and much more than is suspected by students of aesthetics. Hence it becomes necessary for us to enquire into the literary gains secured by the poet through this device and estimate their importance, particularly in view of the total neglect it has suffered at the hands of writers on aesthetics.

3.1 *The essence of all creative art is a freshness, a strangeness which is the mother of surprise*

Most writers on aesthetics agree that the essence of all creative art is a newness, a strangeness, a uniqueness: there should be something in art that has not been noticed and described before. The creative artist, the creative writer may present the same lotus or the cuckoo or the rainbow: but he sees it differently from his own unique viewpoint and he presents it with a freshness which makes it seem unique. Francis Bacon says in his essay "Of Beauty": "There is a no excellent beauty that hath not some strangeness in the proportion". Sanskrit writers, too, have emphasized this: for instance the quality of pratibha the most essential ingredient in the make up of a poet's personality is defined in the line

प्रज्ञा नवनवोन्मेषशालिनी प्रतिभा मता ।

[attributed to Abhinavagupta]

(pratibhā is an aspect of the intellect which projects new and fresh concepts on the mental screen). In support of the theory of the primacy of freshness in creative art, Rājaśekhara quotes these two stanzas in his Kāvyamīmāmsā:—

शब्दार्थोक्तिषु यः पश्येत् इह किंचन नूतनम् ।
उल्लिखेत् किंचन प्राच्यं मन्यतां स महाकविः ॥
अभियोगे समानेऽपि विचित्रो यदयं क्रमः ।
तेन विघ्नः प्रसादोऽत्र नृणां हेतुरमानुषः ॥

[IV chapter]

And Māgha, one of the greatest creative poets in Sanskrit, the author of the epic poem the Śiśupālavadha makes a general remark on the primacy of novelty when describing the Raivata mountain in the IV sarga,

क्षणे क्षणे यन्नवतामुपैति
तदेव रूपं रमणीयतायाः ॥ [17]

adding that this caused surprise in Kṛṣṇa, though he had seen the mountain many times.

And, by definition, this novelty, newness is the basic quality behind the sensation of surprise. This is confirmed by experience and testified to by recent discoveries in neuropsychology: the latter will be taken up for discussion in the next chapter. If novelty is an essential element of all creative art inclusive of literature and it is the quality that provokes surprise, the organic bond between creative art and the sensation of surprise gets clearly established. Wonder may not be the dominant sentiment in any work as seen by a reader: but it has a primary role to play in the process of its creation and this role is fundamental and inescapable: simply and basically, there can be no literature, indeed, there can be no creative art without wonder being evoked, sometime, somewhere.

We saw in the first Chapter that of all the writers on aesthetics in Sanskrit, only Jagannātha and Nārāyaṇa had an idea of the pivotal role played by wonder in the field of literature. While we may not agree with Nārāyaṇa that wonder is the only sentiment there is, he is very much right when he says that an element of wonder enters all aesthetic experience. So too is Jagannātha when he says that wonder is an essential ingredient of *kāvya*. These two independent thinkers stood out of the common herd in this matter and it is unfortunate that the bold lead given by them was wholly ignored by the aestheticians who followed them in time.

3.2 *Wonder opens up the mind of the reader*

The basic difficulty of any creative writer is that though he packs his work with a lot of good things, they are not absorbed fully by the dilettante. It is as if the orifice of the heart through which sensations have to go is too small to permit the flood to enter. Now the strange, new elements in a work seem to be able to open the orifice of the heart wider. The external manifestations of their impact are wide-open eyes and even an open mouth leading us to the feeling that the whole personality is opening up invitingly to welcome in the flood of good things that the poet has put into his work.

That wonder has this orifice-widening effect seems to have been anticipated by our ancients who said

विस्मयः चित्तविस्तारयिता ।

Surprise expands the mind: the stimuli coming in fall on a wider area and are thus appreciated more fully. The analogy adopted here is a little different, of course from that of the heart orifice but the significance is identical—that wonder directly enables the dilettante to savour a work more fully.

3.3 *Wonder helps to secure attention*

An average citizen of today has a hundred things clamouring for his attention: details of family life, worries in the office, civic and national affairs fill his mind: the advertiser with all the art and artifice at his command sets up a compelling clangour which no one can ignore. If literature is to be read at all and appreciated, it should have something which can shut out these powerful rival claimants and help the reader to focus his attention on itself. Elements of wonder with their ability to shock have been found to possess the power to attract and secure reader attention. Newspapers and other mass media of today exploit this capacity of surprise by offering sensational write-ups with shocking head-lines to secure the attention of the reader.

Melvin Konner, the famous anthropologist calls wonder "rapt attention, a focussing for the purpose of elevation". As referred to earlier, even the advertiser, the gossip columnist and the tabloid paper writer make use of wonder to draw people's attention to what they have to say. "Don't read this !" begins an advertisement: naturally everybody will read what follows, which is this: "if you do not care for quality. But if, as we suspect, you stress and value quality, we would recommend you get...... the quality colour T.V. for quality-conscious people". Now what these men offer—material goods which we need or think we need, juicy gossip, slanderous comment—are intrinsically far more interesting to the common man than what the poet plans to give. Works of creative art possess deep and lasting values but often lack surface glamour. Anyone in doubt about the truth of this can study the comparative statistics of sales and readership of classical poetry on the one hand and of pornography and 'who-dun-its' on the other.

But the greatest creative work is of no use at all if it is not read: and if it is to have readership it had better have some elements of (wholesome) surprise. If the subdued notes of great literature are not to be ignored in the pandemonium of the market-place, it had better acquire some additional decibels of wonder.

It is true that this concept has not been recognised and labelled by aestheticians but its value has been clearly grasped by the poets from Bhāsa downwards. Evidence of this lies in the fact that most plays and quite a few epic poems start off with a wonder-ogenic episode. Some of Bhāsa's plays begin with a noise behind the curtain, evoking surprise in the stage-manager who asks

अये मयि विज्ञापनव्यग्रे शब्द इव श्रूयते ।

and he leaves the stage after supplying the answer to his question, being sure that the attention of the spectators has, for the moment, been secured.

Śaktibhadra begins his Āścaryacūḍāmaṇi in a similar manner with a noise prodding the stage manner to exclaim,

अये किं नु खलु मयि विज्ञापनव्यग्रे शब्द इव श्रूयते ।

[Sthāpana]

The answer is provided by the stage manager himself—it is the noise produced by Lakṣmaṇa with the string of his bow to drive off predators from Rama's cottage in the jungle.

In Mudrārākṣasa and Vēnīsamhāra surprise and a certain amount of suspense and tension are created by the dramatic entry of powerful characters in a fit of rage, Cāṇakya and Bhīma respectively, ending the prologue abruptly and sending the stage manager and his wife fleeing the stage in panic. All plays start from the heart of the story, applying the principle of '*in medias res*': but these plays plunge the spectator into the heart of an emotional maelstrom, harnessing forcibly their attention.

Plays are to be seen within the space of a few hours and hence the sustained attention of the spectators is essential for their success. Epic poems are not expected to be read in a single sitting; in fact, they are read over a long period, over a year or more; mostly a canto is read and the work set aside. Hence there is less need for the insertion of passages evoking wonder in them and in point of fact there are not many such passages in the major epic poems. But, still, great poets have given a little of a surprise start to their epic poems. The Śiśupālavadha begins with the dramatic descent of Nārada from heavens in a splash of effulgence causing people to exclaim in surprise "What is this phenomenon?"

गतं तिरश्चीनमनूरुसारथेः प्रसिद्धमूर्ध्वज्वलनं हविर्भुजः ।
पतत्यधोधाम विसारि सर्वतः किमेतदित्याकुलमीक्षितं जनैः ॥ [I/2]

The reader himself may be disposed to ask with the people in surprise "What is all this?" and feel tempted to read on.

Bhāravi begins his epic poem the *Kirātārjuniya* with a forester recounting to Yudhiṣṭhira the many benevolent acts of Duryōdhana done to win his subjects over to his side; this can be guaranteed to evoke surprise in the Indian readers of the classical age who all would know how wicked Duryōdhana could be.

Kālidāsa himself did not see the need for a surprise start for his epic poems and most of the others too followed suit, starting their works with a description of their hero or his lineage in a large number of verses. As stated earlier, plays demanded the sustained attention of their votaries as they have to be enjoyed in a single sitting; moreover the calibre of the votaries of a staged play must be considerably lower than that of the readers of an epic poem who must be determined bibliophiles guaranteed to read on to the bitter end. This fact that theatre-goers may not all be scholars was recognised by the writers of works on dramaturgy who put in a prohibition against the use of involved diction in plays which may go above their heads.

Overall, it will be quite a justifiable claim to say that the ancient Hindus were aware of the part played by surprise in securing reader attention. It is true there is no direct rule recommending the use of surprise to secure this end; it is, however, there to be inferred, as we have done. But there is a very clear rule laying down the primacy of the quality of readability in any work. Kṣēmēndra the polymath of Kashmir says

तत्राप्यनियमो दृष्टः प्रबन्धे महतामपि ।
तस्मादव्यभिचारेण श्रव्यतैव गरीयसी ॥ [II/5]

Though this observation specifically pertains to the construction of verses in a metre, it seems to lend itself to a much wider application; readability is everything in a literary work. The old Hindu aesthetician insisted on this, thus anticipating the eleventh commandment of the modern Moses; "Thou shalt not be dull !" addressed to writers.

3.4 *Wonder makes for greater credibility, lubricating the transfer of experience*

Wonder belongs to the world of children; when we wonder at anything, our years drop away, we become even like children, willing, eager to believe what is presented; the crust of cynicism which age has built around us breaks allowing stimuli to play on our exposed personality and impregnate it with their contents freely, without reserve. Rachel Carson, in many ways the most distinguished and the most committed among those who have thought about this, emphatically states that we continue to be children as long as we wonder and we continue to learn; that we become old when we cease to wonder and not when we reach 60 or 70; that we can never really grow old as we remain young as long as we continue to grow: that cynicism and lack of interest in what goes on around us are the surest signs of senile decay.

If wonder makes us like children in our mentality and thus promotes credulity in us, then, under the influence of this anaesthetic we find our tendency to disbelief suspended for the moment, permitting the sentiment to get transferred to us with ease. The essential role of poetry (as of all creative literature and indeed, of all art) being the transfer of experience from the poet to the reader, if wonder can lubricate this process and render the transfer smoother, it can be hailed as a potent device in the hands of the poet, promoting a heightened enjoyment of his product. We may employ a homely metaphor to explain this. A salesman desires to gain entrance into a house so that he may demonstrate the virtues of a vacuum cleaner but finds it difficult to persuade the housewife to open the door. Now a surprise guest rings the bell and is admitted with tumultuous welcome: through the now-open door the salesman smilingly slips in to start his demonstration. The salesman is the sentiment in the poem finding entry into the heart of the reader difficult: the surprise guest is the passage evoking surprise and it always gets a tumultuous welcome: now through the open door the sentiment can enter without being challenged with the hostess still under the ether of the impact of the surprise guest.

We can, however, have too much of a good thing: while a certain amount of surprise will be accepted and disbelief suspended, in higher octaves it may have just the opposite effect; too great a shock will put up the shutters of the heart securely against all external stimuli. The scientific base of this will be discussed in the next chapter but the conclusion is clear that if wonder is to promote literary delight, it should operate between rather narrow limits, too little being ineffective and too much of it, counterproductive.

Apart from the general resistance put up by all readers to the transfer of sentiment, there is naturally a certain unwillingness on their part to swallow unusual developments like a change of heart in a character or a peculiar act not in character—which the poet finds it necessary to introduce in his work. Creative literature has to be reasonable and convincing as otherwise the reader is unlikely to feel that sense of identification which is universally accepted as a condition for literary enjoyment. It was Mark Twain who said, "Truth is stranger than fiction but it is because fiction is obliged to stick to possibilities, truth isn't."

If fiction (and all of creative literature) does not stick to possibilities, reader-acceptance and reader-identification become more difficult.

But one way poets accomplish this is to spring a surprise on the reader and under cover of the smoke-screen afforded by it, they succeed in smuggling the recalcitrant material into the reader's personality. For with his critical faculties temporarily suspended, the reader is found to accept things which, when he comes out of the ether he may well reject.

In the Uttararāmacarita, the central, axial events are the banishment of Sītā by Rāma and the eventual reunion between them. Now in order to carry the spectators with him, the playwright has to make both these appear reasonable. Having, earlier, built up a case for her banishment, he must have found it difficult to buttress the case for Rāma accepting her back in the palace: indeed, the greater his success in the former endeavour, the greater is his difficulty in bringing off the latter. Every factor he has marshalled in favour of her banishment now acts against the acceptance of the decision to take her back.

Hence, in order to break the resistance of the spectators and render them credulous enough to welcome the reunion of the lovers, Bhavabhūti presents a playlet in his play where the principal characters witness the production of Vālmīki; there miracles aplenty happen and Mother Earth and River Gaṅgā appear on the stage and divine missiles play a role. Particularly evocative of surprise is the scene in the playlet where Sītā is brought by Gaṅgā and Earth from deep down the river up to where Arundhatī is seated, causing a great deal of churning of the waters and the sky is filled with gods and sages. From behind the scenes, is heard a proclamation; "All ye living things, behold this sacred miracle ordained by Vālmīki !" Lakṣmaṇa frequently exclaims "A wonder! A wonder!" at all this, and describes the scene in a verse where he uses the word 'āścaryam'.

मन्थादिव क्षुभ्यति गाङ्गमम्भो व्याप्तं च देवर्षिभिरन्तरिक्षम् ।
आश्चर्यमार्या सह देवताभ्याम् गङ्गामहीभ्यां सलिलादुपैति ॥

[VII/17]

The noise and the succession of effulgent beings and the crowds in the sky and the marvels presented (despite the technological backwardness of the Hindu stage of that day) must have so undermined the critical faculties of the spectators that they would find themselves accepting the idea of Sītā's return to Ayōdhyā. Clearly the adroit playwright conceived of all these noisy scenes of marvel, partly as good theatre in themselves but more pointedly to help him to sell to the spectators the idea of Rāma accepting Sītā back despite the calumny in circulation among his people.

3.5 *Banal everyday objects and sequences acquire a new capacity to interest through surprise*

Poets have to deal with the same objects and living things and sequences which are familiar, often too familiar to us: they cannot conjure up a wholly different world of objects and animals on which to compose, as that would not interest us, being wholly unfamiliar. But the poet manages the situation so adroitly, these banal, everyday things which appear dull and prosaic to us are metamorphosed into things of beauty and of absorbing interest by the alchemy of the poet. This miraculous feat of poets has been observed and recorded by Nīlakaṇṭha Dīkṣita in his Śivalīlārṇava.

यानेव शब्दान् वयमालपामः
यानेव चार्थान् वयमुल्लिखामः ।
तैरेव विन्यासविशेषभावैः
संमोहयन्ते कवयो जगन्ति ॥

How does the poet do it? Shelley provides the answer: poets, he says, remove the film of familiarity from the things around us, with the result that we begin to look upon them with new eyes of wonder. If familiarity breeds contempt, novelty inspires interest via surprise. As the poet cannot create an entirely new world of birds, animals and flowers and he has perforce to deal with the world that is as much available to us as it is to him, the only way open to him is to peel off the film of banality from it, on which it begins to look novel, surprising and therefore interesting to us: from these everyday things at which we do not cast a second glance, which, in fact, we take for granted, the poet can create 'nurslings of immortality' to quote from Shelley, again.

No sensitive reader who has studied the poems of Wordsworth will feel the same way about things in nature; a daffodil or a rainbow will appear coated with glamour to him; even such drab, unpoetical things like field mice may shed their shroud of drabness to the student of Robert Burns. Tamil poets of the Sangam era composed love poems featuring prominently in them such ungainly birds as the crow, the chicken on the dust heap and even the owl. They did not make the owl handsome nor did their crow sing dulcet notes: they pictured them as they are, with all their defects of personality intact, making adroit use of their characteristic qualities in developing the theme of love. But to the one who has savoured these poems, these birds will now appear interesting, full of appeal; the poets have merely removed their drabcoat of everyday triviality, they have not idolised them at all.

Sanskrit poets, too, have made familiar birds and animals vested with a new interest through their alchemy; the deer and the pig and the buffalo and the bee appear imbued with new interest to the reader of Kālidāsa's works. The bee especially, appearing in the first Act of Śākuntala and behaving in a perfectly normal manner is portrayed as a lecherous lothario through the eyes of Duṣyanta and the image lingers in the reader's mind, colouring the way he looks at this guileless workaholic of the insect world, ever after.

Apart from animals and inanimate things, a number of everyday sequences with which we are tiresomely familiar begin to acquire a sheen of freshness and interest when they are presented by great poets. Girls get married and leave for their husbands' homes and this sequence of events is taken as routine in an Indian home and is regarded as commonplace by the on-looker. But after one reads the IV Act of Kālidāsa's Śākuntala, the whole institution takes on a very different aspect, the sequence of events being surcharged with genuine emotion and the chief characters in this homely drama find a conflict going on in their minds, relief and pleasure at the wedding having been gone through fighting for pride of place with sorrow at the parting and, for the girl, fear of the unknown, anxiety at what kind of home she is going to live in for the rest of her life. Many genuine lovers of Sanskrit who had studied the great play have reported the same experience: for when they attend weddings now, they find themselves viewing these events in an entirely new light, with sympathy and interest.

When the seven sages go to Himavān and ask for the hand

of his daughter Umā on behalf of Lord Śiva, the king of the mountains did not rush to reply but looked at his wife Mēnā, obviously seeking inspiratoin from her; and Kālidāsa puts this in the correct perspective that universally, all fathers of girls are very much dependent on the judgment of their wives in the matter of fixing a match for their daughters.

शैलः संपूर्णकामोऽपि मेनामुखमुदैक्षत ।
प्रायेण गृहिणीनेत्राः कन्यार्थेषु कुटुम्बिनः ॥

[Kumārasambhava VI/85]

After reading this verse, we look upon this common trait of men with a new interest and a new significance: this leads us on to view the mother of the girl as much the more important parent in the matter of fixing a suitable match for her and celebrating the wedding, while earlier we perhaps failed to assess her importance adequately. We are not interested in what we take for granted; this is a basic law in human attitudes which when applied to aesthetics yields rich dividends of literary pleasure.

In welcoming guests attending a party, there will always be a difference in the way the host receives men of distinction and the rest: this is in accord with human nature and is not to be dismissed as snobbery. Kālidāsa invests this common trait of man with the gloss of classicity when he shows Lord Śiva Himself displaying a clear difference in the way He welcomes Lord Nārāyaṇa, Brahmā and the run of the minor gods to His wedding reception.

कम्पेन मूर्ध्नः शतपत्रयोनिं वाचा हरिं वृत्रहणं स्मितेन ।
आलोकमात्रेण सुरानशेषान् संभावयामास यथाप्रधानम् ॥ [VII/46]

Most thieves, in real life are found to be seriously deficient mentally and morally; they are dull and uninteresting baring a few exceptions. Śarvilaka's antics in Mṛcchakaṭika are vested with an unusual interest mainly on account of the erudition of the marauder, which prods him to explain the why and wherefore of his actions; his tone is that of a senior professor of technology taking a class in a bespoke university. Similarly the mental make-up of a murderer, a cheat, a gambler, a courtesan appears quite an interesting study after one sees this great social play.

The *ṛṣi* of the Ṛg Vēda, Kavaṣa Ailūṣa, through his sūkta (34) in the X Mandala has succeeded in investing the image of gambler with a new interest through the medium of mild surprise laced with humour and sympathetic understanding. Adroit poets present prosaic objects painted over with a veneer of surprise which demand our interest and attention. As any long poem has to deal with many dull and prosaic things, consider what damage would be done to its readability if this device of surprise is not available to the poet.

3.6 *Surprise being dynamic activates aesthetic enjoyment*

Experimental psychology reveals that emotions vary over a great range in their ability to activate the personality, the level of activation being measured by the range of facial expressions. The range of activation studied varies from sleep representing the lowest point upwards to the high of tension. It is seen from the graph drawn on the basis of the results that surprise, fear and suffering produce the maximum activation; at the next lower level lie love, mirth and happiness while the minimum activation was recorded in the case of contempt and disgust.

So surprise operates at the top of the pyramid and is one of the chief activators of the personality. Now our experience indicates that surprise seldom reigns alone but operates along with or closely followed by other emotions like joy, anger or sorrow. So one of the important roles played by surprise is to activate and render dynamic the perceptions of the dilettante: as a result, he registers the associated emotion of joy, anger or sorrow more sharply and reacts more vigorously to it; the result often is that he gets greater aesthetic enjoyment than otherwise. It is, as it were, a case of emotions vibrating at different wavelengths; wonder vibrates more intensely than most; and it makes the associated emotion too vibrate in tune with itself; this intensified vibration promotes heightened aesthetic impact.

Several examples can be cited in illustration. One great merit of the playwright Bhāsa is his ability to portray characters with a few deft touches, even characters who do not appear on the stage; the best example is Rumaṇvān minister in the court of Udayana in the Svapnavāsavadatta. Udayana is made to believe that Vāsavadatta, his queen had perished in a fire, as part of a grand strategy to restore the throne to him; but knowing his matchless love for her, the wise chief minister Yaugandharāyaṇa realises that all will be lost if the king dies of anguish at the loss of his queen; so he stations Rumaṇvān by the king's side charging him to look after him night and day.

When, as part of the grand plan, Yaugandharāyaṇa is about to hand over Vāsavadatta to princess Padmāvatī to be looked after by her, a stranger comes to that part of the woods and describes in detail the king's anguish and Rumaṇvān's devoted service to him. One verse, particularly is worth quoting as it brings out the sadness of the situation in the uncontrived manner best seen in Bhāsa:

अनाहारे तुल्यः प्रततरुदितक्षामवदनः
शरीरे संस्कारं नृपतिसमदुःखं परिवहन् ।
दिवा वा रात्रौ वा परिचरति यत्नैर्नरपतिम्
नृपः प्राणान्सद्यः त्यजति यदि तस्याप्युपरमः ॥ [I/14]

The chief minister is filled with admiration for the colleague who valiantly and loyally is carrying out an extremely difficult commission; his feelings are expressed as an ejaculation of surprise tinged with awe:

अहो महद्भारमुद्वहति रुमण्वान् ! [Act I]

and the words he adds after this come to carry much greater impact on account of this short passage. We must remember that Rumaṇvān's charge is less glamorous and more onerous than that of most others and the distinction with which he performs his allotted duties compels the admiration of the spectators.

Much later, at the end of the play (without Rumaṇvān appearing on the stage at any time) there is another passage where the personality of this devoted minister gets vividly portrayed through the medium of surprise. The significant role played by Rumaṇvān is pointed out to the grateful king by the chief minister. The king realises how he owes his life to Rumaṇvān who had to act convinced that Vāsavadatta is no more; the king's mental state as well as the personality of the invisible Rumaṇvān are vividly revealed through a surprised outburst of the king which, apparently couched as a condemnation turns out to be a warm tribute.

अहो शठः खलु रुमण्वान् ! [Act VI]

Thus, in both the passages, the sentiment of wonder has been harnessed to intensify the deep appreciation of the chief minister and the king: and the character portrait of Rumaṇvān has been rendered all the more vivid, making the spectators forget that they have never seen this character on the stage.

Love is not something that is slowly developed, it is not an edifice that is built brick by brick. It comes, all together, in a rush, overwhelming the party with a flush of wonder nicely blended with delight and even a little of awe: it is more like a mountain suddenly thrust out by the heaving earth during geological cataclysm. This is the way it overtook Duṣyanta who exclaims in a verse that has justly received the highest plaudits for its peotic quality.

> **अनाघ्रातं पुष्पं किसलयमलूनं कररुहैः**
> **अनाविद्धं रत्नं मधु नवमनास्वादितरसम् ।**
> **अखण्डं पुण्यानां फलमिव च तद्रूपमनघम्**
> **न जाने भोक्तारं कमिह समुपस्थास्यति विधिः ॥** [II/10]

The present writer feels that the very structure of the *śikharinī* metre (in which this celebrated verse has been composed), starting with a short syllable and suddenly soaring to a flight of five long syllables imitates the physical spasm of a surprised person and is therefore most conducive to the promoting of the sense of wonder. Stanzas by Bhavabhūti in this metre nicely blend surprise and sorrow augmenting the latter and leading Kṣēmēndra to pay the tribute

> **भवभूतेः शिखरिणी . . .**

Śaṅkarācārya and other minstrel-saints too have realised the potential of this metre in promoting devotion reinforced by an awe and a surprise at God's limitless qualities.

Talking of Bhavabhūti, we should not fail to take note of the manner in which he makes his hero Mādhava describe the effects of an overpowering love for Mālatī on him. Mādhava's verse (which too has become classic along with Duṣyanta's) records the complex impact of love consisting partly of pleasure and partly of pain served up in a sauce of wonder: this is the verse, put in the melodious metre, *mālinī*:

अविरलमिव दाम्ना पौण्डरीकेण नद्धः
स्नपित इव च दुग्धस्रोतसा निर्भरेण ।
कवलित इव कृत्स्नश्चक्षुषा स्फारितेन
प्रसभममृतमेघेनेव सान्द्रेण सिक्तः ॥ [III/16]

There are several passages in the epic poem Naiṣadha where surprise lends an edge to the passion of love. One of them is quoted here, one reason for its being preferred over the others being that unlike the two verses quoted earlier, this is uttered by the lady in love.

वाग्जन्मवैफल्यमसह्यशल्यं गुणाधिके वस्तुनि मौनिता चेत् ।
खलत्वमल्पीयसि जल्पितेऽपि तदस्तु वन्दिभ्रमभूमितैव ॥

[VIII/32]

Bhāsa is an adept at evoking *karuṇa rasa* by means of simple stanzas with a pronounced tendency to understatement: but despite this, he succeeds in adding a dollop of surprise which sets an edge on the anguished utterance: a good example will be the lament of the blind king Dhṛtarāṣṭra who finds he has lost all his hundred sons together.

रिपुसमरविमर्दं मानवीर्यप्रदीप्तम्
सुतशतमतिधीरं वीरमुत्पाद्य मानम् ।
धरणितलविकीर्णं किं स योग्यो न भोक्तुम्
सकृदपि धृतराष्ट्रः पुत्रदत्तं निवापम् ॥

[Ūrubhaṅga 39]

The rhetorical question in the second half of the verse has an undercoating of surprise—that as the father of a hundred sons, he is destined not to enjoy the ablutions offered by even one of them.

The sorrow of the mother at such a wholesale bereavement is expressed through Balarāma, a partisan of the Kauravas who observes the bandage Gāndhārī wears over her eyes getting damp with the tears she is shedding.

या पुत्रपौत्रवदनेष्वकुतूहलाक्षी
दुर्योधनास्तमितशोकनिपीतधैर्या ।
अस्रैरजस्रमधुना पतिधर्मचिह्नं
आर्द्रीकृतं नयनबन्धमिदं दधाति ॥

[Ūrubhaṅga 40]

The bandage has a special significance: for Gāndhārī had decided to blindfold herself early in her married life in order to please her envious husband who was born blind; this meant she could not look upon the faces of her children, a sacrifice which led people to conclude that she was not very fond of them. Today's copious tears belied this: and Balarāma's surprised observation of this is somehow most tender and moving.

For *Karuṇa rasa*, Sanskrit tradition points to Bhavabhūti whose magnum opus contains many good instances (though some are overdone). Stanzas where an element of surprise underscores the *karuṇa* are I/42, I/44, II/10, III/27 and VII/7, if we wish to make a brief selection.

From the melancholy, let us pass on to the other sentiments: the sentiment of humour getting reinforced by surprise is best exemplified by the verse uttered by Lakṣmaṇa who observes with amusement blended with a little surprise (natural to a member of the warrior clan, especially to one as impetuous as he) the vain efforts of the women of the penance-grove to drive away the deer which behave exactly as spoilt brats: the verse occurring in the Anargharāghava has been quoted earlier.

To the *vira* and the *raudra rasa*, the sentiment of wonder can add considerable clout as both these rasas are expansive and most later day poets are very willing to overportray them. The best examples are found in the Vēnīsamhāra of Bhaṭṭanārāyaṇa, e.g. III/22, III/25, and III/32. (The famous verse uttered by Bhīma spelling out his terrible vow is also very illustrative (I/21).

The sentiment of wonder reinforcing that of fear can best be exemplified by quoting from Bhavabhūti. The description of mountain caverns in the Daṇḍaka forest (II/16) in the *Uttara-rāmacarita*, that in the *Mahāviracarita* from Rāvaṇa describing his own frightening worship of Lord Śiva (VI/14) and those in the *Mālatimādhava* describing the happenings in the cremation grounds will serve as examples. It may be added that fear and wonder are a natural combination and atavistically mankind reacts spontaneously and in a big way to phenomena evoking surprise and a panicky fear from the experience of his cavemen days.

There are quite a few instances of surprise exacerbating disgust (bībhatsa) in Sanskrit. The reaction of Yaugandha-rāyaṇa disguised as an ascetic to the rude, inconsiderate methods of the servants of the princess is one of surprised disgust as he was clearly not prepared for the intrusion of arrogant royalty into the peace of the penance-grove. The verse consists of the simplest words in the language and even though one of the longest metres has been employed, the resultant passage is simple, direct and felicitous and the effect produced is one of dignity affronted.

धीरस्या श्रमसंश्रितस्य वसतस्तुष्टस्य वन्यैः फलैः
मानार्हस्य जनस्य वल्कलवतस्त्रासः समुत्पाद्यते ।
उत्सिक्तो विनयादपेतपुरुषो भाग्यैश्चलैर्विस्मितः
कोऽयं भो निभृतं तपोवनमिदम् ग्रामीकरोत्याज्ञया ॥

[Svapnavāsavadatta I/3]

We can end the section by quoting from Murāri's play where Rāma hurls a verse of expostulation at Rāvaṇa, blending disgust with surprise.

कुले वा शौर्ये वा भुजसमुदये वा तपसि वा
बभूवुर्न प्राञ्चस्त्वमिव भवितारो न चरमे ।
अहो धिङ्मोहस्ते समजनि चिरादेष न खलु
प्रवीराणां पन्थाः दशवदन येनासि चलितः ॥

[Anargharāghava V/13]

3.7 *Wonder helps poet to effect change of direction in a natural and aesthetically acceptable fashion*

In the course of the composition of anything other than a minor poem, the poet feels the need to effect a change of gears for at least three reasons: to effect a change in the course of the plot, in the sentiment and in the atmosphere. Art, like nature, abhors abruptness; and changes have therefore to be introduced in a gradual manner. But, if the poet in trying to avoid abruptness in effecting changes puts in additional material (not needed or justified otherwise) to ease the steepness of the gradient, the artistic value of the work will certainly suffer.

The one device which the harassed poet can use to smooth the gradient is wonder. A surge of wonder is always sudden, never gradual: but, as it purveys wonder, its abruptness is not adversely noticed: in fact its suddenness is part of its attraction. So when a change has to be introduced economically and aesthetically, the sentiment of wonder comes in very handy to bail out the hard-pressed poet.

In the fifth Act of Śākuntala, as noted briefly earlier, all the pleadings on behalf of the poor girl prove in vain and the two boys from the penance grove leave her in the king's court to return home, evidently deciding that they had fulfilled their preceptor's command. To solve the impasse, the royal priest offers to look after Śakuntalā during her confinement and a decision can be taken in the matter on the basis of whether the child displays any bodily marks indicating royal lineage. The king falls in with this but the poet has no use for this prosaic solution. Clearly the stage has been reached when the story has to change direction: Śakuntalā is taken to the higher regions by her mother terminating the first part of the love story: the events unfolding in the VI and the VII Acts leading to the reunion of the lovers fall into a recognisably different track altogether.

The poet therefore introduces this turning point by a miraculous event generating genuine wonder: the priest, overwhelmed with surprise rushes in to report to the king the supernatural phenomenon he had just witnessed: Mēnakā had appeared as a flash of effulgence and whisked her luckless daughter away.

पुरोहितः (प्रविश्य)—देव अद्भुतं खलु संवृत्तम् ।
  परावृत्तेषु कण्वशिष्येषु
सा निन्दन्ती स्वानि भाग्यानि बाला बाहूत्क्षेपं क्रन्दितुं च प्रवृत्ता ।
स्त्रीसंस्थानं चाप्सरस्तीर्थमारात् उत्क्षिप्यैनां ज्योतिरेकं जगाम ।।

[V/30]

Bhāsa's *Svapnavāsavadatta* furnishes a good example of this kind: the dream scene has a number of surprises for the characters: Vāsavadatta who comes to the summerhouse expecting to see Padmāvatī lying in the sickbed is shocked to see the king in the bed: the king, half asleep, is thrilled by her touch and recognises her though he is under the impression that he is dreaming: he gets up in a hurry on seeing her trying to run away and gets a knock on the door-post: she vanishes leaving the king puzzled as to whether all this is a dream or reality. The dream scene is obviously important in the design of the playwright who has named his play after it: what is its real importance? The dream, in fact, is not a dream at all: the king sees his queen (supposed dead) in reality but to his mind from which the mists of sleep have not quite cleared it seems a dream. So what can be the significance of this illusory dream?

Firstly, as the king himself is not very sure it was all only a dream, hope begins to sprout in his breast that the queen may be alive, after all. For the king driven to despondency on the supposed death of his beloved queen, this half-hope acts as a tonic: he is spurred to heroic action from a listness inanity. Eventwise, this is the time (accidently) chosen by his military planners to launch a counter attack on the hated Āruṇi. The call to action finds the king spoiling for a fight: he leads his army to a great victory and regains his lost kingdom. Hence the dream sequence acts as the turning point in the story and the many surprises that inhere in it smooth the process of change, rendering it aesthetically convincing.

Sentiment being the heart of a creative literary work, a change in the sentiment is a thing that has to be worked out very carefully by the poet if he is to bring conviction to the reader. Usually this is accomplished through the medium of surprise. We shall examine the mechanics of it by studying two examples from the Vēṇīsamhāra.

After developing the heroic sentiment in the first two Acts, the playwright introduces Aśvatthāman in the lowest nadir of gloom at the news of his father's death. He yet does not know the manner in which his father came by his death: so it is pure anguish at the death of a father who had been everything to him. In his hour of sorrow, Aśvatthāman does something no one who knows his blood-thirsty belligerance would have expected him to do. To astonishment of everyone he formally lays down his arms in a gesture of renunciation. This surprising development, so out of character in Aśvatthāman heralds the major change of sentiment from the pervasive *vira* to *karuṇa*.

Aśvatthāman now proceeds to wallow in self-pity: he curses himself as a loveless son: for, while his father had laid down his life on hearing of his son's death (which later proves a false news) he himself continues to live after hearing of his father's death. And he asks his late father why he threw away his life for the sake of such an ungrateful son.

Hereabouts a voice is heard (presumably Duryōdhana's) pointing out that Dhṛṣṭadyumna, after killing Drōna through chicanery is walking back to his camp unscathed, with all the Kauravas looking on. This rouses the sleeping fiend in Aśvatthāman: the details of Drōna's killing are supplied by the charioteer: his rage, never much under control in the best of days now boils over. He had just renounced his arms in a formal gesture, after many austere pronouncements: now impetuously he takes them up. The characters and the spectators who were witness to the farewell to arms so unctuously proclaimed by him are now surprised at the alacrity with which he seizes his weapons of war.

The provocative pronouncement relating to the killer of Drōna and the resumption of arms by the son—these acts of surprise succeeding each other in such a short space of time signal a violent change of sentiment. For pathos yields place to a consuming rage laced liberally with a braggart type of heroism: he is spurred on to mouth those splendid verses which raise the work from the humdrum level to that of great literature. From out of them, we can pick verses 22, 23, 25 and 32 of the third Act of the play as fair samples. The switches of sentiment would have appeared unnatural and abrupt had it not been for the smoothening effect of the surprise-laden episodes. Of the two, the more unexpected switch is the earlier one from the prevailing sentiment of heroism to that of melancholy and appropriately the more surprising of the two episodes, the renunciation of arms by the warlike youth heralds it.

The above are examples of change of sentiment where the new sentiment is also a desired one put in there by design as it has a part to play. We can see two examples of change where the sensitive poet provides it only as a relief to a sentiment that has been continually nourished over a length of time. The first occurs at the end of the I Act of Śākuntala, a long Act replete with the sentiment of love expertly evoked. At a point indicated by the sense of balance and propriety (*aucitya*) of the master, a situation is created, providing tension and excitement: for the army of Duṣyanta drives the animals of the penance grove to a panic and the ascetics run to him for succour. This sudden intrusion of an element of panic with its strong element of surprise provides welcome relief from the sustained love-making of the past hour.

The third Act of the same play—almost equally long—is wholly taken up with the developing affection between the lovers.

Kālidāsa, who can judge these things to a nicetv decides that enough is enough and proceeds to provide relief through the device of surprise, incidentally solving another problem, too.

When the lover is sentimentalizing in the bower of creepers which has just been vacated by the lady, a voice is heard, shrill with fear, announcing the onslaught of ogres inspiring terror in the hermits in the grove. The picture is painted with the aid of words selected for their sound echoing with the sense.

सायन्तने सवनकर्मणि संप्रवृत्ते
वेदीं हुताशनवतीं परितः प्रकीर्णाः ।
छायाश्चरन्ति बहुधा भयमादधानाः
संध्यापयोदकपिशाः पिशिताशनानाम् ॥ [III/26]

Apart from providing welcome relief to the reader, this episode furnishes an excuse to Duṣyanta to extend his stay in the penance-grove, a consummation devoutly wished for by the love-lorn king.

The third kind of change which is aesthetically effected with the aid of wonder is the shift in the atmosphere. When the stage is set for a particular atmosphere, it is impossible to change it in the middle of a scene: and it would be the height of absurdity for the stage hands to enter the stage while a scene is being enacted, with a set of props in hand. The best way is to suggest the change through the dialogue: Śaktibhadra uses this device in his play the Āścaryacūḍāmaṇi.

The play opens with a very good verse by Lakṣmaṇa which quickly helps to create the atmosphere of a penance grove where hermits practise austerities: he then utters a few words in prose which set the seal on the portrait of a calm, passion-free atmosphere. Now the poet has to introduce Śūrpaṇakhā within a few short moments and she represents an acutely disturbing force, a bull in a china-shop, in the calm surroundings. So the poet calls upon the sensation of wonder to help him to smooth the gradient: he makes the devout Lakṣmaṇa register surprise with the words,

अये अरण्यविरुद्धेयं आकृतिः ।

[Act I]

the first word '*ayē*' being a standard ejaculation in Sanskrit. He then recites a verse expressive of wonder for he is puzzled as to whether the girl walking up is human or divine: he actually uses the word *āścaryaratna* to describe her exquisitely beautiful form. This is the verse:

> अस्यातिमात्रायतलोचनस्य नतभ्रुणः कम्रपयोधरस्य ।
> आश्चर्यरत्नस्य विलासयोनेः किमाकरो द्यौर्नु वसुन्धरा नु ॥
>
> [I/6]

The injection of a surprise element helps the poet to effect a change of atmosphere, artistically, without having to change the physical props on the stage.

3.8 *Wonder brightens the narrative, it lights up the dull patches*

In two earlier sections we have examined the signal service wonder performs in making banal, everyday objects and sequences interesting and in activating and vivifying other sensations with which wonder is associated. In this section, we propose to discuss the role which wonder fills in rendering dull patches innocuous, in taking away the smothering effect of long descriptive passages or routine sequences which the poet has to accommodate in the interests of maintaining continuity of the story or of fulfilling some requirement of an epic poem. If surprise vibrates, as we saw it does, with greater intensity than the other sensations it cannot coexist with dullness: surprise, by its very nature goes with thrilling new experiences and represents aesthetically the very opposite of the twice-told tale, the insipid description, the bland, the banal, the prosaic.

We had occasion to note that books on dramaturgy lay down that a surprise sequence should be put down at the stage of the denoucement in any play.

> कुर्यान्निर्वहणेऽद्भुतम् ।
>
> [Daśarūpaka III/33]

The point of this directive, of course, is that the spectators may take the ending of the play for granted and lose interest in the final Act. Indian plays were based on plots drawn from the two famous epics or the Kathāsaritsāgara and the spectators all could be expected to know the course of the story from start to finish. In such a situation, the directive becomes meaningful as otherwise, the actors in the last Act may be playing to an empty theatre.

Striking examples of the way this directive has been implemented can be found in the Vēṇīsamhāra and the Janakīpariṇaya. In both the plays the plot is well known and the spectators would be in a position to anticipate how the play will end, as the sources of the plot are the two great epics popular even among the illiterate Indians. In the former, the playwright creates a situation at the end where Bhīma bathed in the blood of Duryōdhana is mistaken for the enemy: everyone jumps to the conclusion that the *Pāṇdava* cause is now hopelessly lost, the women resolve to enter the fire and Yudhiṣṭhira gets ready to have a last duel with his hated cousin when the mistake is corrected by Bhīma himself and there is joy everywhere. But the playwright has succeeded in making everyone to sit up and take notice.

In the second play, Rāmabhadra Dīkṣita makes the vengeful Śūrpaṇakhā go in disguise to Ayōdhyā and unfold an amazing fabric of calamities befalling Rāma and his kin, before Bharata who naturally decides to immolate himself: the considerable suspense is dissipated by the timely arrival of Hanumān with the news of Rāma's triumphant return.

As for the point made earlier in this section that surprise is employed by good poets to enliven dull patches, we can cite some good examples particularly from the epic poems where such dull passages may well occur. In the V sarga of the Raghuvaṃśa, the poet spends a certain amount of time describing Aja's journey to Kuṇḍinapura to participate in the *svayamvara* there. As a relief, (and there does not appear to be any other purpose served by the episode) he introduces the incident of an elephant hit by Aja turning into a *gandharva*, a supernatural event evoking surprise.

But Kālidāsa is not given to excessively long descriptions: Śrīharṣa, undoubtedly is. He was clearly conscious of this tendency in himself and he provides, thoughtfully, some relief for the harassed reader. In the first canto itself after apparently interminable descriptions, he inserts a verse where Nala expresses wonder at the golden splendour of the swan.

न जातरूपच्छदजातरूपता द्विजस्य दृष्टेयमिति स्तुवन्मुहुः ।
अवादि तेनाथ स मानसौकसा जनाधिनाथः करपञ्जरस्पृशा ।।

[I/129]

But in Naiṣadha the most amazing unit is the VII canto where Nala, himself remaining invisible, describes Damayanti in nearly a hundred verses! But, for the determined reader who has managed to traverse this vast expanse, the poet offers relief by stating at the end of the canto that Nala wished to reveal himself and then inserting a passage at the very beginning of the next, portraying the astounded reaction of Damayanti and her maids to the sudden appearance of Nala in their midst.

3.9 *Man, atavistically, accords the highest priority to surprise-evoking stimuli*

The history of human civilization counting its beginning from the day he started living in settlements may not be more than 10,000 years old. But the epoch when man hunted for a living in dense jungles contending against a hundred dangers extended over hundreds of thousands of years. Perceptive writers like Desmond Morris do not think very much of the impact of civilised living on man's thinking and habits and pattern of living in his "Naked Ape", Mr. Morris has demonstrated how the urges of a highly sophisticated clubman of Newyork are exactly those of the higher animals, no better and no different. It would seem that biologically these 10,000 years of civilisation have been but a moment in man's evolution, much too brief to have had any major impact on him. And the millions of years he has been evolving from the higher animals and the long epoch during which he followed hunting as a career have set up a strongly-impressed and long-lasting pattern of behaviour in him.

It is easy to see that during these long epochs of living in the forests as an animal and a hunting man, he would have learnt to react with the deepest concern to surprise-evoking stimuli invading his personality from the outside world, so full of dangers: these stimuli might indicate a sabre-toothed tiger stalking him or a snake in the grass athwart his path or a forest conflagration spreading his way; and failure to attend to these stimuli and act with alacrity may well mean a quick and violent death for him. These surprise stimuli may also mean a new source of food, a fresh refuge or an unlooked-for friend. Either way, these stimuli evoking surprise must have proved repeatedly of the primemost significance to him over long epochs. This naturally has implanted in his personality a strong tendency to accord the foremost importance to surprise stimuli: his senses, his nerves, his brain and his endocrinal glands have all been trained to react sharply, on the highest priority basis, to these stimuli evoking surprise. And, quite obviously, his evolutionarily short urban career where such life-and-death sequences are much rarer could have had but little influence on these reactions.

Hence, atavistically, man reacts with much greater readiness to stimuli causing wonder: his system accords the highest priority to them, to the exclusion of others, even without his consciously willing it. Surprise stimuli emanating from literary sources (being no different from real life stimuli at the initial impact) therefore command a priority of reception and attention in the reader's personality to the exclusion of others. Considering the number and the strength of the distractions man is subject to, one realises the value of surprise in the hands of an adroit poet who has something valuable and interesting to communicate but is unable to secure reader attention.

3.10 *Certain elements of surprise born of audacity, perversity, iconoclasm can purvey vicarious delight*

Many of us would like to hand out audacious claims and mischievous interpretations: we may get into the mood to break some idols, if only to get some attention: but we do not get round to doing it actually, for lack of opportunity, or more often, for lack of courage. So, when someone does it in our knowledge, we derive vicarious enjoyment out of it. Admittedly audacity and perversity are only two of the many excitants of surprise we have examined and hence the scope of this section is limited to the cases coming under them: that way, this is not a general and universal literary advantage claimed for surprise but within these limitations it certainly promotes reader pleasure and hence merits distinct categorization and discussion in this part of the work.

We have already referred to the rueful rumination of Duṣyanta at the antics of the bee: we, happily are in the position of enjoying the antics of the bee as well as the hero's sense of deprivation, being held back by no such moral misgivings as hamstring the king. It is said, (probably on paltry evidence) that man is essentially polygamous (and woman, by the same count, polyandrous) by instinct and is held back from giving expression to this instinct by social taboo. But it is undeniable that man derives pleasure from reading about others' promiscuity: and Amaru's romantic characters like the one who duped two girls by making love to them simultaneously without each knowing about his attentions on the other make pleasant reading as also the other situation where constancy is held up to ridicule in the poem quoted earlier, beginning with the words,

इन्दुर्यत्र न निन्द्यते

These verses are universally popular, not excepting the puritans who overtly condemn what they privately devour. The verses mouthed by Nārada in Bālacarita, confessing to a love of mischief in a highly regarded divine sage will be go very well with the gallery. A certain harmless iconoclasm is devoured eagerly by the lower echolons of society in all ages. And the remarkable fact is that despite the generally prevalent aura of reverence in the classic age, there were, too some Sanskrit poets who would pull down some idols in order that they might purvey delight.

3.11 *Surprise, the prime constituent of Jagannātha's 'beyond-the-world' concept*

Among the many definitions of poetry attempted by Sanskrit aestheticians, the one by Jagannātha Paṇḍita set forth in his *Rasagaṅgādhara* stands out as highly original and appropriate. The passage in which it occurs is worth quoting here:

रमणीयार्थप्रतिपादकः शब्दः काव्यम् ।
रमणीयता च लोकोत्तराह्लादजनकज्ञानगोचरता ।
लोकोत्तरत्वं च आह्लादगतः चमत्कारत्वापरपर्यायः अनुभवसाक्षिकः जातिविशेषः ॥

[I (Kāvyalakṣaṇa)]

Jagannātha thinks that poetry should yield a meaning that is pleasing: and this pleasure should spring from a quality that is beyond the world, interpreted in terms of wisdom. The key word in this is "beyond-the-world" (*lōkōttara*): unless this word is correctly and fully understood, Jagannātha's definition cannot be evaluated.

Jagannātha himself offers a reason why the pleasure has to be *lōkōttara*. There are many statements consisting of Sanskrit words which give pleasure to the listener, like "I like you very much", "Your wife has just brought forth a male issue" and "I shall present you with considerable wealth"; they are statements which generate great pleasure in the one to whom they are addressed, undeniably; but they are not poetry; the pleasure they generate is not literary pleasure, it is of the world, not beyond the world. So the word *lōkōttara* has been employed in order to keep out such transactional passages as the above from the scope of the definition.

Jagannātha gives a further hint regarding the scope of the significance he attaches to the word *lōkōttara*: according to him, it is synonymous with *chamatkāra*, which means the quality of flashing and is generally understood to mean wonder. This is an original contribution of the great aesthetician and his recognition of the pivotal importance of wonder in the enjoyment of literary pleasure proclaims his ability to think far in advance of his times. However it has to be pointed out here that Jagannātha should have gone farther than this and indicated the full significance of the highly suggestive word he had thought up, this *lōkōttara*: by merely indicating that it is synonymous with wonder, he runs the risk of admitting as poetry merely transactional statements which evoke surprise in the listener and which are certainly not poetical: to an impecunious suppliant who came to a king expecting food and perhaps a present of Rs. 100 if the king says, "I shall present you this gold flower studded with gems" this statement will cause not only pleasure but considerable surprise: but it is clearly not classifiable as poetry.

Hence it becomes necessary now to delve deeper into the scope of the signification of the word *lōkōttara*. *Lōka* literally means what is perceived by the senses and by derivation has come to refer to the world we live in: *Uttara* is beyond: so the word *lōkōttara* means beyond what is perceived, beyond the world. Now going beyond mere etymology, this word has generally been interpreted to yield meanings like 'metaphysical', 'non-material'. Hence we can assume that poetic experience goes beyond physical sensations into the region of the mind and the spirit: it crosses the territory of everyday transactional experience, the concerns of the body, the need for want-fulfilment and picnics in the parkland of subtle sensations. It involves, not surface appearances and gross relationships but the inner life of things. It habitually deals with the inner drives behind every day experiences. While the raw material of all poetry has to be the world of physical objects and relationships, the concern of the poet is not merely to photograph or record them as they are but look into, under and beyond them for the subtler essence which informs and directs them. *Uttara* in the word *lōkōttara* stands for these prepositions "into," "under" and "beyond" and is the operative part of the entire definition.

A little reflection will convince the gentle reader that the *uttara* concept ensures a considerable element of surprise turning up in any work of poetry: what is perceived, on the surface is very familiar: a glance into the secret heart of things, a gaze with the head raised at realms beyond what is ordinarily seen are certain to disclose unusual aspects, evoking wonder. We have seen how the photograph of the underside of a cockroach (than which there can be nothing more repellent, unpoetical, banal) surprised thousands of intelligent readers. So the uttara concept has a strong element of surprise ensconced in it, though it is very comprehensive, accommodating many more things and is not confined and delimited by wonder. To this extent we may make bold to disagree with the master—and assert that *lōkōttara* is not synonymous with wonder, it is bigger than that; but we owe a great debt to him for recognizing the significant part that wonder plays in the *lōkōttara* concept.

For a heart-deep comprehension of Jagannātha's concept of beyondness, one should study a great work of creative literature—which instantly lights up the obscure corners of this detailed theoretical discussion. If we take Kālidāsa's Śākuntala and examine it from the viewpoint of the axioms elaborated earlier in this section, we see clearly what is meant by beyondness. The love between the king and the hermit girl when initially fed by physical allure fails to get consummated: they, then, resort to other than physical means; while the king eats his heart out in repentance, Śakuntalā performs austerities in the Hēmakūṭa and the union that takes place after these is indissoluble and productive of not only lasting happiness but the greatest good to the world. This view which we owe to the late Rabīndranāth Tāgōre clearly emphasizes the uttara concept of transcending the physical. The king we see in the early Acts is a playboy with more than a bit of a lothario in him, despite his *rājarṣi* image: but he matures during the VI Act and emerges with an enriched inner life from the tunnel of heartache and critical introspection.

Śakuntalā too has grown wiser from the light-hearted girl of the woods apt to skim the surface of life: deep anguish, the mortification of a rejection by her lover, an unpleasant present and a wholly bleak future have rebuilt her personality to a nobler design. With such enriched, ennobled inner personalities they enter matrimony for their own fulfilment and for the good of the world. Such a view which is certainly beyond the everyday estimate of married life as legitimised sex is the true poetic perspective.

Kumārasambhava, too, illuminates a similar concept: the love that spring up between Lord Śiva and Pārvati is based on physical attributes and it comes to no good at all. Pārvatī performs her celebrated penance to get Him: but the Lord, too, performs penance, presumably to get her: but as the heart of Almighty God is not open to man to read, the poet puts up his hand and remarks,

केनापि कामेन तपश्चचार । [I/57]

clearly throwing a hint by the use of the word kama, that he who runs may read. The marriage that ensues is everlasting and productive of the greatest good to the gods and men.

This beyondness has little to do with the nature of the characters or the atmosphere of the work: all great works of literature whether they are laid in Himālayan bowers or the ghettoes of Chicago will be found to be preoccupied with the subtle inner life of things, beyond the gross, the earthy, the external, the physical. And this focussing on the beyond ensures a fuller play of the sense of wonder which is fed and nourished by the unknown, the unusual.

3.12 *Surprise enables the portrayal of a fine excess of sentiment*

Keats said in one of his letters that poetry should surprise by a fine excess. The present writer has applied this principle to the portrayal of sentiments in Tamil Sangam poetry* and he feels there are many important literary gains realisable by a poet who proffers a fine excess of sentiment. The principle is applicable to all literature and the present writer is working on a book discussing its application to Sanskrit literature. The excess referred

*Fine Excess of Poetic Sentiment (S. Visvanathan & Co. Madras 31) 1985.

to is in comparison with the level of sentiment met with in similar life situations.

Some of the advantages of such portrayal to a fine excess are that it compensates for the loss of sentiment in the process of transfer of experience from the poet to the reader, that it makes the voice of the poet heard by furnishing the additional decibels to drown the din of daily life. A fine excess serves to tense up inter-personal relationships so as to bring out their strength and weakness and draw attention to the role they play. If poetry is energised speech, the energy is provided by the excess of sentiment: this extra provision of sentiment raises the poem to the point of incandescence where it sheds light and becomes more than noticeable. Many other literary gains are discussed in the book which examines this aesthetic theory for the first time.

But runaway sentiment will ruin any work of art: excessive excess should be avoided like the plague by all artists including the poet. All great art has to function within some limits: this aesthetic theory lays down that this excess of sentiment has to be fine, it should not overleap the boundaries set by art. This theory actually, therefore, sets two limits for the portrayal of sentiment: the lower which should be higher than the level of emotion seen in life situations of a similar type and the upper limit set by artistic sensibility. The factors rendering this upper limit necessary have also been examined in detail and a closer look given to these artistic limits themselves, in the book referred to.

The sense of wonder, being more dynamic, vibrating with greater intensity than most others can prove a handy device in the hands of the poet when he attempts to portray a sentiment to excess. A producer of a play can call upon a number of devices like music, specially designed dress and equipment for the actors and scenic stage effects to help him in his task: the painter has colours of a very wide range and an array of brushes to help him to create art. But the writer has to rely only on words as the sole tool with which to evoke artistic reaction: hence a device like the sense of wonder which intensifies the vibration of the associated sentiment comes in uncommonly handy to help the poet to strike up those extra decibels or the additional frequency needed.

An excellent example can be cited from Shakespeare's Romeo

and Juliet where in Act V, Scene iii Romeo breaks open the door of the monument where the body of Juliet is kept. Romeo is in extreme anguish when he sees that Juliet is beautiful even in death: he cries out in wonder.

"—Ah, dear Juliet
Why are thou yet so fair? Shall I believe
That unsubstantial death is amorous;
And that the lean abhorred monster keeps
Thee here in dark to be his paramour?"

Romeo must have seen how death contorts and renders hideous the faces of people: his wonder at the beauty of Juliet in death somehow intensifies the impact of his sorrow on the reader.

Kali, the spirit of evil makes many perverse statements in a cynical vein in the epic poem, the Naiṣadha but when he starts talking about the hypocrisy of ascetics and their capacity to apply double standards, Kali's voice gets shrill with a surprised indignation. For he exclaims, "The ascetics who are short-tempered (as evidenced by their widely known proclivity to curse all those who offend them) go about teaching the world the need for the control of temper! They are poor and preach against greed but they teach alchemy through which one can get rich quick!"

अक्रोधं शिक्षयन्त्यन्यान् क्रोधना ये तपोधनाः ।
निर्धनास्ते धनायैव धातुवादोपदेशिनः ॥ [XVII/79]

Through this statement where there is a nice blend of surprise, indignation and contempt, Kali is able to convey an excessive censoriousness, an irreverence, an iconoclasm towards established beliefs.

Kālidāsa makes Duṣyanta exclaim in consorious disapproval of the hard-hearted, pitiless attitude of Kaṇva who engages the delicately-nurtured Śakuntalā in such toil around the ashrama as watering the plants. Duṣyanta has just seen the girl for whom to develop so much solicitude in so short a time would look improbable: but the surprised exclamation of the king succeeds in bringing out his excessive infatuation for her which largely explains this unbalanced observation of his:

इदं किलाव्याजमनोहरं वपुः तपःक्षमं साधयितुं य इच्छति ।
ध्रुवं स नीलोत्पलपत्रधारया शमीलतां छेत्तुमृषिर्व्यवस्यति ॥ [I/18]

The sense of wonder, when evoked, may perform the task of helping the poet to portray sentiments to excess on account of its extra vitality, its higher frequency of vibration: but, by the same token, it may overperform this service resulting in unbridled excess: the question whether the sense of wonder helps the poet to keep the excess within limits, however, can be answered with a positive yes. If the poet knows how to handle wonder, he would take good care to make it operate within limits: too little of it will fail to attract attention while too much of it will excite the critical sense of the listener and prove counterproductive. This controlled evocation of wonder will solve the problem of excessive excess. The limits within which the sense of wonder is effective will be discussed in the next chapter, in terms of a theory of 'moderate discrepancy' developed by neuro-psychologists in recent times.

3.13 *Surprise engenders puzzlement which challenges the mind and engages it, furnishing delight*

This category needs little explanation. As novelty is of the essence in the build up of surprise, what is new, not met with before may puzzle the mind: and the mind is challenged to clear up the matter: when the mind is challenged and is made to focus on something, there is delight produced. Clearly all cases of surprise do not have an element of puzzlement: there is none where the hero is surprised at the beauty of the heroine. It arises wherever there are elements in the situation not explained by the recorded facts—as in verses 8, 10 and 12 of Act VII of the Śākuntala and the prose passages introducing them. Again, such puzzlement is experienced in the verse in the Kṛṣṇakarṇāmṛta (quoted earlier) where Rādhā churns assiduously for quite some time but there is no resultant butter and Kṛṣṇa milks for a length of time but no milk collects in the pitcher: the mystery is solved when the poet reveals that these lovers with their minds absorbed in the contemplation of each other had been trying to churn an empty vessel and milk a bull!

Similar instances can be seen in the XIII Canto of Raghuvamśa and less frequently in the many imitations of this device of Rāma flying over most of India in the aerial vehicle, the *Puṣpaka*, in his return journey to his capital after killing Rāvaṇa. The classical verses in XIII canto of Raghuvamśa which evoke a puzzled surprise are 2, 9 and 54 to 58, mainly on account of the unique angle of vision adopted here. There are similar verses in Śivalilārṇava of Nīlakaṇṭha Dīkṣita, too.

Just as a change of the physical angle of vision engenders puzzlement, so too does a shift in the mental angle; when Rāma destroys the ogres in the Daṇḍaka and enables the ascetics to pursue their austerities in peace, the news is reported to Rāvaṇa as a great calamity (as quoted earlier). This causes a momentary puzzlement to the orthodox, simple minded reader. So too may the utterances of Rāvaṇa, perversely running down virtue and lauding evil as in verses V/17 and V/27 of the Āścaryacūḍāmaṇi. Stark contrasts too as discussed in an earlier section (in Chapter II) may harbour elements of puzzlement. When a confused sequence is further confounded as in many instances in the Mudrarakshasa and the *Jānakīpariṇaya*, puzzlement inheres in the situation, as also when the poet himself or a character says something quite opposed to what is expected, so as to secure a better effect.

Wherever there are elements of mystery and the reader can be offered a puzzle, his mental faculties are challenged and gripped by them: this powerful engagement of the mind produces pleasure, as in the well known cases of mystery novels and crossword puzzles and in the much less known cases of mathematical and scientific problems.

3.14 *Surprise furnishes a magic attic for us to escape into from the troubled world we live in*

Most of us when we were very young had a favourite hideaway to run to when things became too sticky: the hideaway may be a barrel or an attic or even a large card-board box in which a gadget had arrived. After we grow up we are deprived of such a chance and much of adult frustration may be traced to this.

Most of us live uneventful, drab lives and there arises a need in us to experience thrilling new adventures. In most cases such adventures do not happen: and if they do happen, most of us would find them to be unpleasant—we may get hurt, we may get killed. So the best plan is to read about other peoples' adventures and vicariously participate in them.

But it is not merely thrill and adventure that we crave for. Wonder creates for us an expanded variegated experience which our everyday life cannot offer. When we read of Lord Viṣṇu's incarnation as a boar on whose horn the earth was suspended a tiny, negligible ball, we find our horizons recede away leaving us citizens of a much larger world.

Reality is a confining prison: and too long an exposure to it makes man restless. Wonder (may be for the moment only but still what a relief!) emancipates us from this prison and enables us to taste the joys of freedom. Even after we go back to everyday reality we cherish some of the joy we have had and we create more and more opportunities for us to savour this joy by turning to great books which purvey wonder.

There is a certain widespread feeling against such 'escapist' literature: there are psychologists and others declaiming against it for the reason that this tendency to escape represents lack of courage and one should fight against it if one is to preserve mental health. It may be true that such a tendency to seek escape routes, if allowed to become a habit may ruin mental health. But admittedly life today is full of tensions, frustrations and even positive tragedy: it is far better to seek relief in literature and art and allow wonder to act as an emollient for the bruised soul than find solace in alcohol and drugs. And apart from providing temporary relief from vexing problems, the sense of wonder when evoked can enlarge horizons, elevate the level of thinking and feeling, take the mind off from a morbid preoccupation with bodily and material problems. Life in a modern city has a tendency to revolve in a very limited circle and years of living such a life delimits the mind and cabins the soul: it is far better to escape now and then into the perfumed world of wonder where there are no cribs or fetters confining us: the world may be unreal but the pleasure is real and a little of it rubs off on us so that even on our return to the prison house, it lights up our banal lives.

Chapter 4

LIGHT FROM MODERN SCIENCE

4.1 *The two fresh thinkers*

Thoughtful students of Sanskrit poetics would have noticed two different trends of thinking on the subject of wonder among the aestheticians. One is that wonder is a minor sentiment, to be classified with the sense of humour and the sense of disgust: this view is held by all the aestheticians except Nārāyaṇa and Jagannātha: the latter two seem to regard wonder as a basic and universal ingredient in all literary works: for Nārāyaṇa, it is the king of the sentiments, holding sway over all the others; for Jagannātha, wonder plays a pivotal role in the literary pleasure generated in the reader's mind.

The first school allotted a very secondary role to wonder: and as a corollary dismissed it after the most cursory attention. Ācārya Nārāyaṇa's view consisting of three lines (1½ anuṣṭubh stanza) as reported in the third person has come down to us via Viśvanātha: it is most unfortunate that the complete work of this original thinker has not been preserved. We have already discussed Jagannātha's view in some detail. It is to be remarked with considerable anguish that no writer since has thought fit to pursue the line of investigation suggested by these two astute thinkers.

The importance of wonder as a ubiquitous and effective poetic ingredient has been grasped by the greatest poets in Sanskrit who have made extensive use of wonder in their works: an overwhelmingly major part of this work has been devoted to create an image of the significance of the sense of wonder. Now it is proposed to study some relevant discoveries of modern neuropsychology and apply them to Sanskrit aesthetics, to sharpen our comprehension of the role played by wonder in creative literature. It will be found, as a result of such an application, that the view of these two thinkers is much nearer the scientific position than that of the majority of writers. It is amazing to think that these two writers, without the help of science and in the teeth of the universally held view of all the rhetoricians before them could pursue a wholly independent line of enquiry and boldly set down their thoughts in writing.

4.2 *Light from Neuro-psychology*

Now let us turn to science and examine what very recent neuropsychologists have to say in the matter. The phrase 'in the matter' does not mean the sense of wonder or the field of aesthetics specifically. The discoveries pertain to the impact of stimuli on the human personality and the process of their absorption—not, particularly, literary, or artistic stimuli. In the last half-century, there is a growing consensus of scientific opinion on the way new stimuli are reacted to, based on a number of very interesting experiments conducted primarily in the new world. Let us get an idea of this consensus briefly, using the minimum of technical terms.

When we come across facts and figues, when we undergo experiences, we selectively absorb some of them, storing them in the brain in the form of patterns called schema. Now, when a new stimulus assails us, let us say, through our eyes, at the first impact, a quick comparison is made between the pattern of the incoming new stimulus and the established schema in the brain. If it is totally unrelated to the schema, the system may become indifferent to it: so too may it lose interest if it is wholly in conformity with one of the schema. But, if there is a moderate degree of discrepancy in the new pattern as compared to the schema, the brain gets interested in the new stimulus but is puzzled by it too: when it is not able to identify, immediately, any pattern similar to it in the established schema but is unwilling to dismiss it as wholly identical to one of the schema or radically different (and therefore is of no interest to it), then, a state of alertness, attention and arousal is quickly set up in the personality. This alertness, attention and arousal may help the system to effect a mental reconciliation of the mismatch either by creating a new schema or extending an existing schema: it may, sometimes, be further helped by new stimuli coming in. On this mental reconciliation being effected, the puzzlement is resolved, generating a sense of pleasure. If, despite the arousal and attention, the mismatch cannot be reconciled, then fear and anxiety arise, not pleasure.

4.3 *The concept of moderately discrepant stimuli*

It may be noted from the above that too familiar a stimulus does not produce the puzzled state when arousal and attention are caused: similarly when a wholly unfamiliar stimulus, bearing no relation to any of the schema in the brain impacts the personality, it disregards it and no puzzlement accompanied by alertness and attention is produced. So the condition that the new stimulus evokes these states of puzzlement, alertness, attention and arousal is that the stimulus must be tantalizingly discrepant from the schema—sufficiently different to excite curiosity and offer a challenge but not so radically discrepant that all challenge is discouraged and interest stilled.

Donald Hebb, a brilliant Canadian researcher to whom we owe many of these ideas showed* that infant chimpanzees would exhibit extreme fear when presented with a snake or the death-mask of an adult chimpanzee or the cadaver of a chimp foetus. These chimpanzees had had no experience of these objects before and hence no conditioning of any kind with regard to them. There was no reason to believe that these fears were the result of the usual learning process. According to D. Hebb, these fears were due to the fact that the stimuli emanating from these objects were discrepant from the schemata acquired perceptually: they coult fit into none of them even after a process of comparison and analysis. It could be observed that after the initial puzzlement accompanied by attention and arousal, the system found that the mismatch could not be reconciled: hence fear was generated. Other experiments confirm that it is not the fearful nature of the object but its unfamiliarity that causes arousal and the subsequent fear. It is always the irreconcilable discrepancy that causes fear.

Now, if we apply these scientific findings to the field of aesthetics, we can see clearly that, on being presented with moderately discrepant stimuli (literary stimuli not being excluded from their scope), the human system would respond with a puzzlement followed by alertness, attention and arousal. Puzzlement is the direct cause of surprise: elsewhere we have quoted Konner as saying that surprise is rapt attention. So there is no doubt at all that if the stimuli are neither too familiar nor too radically

*Donald D. Hebb "On the nature of fear" Psychological Review 53 (1946)

different but moderately discrepant from our recorded experience, they cause surprise at the initial impact: and surprise throws a challenge to the organism which gets sufficiently interested in the new stimuli to get alert and attentive and to get aroused.

With the aid of the newly aroused attentiveness and perhaps of additional stimuli impacting the system, the stimuli are subjected to a closer examination and analysis: and the system may be able to find a schema which can either be altered or extended to accommodate the new stimulus, thus removing the cognitive mismatch. On the removal of the mismatch and the absorption of the new stimulus, there is a feeling of relief and ressurance and, as a consequence, a sense of pleasure established in the system.

The careful reader would have noted that whatever the nature of the stimuli, whatever is their emotional hue, on the rectification of the mismatch there is always a resultant sense of pleasure. This means that even if the new stimulus conveys an unhappy experience its absorption produces a sense of reassurance and pleasure. The pleasure is owed to the cessation of the uncertain groping to discover a matching schema: the initial inability to interpret the new stimulus in terms of recorded experience causes a certain discomfort and the eventual success in the process of interpretation and absorption removes this discomfort, causing an upsurge of pleasure. The emotional contents of the new stimulus which may be sad and which will have their own impact on the system elsewhere do not quench out this basic satisfaction at the matching and the absorption.

4.4 *The theory of Moderate Discrepancy*

This new theory of aesthetics that can rightly be called, the 'Theory of Moderate Discrepancy' explains the pivotal role played by surprise in the aesthetic process. Surprise is invariably caused at the first impact of literary stimuli and that is the guarantee that the system gets interested in them and gets aroused, alerted and attentive to them. It is the initial puzzlement at the tantalizing new stimuli (generating surprise) that challenges the system and compels it to pay attention to them. Hence surprise has a pivotal role to play at the initial stage of impact, ensuring that the incoming stimuli (consisting of scenes and sounds) are attended to with care and interest. With such care and interest, the system is usually able to match the new stimuli with some schema recorded in the brain and delight ensues accompanied or followed by the specific reaction to the emotional contents of the stimuli: this last represents the registration and enjoyment of the different sentiments or rasas. It is therefore clear that surprise is registered and experienced before the sentiments are relished. We shall examine this more closely a little later.

Incidentally it may be noted that this new theory, provides a possible solution for one of the unsolved problems of aesthetics. The existing theories of rasa etc. do not explain how tragedy produces a sensation of pleasure in the reader. The new theory shows that the pleasure the reader gets is not on account of the emotional contents of the stimuli but as a result of the matching with the established schema. In other words, the pleasure (at least in the first phase) is owed to the fact that the stimulus bears some relationship to the recorded experience of the reader on account of which the system is able to accommodate it: it is also due to the fact that it contained some elements of surprise or puzzlement which were removed on closer examination. What happens on absorption and as a result of the impact of the emotional contents (like sadness, anger, love) of the stimulus is however far beyond the scope of this work.

Again, incidentally, it can be seen that the system registers pleasure only on the mismatch being removed and the system is able to identify a schema in itself which bears a certain relationship with the stimulus. It therefore follows that the larger the number and the wider the range of the schema recorded in the brain, the greater is the likelihood of the system solving the mismatch and the shorter the time needed for it. As the pleasure we are talking about is realised only as a result of the removal of the puzzlement and the accommodation of the new stimulus by identifying a related schema, it is clear that people of wide experience and scholarship are more likely to reap rich harvests of such pleasure than the vegetables, the stay-at-homes with no worthwhile range of experience, who do not read much. Such pleasure is the least in the case of children: that explains why children love bizarre tales involving supernatural phenomena where ogres appear as characters: they have so little of recorded schema that they have got to be continually surprised by unlikely events to feel joy: this joy they feel is not, of course, true literary pleasure, it is more of the nature of titillation and excitement.

Even among adults who have travelled widely and have an extensive schemata, it is easy to see that in the case of a trader of little mental ability, the schema are likely to be of a type that cannot find a ready relationship with much of the stimuli from literary sources. Hence such people are found to register little enthusiasm for literature. It is not merely enough to have extensive schema, it is necessary that the schema are of a higher calibre than those experienced by a man of the world with little intellectual curiosity and maturity.

4.5 *The poets' problem*

There are at least two implications flowing from the earlier discussion on the main features of the theory of moderate discrepancy. One is that sufficient attention and arousal are not induced by stimuli which are either too familiar or too unfamiliar. Clearly, overly familiar stimuli, being of a pattern very similar to the recorded schema, are assimilated straightaway without causing any puzzlement and consequently any alertness, attention or arousal: there can be little pleasure in this as there is no puzzlement to unravel. So passages which present very familiar images will not be able to arouse any surprise at all.

Now, poets have to deal with the same world of beings and things as we do and they use much the same vocabulary as we do, as Nīlakaṇṭha Dīkṣita states (The verse from his Śivalīlārṇava has been quoted earlier).

It cannot be otherwise: strange new worlds peopled by strange men and beasts and cockroaches the size of eagles will not interest us adults. In fact unless the poet presents his characters in moods recognizable by the readers as similar to the ones they themselves have, enabling them to identify with the characters, the work will not interest the readers. And the work of mature poets is peopled by familiar animals (often domestic animals like cattle and sheep) birds like sparrows and parrots and peacocks and trees like the banyan, not by gigantic condors that can lift whole houses and beanstalks that grow to the high heavens. So here, there is a first-class conflict for a poet: while he has, inevitably to deal with very familiar things in his work, these familiar things do not evoke surprise without which it is not possible to enlist reader attention.

Poets resolve this conflict, each in his own individual manner using one or more of the excitants we have discussed in Chapter II. Poets, however, take great care to limit the use of these excitants to produce just that degree of surprise required to enlist reader attention and no more: the point is to avoid prolonged evocation of surprise, as this has the effect of postponing the reconciliation of the mismatch which is the desired end-product. The essential guiding principle is that the sense of wonder while very useful in small doses becomes counter-productive in prolonged spells of evocation.

4.6 *Evils of overevocation of wonder*

The gentle reader is invited at this stage to recapitulate quickly the many methods through which wonder is evoked, as discussed in Chapter II; this may be done from the limited viewpoint of the duration of time over which surprise rules. It is easy to see that where surprise is sought to be evoked through verbal tricks, the duration must be very short and the extent of surprise evoked, very limited, indeed. Attempts at prolonged evocation of surprise through verbal jugglery may well lead to a sense of disgust being produced. Many of the excitants discussed provide a sharp and short-lived puzzlement as in the cases of patakasthana, to be relieved in a minute by the subsequent passage. It may be seen that many of the excitants discussed depend upon psychological twists and perversities of mind: the surprise caused by them is not allowed to last long as the reader is quickly led on to a realisation of how natural they are, given the basic drives of the characters involved. In the cases of human foibles being superimposed on birds and beasts, the surprise is only momentary as we quickly recognise the all-too-familiar failings of our species despite their unlikely habitat.

The present writer is here tempted to cite a joke which depends on surprise being evoked—but notice how quickly the surprise is resolved, after it has served its purpose. A long-time spinster announces to a group of similarly-placed women that she had advertised for a husband: the listeners are immediately interested: one of them asks: "Was there a response?" "Plenty! I got hundreds of letters—all from ladies".

At this stage, surprise is definitely evoked and vague forebodings of an orgy of lesbianism are smelt in the air, until the lady adds, "They all say: 'you can have mine'."

The surprise is resolved by what the psychologists term a discharge—a discharge of laughter here. The surprise evoked by the uniform gender of the correspondents (in the last but one sentence) has a sway of perhaps less than 10 seconds, till the punch line is said. But the punch line undoubtedly ends the sway of surprise as all the listeners (of the joke), if male would be aware of the general critical opinion women have about their husbands.

The life-span of a flash of surprise should necessarily be short: it should serve its purpose within that fleeting moment and quickly yield place to a sentiment, like love or heroism or pathos that can safely be evoked for a longer time. We have seen such quick-fire surprise fusillades being used to excellent advantage by the great playwrights: notice how, at the start of a play they grip the attention of the spectators by throwing up a surprise—but observe, also, how quickly that leads them on to the main sentiment of the play. We have seen how even the more slow-paced works like epic poems, intended to be read over a long spell of time, may begin with a surprise as the Śiśupālavadha but here again the surprise quickly yields place to the main sentiment chosen by the poet.

If surprise sets up a state of altertness, attention and arousal, a prolongation of this state will surely lead to fatigue of the nerves. This is an important reason why great poets do not evoke surprise over long periods. Another reason, of course, is that during the sway of surprise, the reader is denied the first flush of pleasure resulting from a reconciliation of the stimulus—schema mismatch. A third reason is that prolonged evocation of surprise makes the characters less and less familiar, rendering identification of the reader with them more difficult: this identification, called *tanmayībhāva* in Sanskrit is a very vital condition for the work to be enjoyed. For these three reasons, surprise can never be made the main sentiment (*aṅgī rasa*) of a work. There is yet another reason why it cannot function that way—and readers will agree, after the next few pages, that it is a shatteringly conclusive reason.

4.7 *Wonder, not a sentiment*

We referred, earlier, to two implications flowing out of this new theory in aesthetics: let us now discuss the second. This implication is of fundamental importance: for, quite simply, it has the effect of taking away wonder from the group of sentiments: wonder is a sensation that is felt before any of the sentiments can be experienced and, for that reason can be called a pre-sentiment though the word means a very different thing as used today. There is a phase difference between the stage at which wonder is felt and that at which the sentiments are experienced. This should be examined in some detail.

When new stimuli impact the system with moderate discrepancy and a quick look does not reveal to the system any similarity between their pattern and that of the impressed schema, there is perplexity and surprise and a tensing up and a rapter attention and arousal. This is a very distinct preliminary stage at which only surprise has sway: the elements of love or heroism or pathos are yet to be scanned and assimilated. To use a loose metaphor, only the packaging has been studied, not the contents yet.

When, after examination (and perhaps the impacting of new stimuli) the system finds it possible to assimilate the discrepant pattern by either changing the existing schema or enlarging it, the perplexity is at an end and there emerges a state of relief and pleasure: at this stage the sentiments in the stimuli have their play, acting and being acted upon by the stored-up experience. Clearly therefore there is a phase different between wonder and the sentiments: the former plays its role before and the latter, during and after the process of assimilation: the stage of close examination and analysis by the system, of the incoming stimuli acts as the water-shed dividing these two categories. As we are concerned with wonder in this work, we can state confidently that wonder is a sensation that has a considerable role to play at the stage of impact of stimuli and before the stage at which sentiments make themselves felt: if it influences the literary delight felt after assimilation it would mainly be on account of its ability to intensify the vibrations of the sentiments with which it is associated. It may be observed that the other advantages cited in Chapter III mostly operate at the preliminary stage of securing attention and do not relate to literary delight directly.

We can represent the transaction in the form of a diagram to make the stages clear.

A	*B*
Stimuli impacting system	Puzzlement, tension, alertness, attention and arousal (The stage at which wonder has play)
	C
	(Reconciliation of mismatch, assimilation, relief, generation of sentiment and rise of delight)

We made a point in Chapter 3 and reiterated it in the passage above that wonder has its major influence in the production of delight only through its propensity to intensify the sentiments (and it is the sentiments that directly generate literary delight). While, from the end-result, one can subscribe to this view, a close look at the whole transaction, keeping in mind the basic nature of wonder, will reveal that wonder essentially influences the dilettante rather than the sentiments. By making him more alert, more aroused and more receptive, wonder ensures a better reception to the sentiments. To use the analogy of guests visiting a house, wonder accompanying them and registering itself at the gate—lodge ensures that the host receives the guests more warmly: wonder itself is not among the guests, it does not enter the house: it may make the guests a little more interesting to the host and therefore more welcome: but the main contribution it makes to the situation is in making the host more receptive to the guests visiting him.

We have derived the concept that wonder is a sensation that is experienced prior to the sentiments, that there is a phase difference between wonder and the sentiments, from the published observations of neuropsychologists. Fortunately, it is possible to demonstrate this from an analysis of our own aesthetic experience, thus confirming the theory.

4.8 *Proving the phase difference between wonder and the sentiments*

For this purpose, we should take passages where wonder is associated with one of the sentiments like love or pathos. Our first example will be the verse in Act II of Śākuntala recited by Duṣyanta: it has been quoted once but is again reproduced here on account of the importance in this context:

अनाघ्रातं पुष्पं किसलयमलूनं कररुहैः
अनाविद्धं रत्नं मधु नवमनास्वादितरसम् ।
अखण्डं पुण्यानां फलमिव च तद्रूपमनघम्
न जाने भोक्तारं कमिह समुपस्थास्यति विधिः ॥ [II/10]

The first three lines are a glowing description of Śakuntalā's unsophisticated beauty portrayed by a wonder-struck Duṣyanta who, no mean a connoisseur of feminine comeliness himself, confesses openly elsewhere, that he has not come across so much loveliness among the women of his own palace. The beauty is so great and the wonder so enveloping, the description takes on an impersonal tone till the end of the third line: it is like someone admiring the Fujiyama or the Taj Mahal with no desire (there being no likelihood) to own it. This is the stage where Duṣyanta does not project himself in active relationship with the girl: this is the stage of impersonal admiration for a thing of beauty. Even though he has been in the penance-grove for sometime now, her beauty still strikes him as part of elemental nature: he has not yet got round to the state when he can take her beauty for granted. Further, it is permissible in literature to stylise and segregate these different moods to enable the reader to savour them the better. So then, after a distinct spell of impersonal admiration liberally laced with wonder, he comes down to the personal question: who is the lucky man whom Fate has nominated to be the enjoyer of all this beauty? Clearly at this stage there is an unexpressed but definitely hinted-at longing that the lucky nominee should be he, himself. All aesthetic relish is personal and at this point, clearly the stimuli have been assimilated into the system where ego has a domineering role and have been related to the self. So the sentiment of love with its related ideas of the enjoyer of the object of love has taken hold, at this stage, at the end of a noticeable phase after the impact of the sensation of wonder.

4.9 *A second example*

A second example can be cited showing how the associated sentiment of pathos is phased measurably after the impact of the sensation of wonder. It occurs in the Ūrubhaṅga, recited by Balarāma describing Gāndhārī's reaction to the news of her son's death: this beautiful, evocative verse has been quoted earlier.

In the poem, Balarāma notes that the bandage Gāndhārī wears over her eyes—has in fact been wearing for decades—is wet with tears and the first impact of this on him generates surprise. The reason for the surprise is a little unusual: Gāndhārī had decided years ago to bandage her eyes to please her blind husband who was the personification of envy: this she did to please her husband, overcoming a mother's normal desire to look upon the faces of her sons. So the world and Balarāma too along with the rest had long labelled her away in their mind as a loveless mother whose wifehood had completely eclipsed her motherhood. Now when he saw the very bandage, the symbol of an all-encompassing wifely loyalty getting wet with tears at the demise of her son Duryōdhana, he was puzzled and surprised as the stimulus of the wet bandage did not match the schema of a loveless mother inscribed in his mind.

After registering a shock on account of the unexpectedness of the reaction, Balarāma's mind examines the stimulus more closely and compares it with the different schema inscribed in it. The mind finds readily a hundred recorded cases of mothers loving their children to distraction: for has it not been said,

> कुपुत्रो जायेत क्वचिदपि कुमाता न भवति ।
>
> [Dēvyaparādhakṣamāpaṇa stōtra of Śaṅkara, verses 2, 3 & 4, common refrain]

In fact the image of a loving mother sacrificing her all for her child is beautifully burnished in the schemata of everyone who has lived in the midst of men. And there is little difficulty in Balarāma's mind assimilating this new stimulus as an extension to the hundred schema of loving mothers already inscribed. So now two powerful facts arise to nourish the sentiment of pathos: that Gāndhārī had assumed the bandage not out of lovelessness for her children but only in her excessive zeal to please her husband, thus stifling the normal desire of every mother to fulfil herself by looking on the faces of her children; and that the death of Duryōdhana now is a blow she is finding very hard to bear.

In other words, the initial surprise was occasioned by a surface appraisal of Gāndhārī's attitude: it is clearly an early reaction. On more careful analysis and deeper examination, the system finds Gāndhārī to be, after all, like all the mothers in the world and the bandage she wears is a symbol of the sacrifice of her natural and powerful motherly instinct (as much as a symbol of her wifely loyalty). The system takes in the very obvious fact that Gāndhārī is deeply affected by the news of her son's death: these combine to nourish the sentiment of pathos which is registered and experienced after a phase difference, it is savoured distinctly after the impact of surprise.

From a different point of view, it can be stated that Balarāma's surprise is based on a misapprehension that Gāndhārī does not love her children as other mothers do. The sentiment of pathos arises after the misapprehension is cleared and the truth is realised (that she is as loving a mother as any other). Mistakes and misapprehensions arise as a result of hasty judgment and are temporary: truth lies at the bottom and may take a little time to reach but it is permanent, it rules for ever.

This kind of analysis done on the other examples quoted in the work, too, will reveal the phase difference between the sense of wonder and the sentiments. Where suprise is caused by the audacious, perverse or amoral statements of characters like Rāvaṇa, the surprise is owed to the flagrant breach of *dharma* underlying them. Further examination reveals a number of characters we have read about and persons we have known (as inscribed in the mental schema) who love the 'bad-guy' image and who would regard a dharmic image as too 'sissy'. It also strikes us that this throwing overboard of moral principles accepted by all decent men is at the root of their tragedy: these thorough-bred villains have a completely different set of private morals which run counter to the universal moral law: hence surprise vanishes to be replaced by a sense of pathos in some cases or by a sense of disgust in occasional instances. In all such cases, surprise is only a preliminary reaction, followed by a cogitative phase after which the sentiment begins to appear.

When a new twist is given to an old concept, there is the initial gush of surprise, as in the case of Purūravas' remark that love arrives at its consummation, not in spite of the sufferings undergone by the lovers but precisely on account of them. But a little thought and a study of our mental schema would indicate that it is these sufferings that purify, strengthen and elevate an infatuation into love, that these troubles undergone and battled against together, shoulder-to-shoulder actually mature them, bring them together more closely and make them more determined. It has been so in the past and it shall be so for evermore, given the fundamental urges and foibles of mankind. So the sentiment of love with a growing respect and affection for the lovers develops after this process of comparison and cogitation, establishing a clearly marked phase difference between the sentiment and the sensation of wonder.

An example can be cited from life to prove this phase difference separating the impact of surprise and of emotions like sorrow and joy. When great tragedy strikes a person the first impact which is one of overwhelming surprise knocks him or her unconscious. On recovery, the system starts examining the detailed implications of the sudden stimuli and sorrow is registered. That it is the shock of surprise that was behind the fainting fit and not the sad contents of the tidings is proved by the fact that sudden good news too has the same initial effect. So, while surprise is the first sensation to be registered, there is a certain timelapse and a process of suspension of consciousness followed by a spell of close analysis and comparison with the established schema before the emotional reaction is registered. Literature being true to life, readers get an initial impact of surprise, followed after an interval of time and fresh activity in the brain, by the onset of sentiments, thus marking off surprise as a sensation distinctly different from the sentiments.

4.10 *Wonder, basically different from the sentiments*

This fact that the time difference during which a vital process of examination, analysis and comparison with the schema has to go on constitutes important evidence that wonder is not a sentiment but a sensation that is basically different from the sentiments. There is yet another piece of evidence marking off wonder from the sentiments and making it a distinctly different sensation, altogether.

Wonder, as we have seen, arises on account of unfamiliarity, if there is discrepancy between the stimulus and the schema—which signifies that at the first impact there are some unusual features about the stimulus which make it look different from the recorded previous experiences. Thus unusualness, uniqueness, unfamiliarity are the very stuff of which wonder is made.

Sentiments like pathos and love thrive on identification which can happen only if the stimulus displays familiar features on closer examination—features which can help to relate the stimulus with some schema already inscribed, representing an experience undergone. Unless this linkage with a previous experience is effected, there can be no sentiment. Hence sentiment subsists on recognition of similarity and on familiarity: unless a stimulus can be shown to be related to a familiar experience and therefore is not unique, it cannot evoke a sentiment.

Thus wonder which depends on unfamiliarity is fundamentally different from the sentiments which subsist on recognizability. This unfamiliarity which is the initial reaction evoking wonder has to be replaced by recognition of familiar, related features in comparison with the schema, before a sentiment can be evoked. Wonder has to be destroyed before a sentiment can be born. They are generated by two states of the mind which are basically opposed to each other; therefore they cannot co-exist; and they lay claim to be recognized as two distinct classes of reaction.

SELECT BIBLIOGRAPHY

1. "On the nature of fear", Donald O. Hebb, Psychological Review 53 (1946) p. 259-76
2. Merrill-Palmer Quarterly of Behaviour and Development (18) 1972, p. 349-65 and p. 327
3. Psychological Review 77 (1970) P. 16-31
4. Scientific American 192 (1955) p. 74-76
5. The origins of intelligence in children, Jean Piaget (1963) p. 72
6. The Tangled Wing, Melvin Konner (Penguin)

INDEX OF ŚLOKAS

SUBJECT INDEX

CORRIGENDA

Page	Para/ Verse	Line	For	Read
v	2	12&14	*sthāyibhāva*	*sthāyibhāva*
1	1	1	जाति् भाजो	जातिभाजो
2	4	4	मनोरथावाप्तयु	मनोरथावाप्त्यु
3	1	3	कृति	कृती
4	2	7	ike	like
11	2	12	ensures	ensues
14	2	2	भुजटूयेन	भुजद्वयेन
16	1	2	मजोगतमाधिहेतुम्	मनोगतमाधिहेतुम्
21	2	1	व्यथमानामद्दंहत्	व्यथमानामद्दंहत्
22	1	2	वजनास	जनास
22	4	9	one-rākṣasa	one rākṣasa
23	2	3	सामर्थ्यानिामिन	सामर्थ्यानिामिव
24	2	3	उपयुषि	उपेयुषि
25	1	3	वेषमशेष भीषणमहो	वेषमशेषभीषणमहो
27	3	4	दशशु	दशसु
28	2	4	क्षरत्कीलालाभ्य:	क्षरत्कीलालाम्भः
29	1	1	लक्ष्मींश	लक्ष्मीश
			मेरूधन्वेति	मेरुधन्वेति
30	1	3	तीताम्बरं	पीताम्बरं
30	2	2	वित्तेश भवनीभत्तेः	वित्तेशभवनभित्तेः
34	1	1	जिह्नः	जिह्मः
37	2	2	खट्वाङ्गदेरिव	खट्वाङ्गादेरिव
39	2	3	तत्तसहेतुमपि	तत्तासहेतुमपि
40	1	4	तोन्व्यास्तिष्ठतु	तन्व्यास्तिष्ठतु
43	1	3	जलिपतं	जल्पितं
43	3	1	भुवामवनेतुमेतद्	भुवामपनेतुमेतद्
45	1	3	गेणैर्मा	गुणैर्मा
45	2	3	मौक्तिकरसः	मौक्तिकसरः

46	1	1	लोलांशुकस्य	लीलांशुकस्य
47	1	2	शौर्यं तत्	शौर्यं हि तत्
52	1	2	घट्टयन्ति	घट्टयामि
53	2	2	स्नवसि	स्वनसि
54	1	3	दुष्करमेतादित्य	दुष्करमेतदित्य
54	2	1	दृष्टैव	दृष्ट्वै
54	2	4	मन्तहृसिल	मन्तहृास
56	1	3	मालयति	माल्यति
56	2	3	यत्प्रादुर्भवनाद्रवन्ध्य	यत्प्रादुर्भवनादवन्ध्य
56	4	1	भरतकपरिधस्पर्धि	मरतकपरिघस्पर्धि
57	1	1	निवपिणीयं	निर्वापिणीयं
59	1	2	द्लुवनवलयं	द्भुवनवलयं
59	1	3	विहितवसतिकैलासाग्रे	विहितवसतिं कैलासाग्रे
59	4	1	नग्निस्तृप्यति	नाग्निस्तृप्यति
60	1	2	पुष्पगन्धि:	पुष्पगन्धी
60	1	4	तमात्रप	तमातप
61	1	3	लङ्का	लङ्कां
62	2	3	वलकलेनापि	वल्कलेनापि
66	1	1	दिशे	दिशि
67	1	1	कोणवपुरी	कोणपपुरी
67	1	4	जलपन्नित्यनिलात्मज:	जल्पन्नित्यनिलात्मज:
68	1	14	monkeys in-the-street	monkeys-in-the-street
70	1	1	नवपरिणयलज्जाभूषणं	नवपरिणयलज्जाभूषणां
70	1	4	प्रमथभुखविकारै:	प्रमथमुखविकारै:
			गुढम्	गूढम्
73	5	1	खावुदिते	रवावुदिते
77	1	1	स्मशानेएवाक्रीडा	श्मशानेष्वाक्रीडा
77	2	1	कलोराणि	कठोराणि
78	2	3	दक्षिण्यवा-	दाक्षिण्यवा-
87	2	2	शड्क्तानिव	शाद्वलानिव
89	1	2	क्षितिभूद्गणे	क्षितिभृद्गणे
90	1	2	स्फुरदीन्दुमध्ये	स्फुरतीन्दुमध्ये
92	2	1	दुष्यन्तमभ्युद्यतं	दृप्यन्तमभ्युद्यतं
92	4	1	Hanumānnāṭaka	Hanumannāṭaka

92	4	2	hernessing	harnessing
93	1	2	शाखामगम्	शाखामृगम्
93	1	3	आस्तेऽवापि	आस्तेऽत्रापि
97	1	4	क्षमानन्दिनीमर्पयन्	क्ष्मानन्दिनीमर्पयन्
99	1	4	दाखन्तः	दारवन्तः
101	2	7	in effect.	in effect,
104	1	4	निषेक्त	निषेवत
105	4	6	range	rage
111	1	3	प्रगुणितमनुजेनादरा-त्तीक्ष्णमक्ष्यः	प्रगुणितमनुजेनादरात्तीक्ष्णमक्ष्णः
112	2	1	प्रिस्फुरिताधराः	प्रस्फुरिताधराः
112	2	2	अनुक्तैक्व	अनुक्त्वैव
113	1	1	fling	fixing
119	1	1	प्रातः	त्रातः
125	1	3	मदपराछाश्च	मदपराधाश्च
125	2	4	जहिपः	जीहपः
133	1	1	लब्ध्या	लब्धया
133	2	8	rākṣasa	rākṣasa)
133	2	3	यवयिसा	यवीयसा
137	1	4	शिशुनां	शिशूनाम्
139	5	6	glory	gory
140	2	3	किंचित्किंचिब्दुध	किंचित्किंचिद्बुध
142	3	1	मेघः :	मेघः
144	1	4	इत्यद्भुतम	इत्यद्भुतम्
147	1	1	जेतुम	जेतुम्
153	1	5	ashamed to	ashamed of
155	2	2	लोकश्चिरमुच्छमुत्सकः	लोकश्चिरमुच्छमुत्सुकः
157	2	10	pratibha	pratibhā
160	4	2	manner	manager
167	4	2	baring	barring
170	2	5	earth during	earth during a
172	5	10	cavemen	caveman
175	3	8	To astonishment	To the astonishment
180	2	8	living in his	living; in his

185	2	2	spring up	springs up
187	1	6	are	art
187	5	1	consorious	censorious